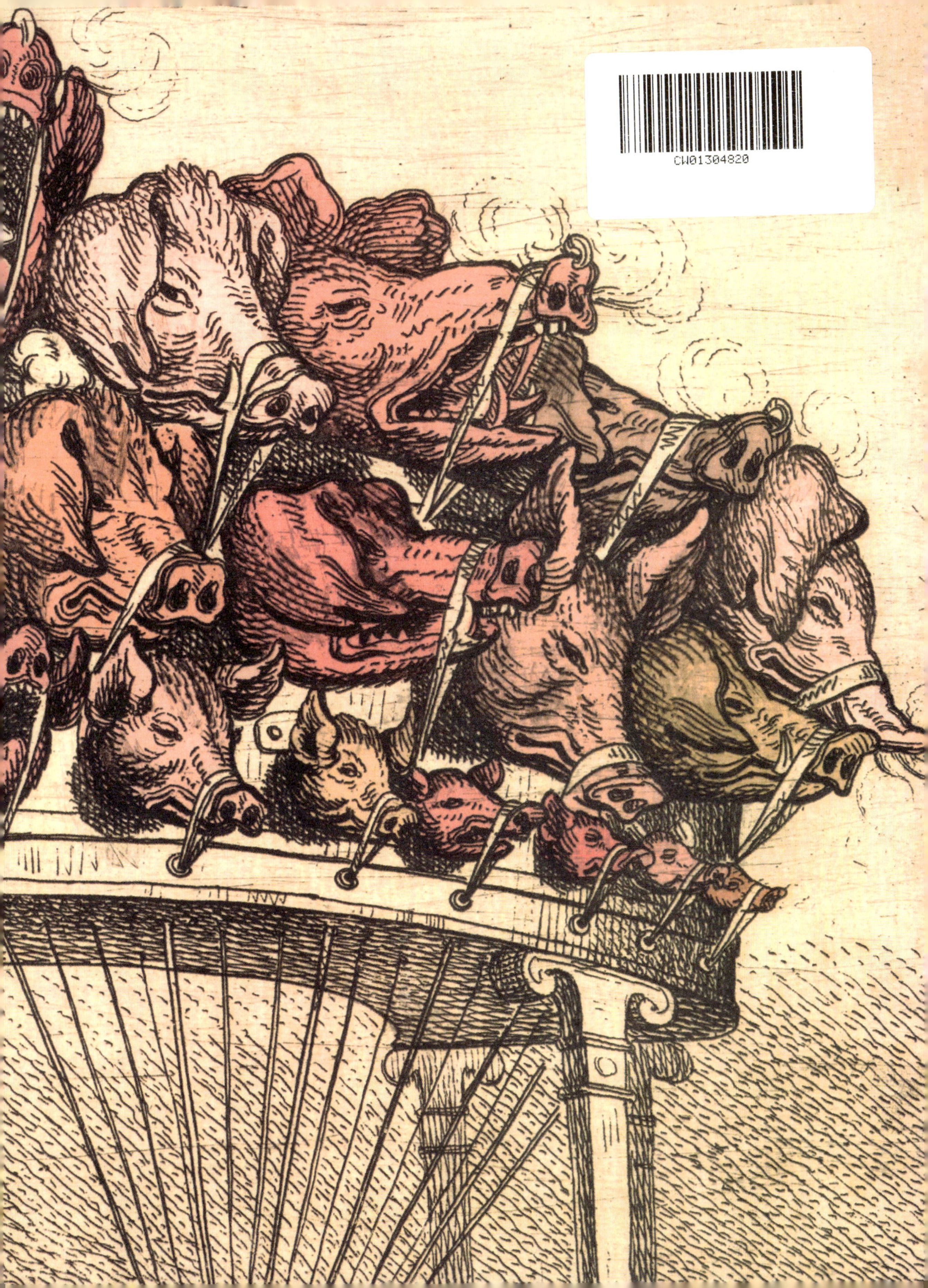

THE
MADMAN'S
ORCHESTRA

THE MADMAN'S ORCHESTRA

*The greatest curiosities from
the history of music*

EDWARD
BROOKE-HITCHING

SIMON & SCHUSTER

London · New York · Amsterdam/Antwerp · Sydney/Melbourne · Toronto · New Delhi

MMXXV

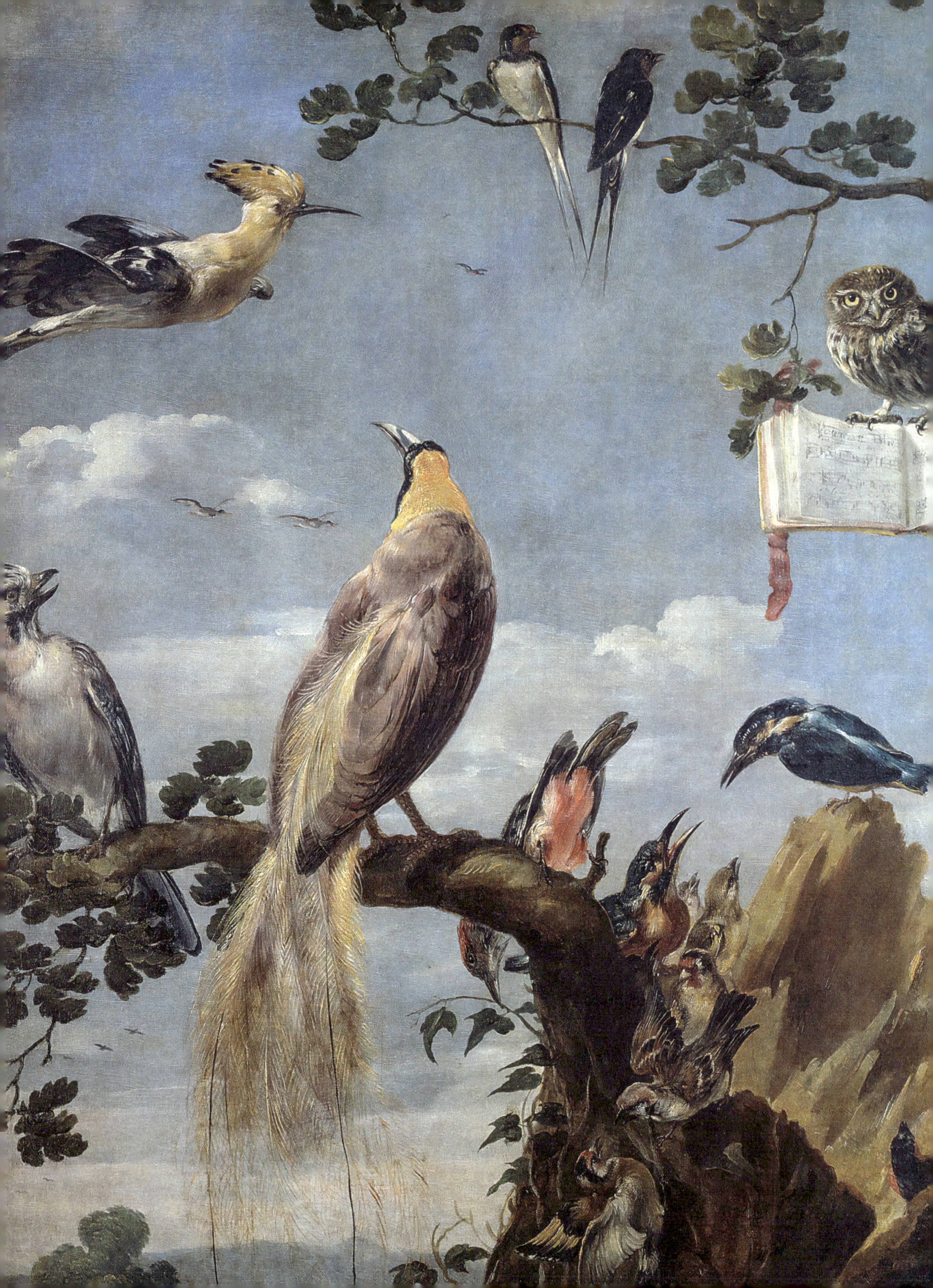

For Emma and Franklin, composed *con amore*

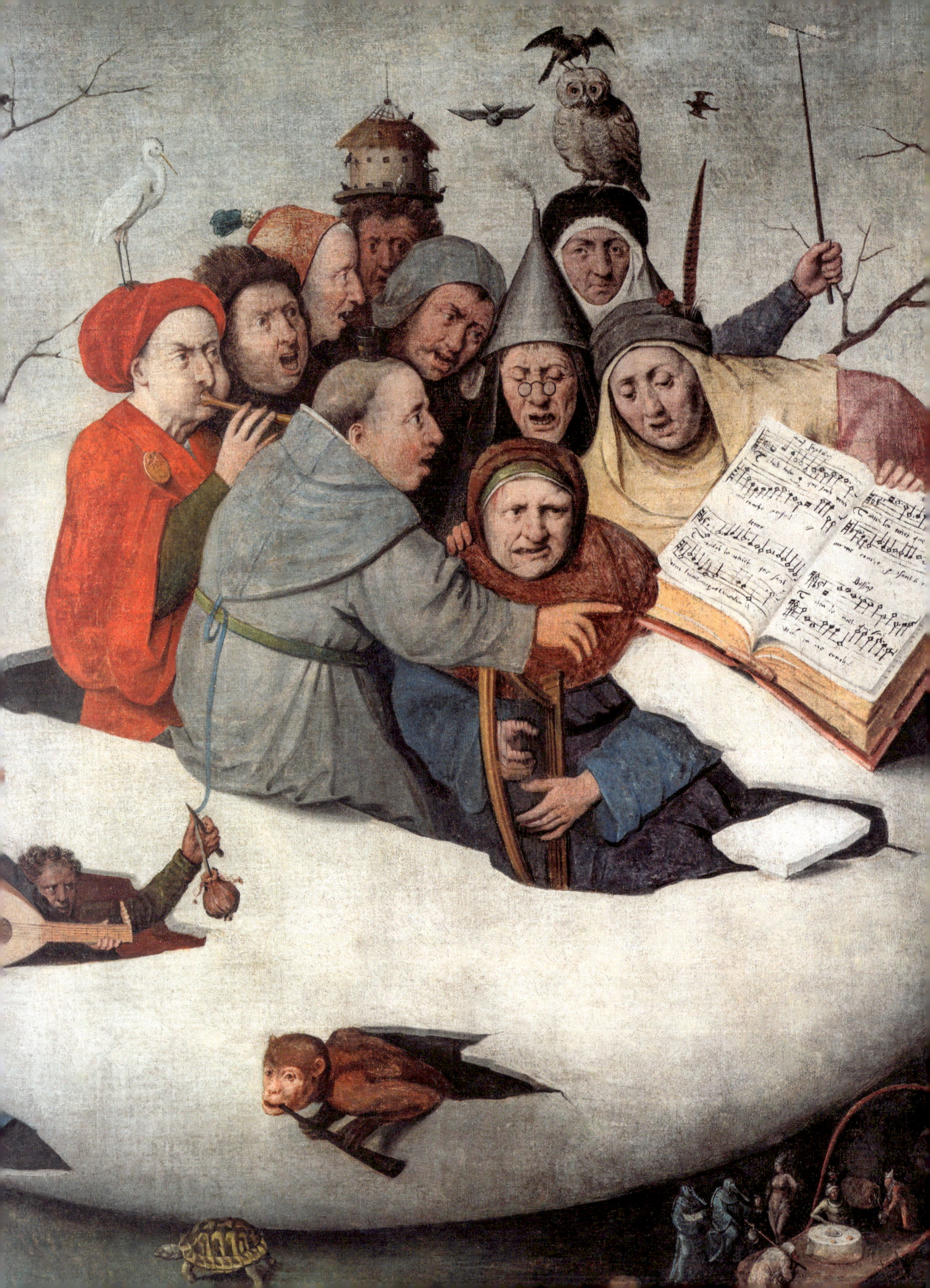

CONTENTS

8 INTRODUCTION

14 SOME UNUSUAL MUSICAL TERMS

16 MUSIC OF THE UNIVERSE

40 CURIOUS INSTRUMENTS

78 COMPOSERS ON COMPOSERS

80 VISIBLE MUSIC

112 LOST MUSIC FOUND

130 SOME MUSICAL UNAPPRECIATION

132 CRYPTOGRAPHIC MUSIC

152 MUSICAL DISASTERS

166 SOME CURIOUS COMPOSER INSTRUCTIONS

168 EXPERIMENTAL ODDITIES

200 MUSICAL HOAXES

218 DECOMPOSITION: SOME CURIOUS DEATHS IN MUSIC HISTORY

220 THE HORNED SECTION; OR, THE DEVIL IN MUSIC

242 SOME FINAL WORDS OF GREAT MUSICIANS

244 SELECT BIBLIOGRAPHY

246 INDEX

254 PICTURE CREDITS

255 ACKNOWLEDGEMENTS

PAGE 1: *A devil playing a monk's head like a set of bagpipes, 1535.*

PREVIOUS SPREAD: *Frans Snyders's* Concert of Birds, *1629-1630.*

OPPOSITE: The Concert in the Egg, 1561, *by Gielis Panhedel (1490-1547), a follower of Hieronymus Bosch (1450-1516).*

INTRODUCTION

In 1964 an Englishman named Ray Stanton King – who would go on to become chairman of the City of Oxford Conservative Association – spent four months sitting in various hotel bathrooms at night, dangling a microphone over the basins to record the gurgling of drains. From these recordings he composed the 'Sink Symphony', a five-minute-and-three-second medley of British hotel plumbing. Not only did the musical piece win Mr King the British Tape of the Year award, but also the Grand Prix at the International Tape Recording Contest in Lausanne, Switzerland.

Whether or not Mr King's composition is 'good' music is not for me to say (although I do have sniffier feelings about the symphony he composed the following year from tapes of people blowing their noses). I can, however, be firmer about the musical performances of an Edinburgh-based orchestra with whom I spent one summer exactly twenty years ago. The Really Terrible Orchestra, also known as the RTO, is officially the world's worst orchestra. It was founded in 1995 by the author Alexander McCall Smith and financier Peter Stevenson, both amateur musicians of limited ability who simply wished to perform music for the fun of it. The RTO sold out London's Cadogan Hall in 2007, and the New York Town Hall on their (single-date) 'world tour' in 2009. Audiences are handed a glass of wine *before* the performance as a form of anaesthetic.♪

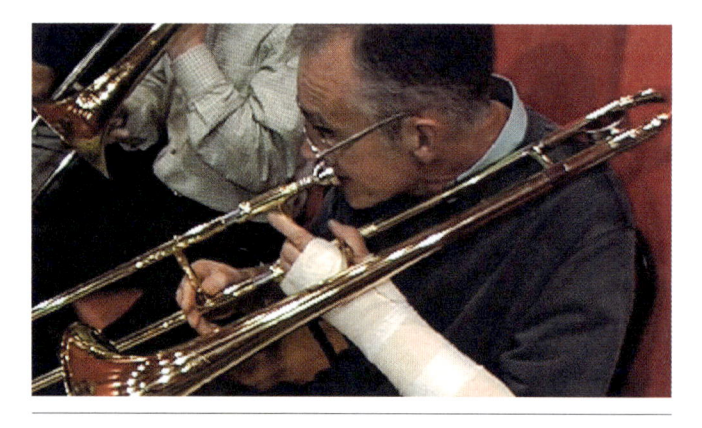

LEFT: *A member of The Really Terrible Orchestra, which enjoys the official designation of being the world's worst orchestra.*

♪ In the first of the raft of foot-*notes* (geddit?) throughout this book we can immediately provide a related song recommendation here in the form of 'The Most Unwanted Song' (1997), an attempt to make the most hated piece of music that includes bagpipes, cowboy music, an opera singer rapping and a children's choir urging the listener to 'do all your shopping at Walmart!' The artists Komar and Melamid, and composer Dave Soldier, also included 'The Most Wanted Song', which drew on elements most favoured in a musical opinion poll, but 'The Most Unwanted Song' bizarrely became the more popular of the two.

Along with the neurological hazards of attending months of rehearsals and the grand public performance of the worst orchestra in the world, the experience also gave me a crashing introduction to the eccentric side of music, and the germ of the idea for this book. While many histories of music – quite sensibly – focus on the important, the revolutionary and the classically revered, the idea with this book is to take a tour down the murky alleyway that veers around the side of that respectable institution and through the stranger areas of music history, collecting almost worryingly weird pieces that each have an intriguing story to their composition. For every Für Elise or *Eine kleine Nachtmusik*, for example, there is a 'Helicopter Quartet', requiring each string player to perform in a different aircraft circling the audience (see page 197); or the sixteenth-century lute duet that requires the players to share the instrument while one is sat on the other's lap (see page 179); or Scelsi's 'Four Pieces, Each on a Single Note' of 1959, which pairs neatly with the horrifying 'Rick Astley's "Never Gonna Give You Up" But All the Notes Are C' (see page 184). For every standard orchestral instrument like the oboe, clarinet and tuba, a madman's orchestra instead might incorporate the rat-bone witch flute, the fire organ, the hog harmonium, the perfume organ and the toothier alternative to the theremin known as the badgermin (see Curious Instruments, page 40).

While searching for musical curiosities across history, genre and geography,♪ pools of strange stories began to coalesce into

A rare surviving example of a heksenfluit, *or witch flute, carved from rat bone c.1890. According to folklore, the instruments were played as a form of enchantment by diabolic pipers, similar to the legend of the Pied Piper.*

♪ Some of the most fascinating musical curiosities occur when two cultural worlds collide. A most beautiful example is the short song 'Chemirocha III', one of over 40,000 recordings of African folk music made by the English ethnomusicologist Hugh Tracey (1903-77) while working at a tobacco farm in Southern Rhodesia. The story of 'Chemirocha III' is particularly fascinating. During the Second World War, the Kipsigis tribe of the Great Rift Valley of Kenya were visited by Christian missionaries, who played them gramophone recordings of the American Country singer Jimmie Rodgers (1897-1933). When Tracey visited them in 1950, he found the tribe had amalgamated Rodgers's musical style with theirs, and incorporated Rodgers himself into their mythology, believing him to be a half-man, half-antelope faun. 'Chemirocha', which is strummed country-style on an instrument called a *kibugandet*, is how they pronounced 'Jimmie Rodgers'.

9 | Introduction

Verkhünder des Thrüümphs.

their own strange chapter themes. 'Musical Hoaxes' (see page 200), for example, gathers forgeries, mockeries, lies, jokes and frauds of melody, climaxing with the tale of the female pianist who appears to have perpetrated one of the most expansive deceits in the history of the recording age. Elsewhere, for those wishing to tell their cheese paradiddle from their side flamadiddle, there is 'Some Unusual Musical Terms' (see page 14) to explore. To find out which sheet music carries the composer's instructions to push their piano through a wall and 'to keep pushing in the same direction regardless of new obstacles'; or to bring 'a bale of hay and a bucket of water onto the stage for the piano to eat and drink'; then 'Some Curious Composer Instructions' (see page 166) can provide some answers. 'Musical Disasters' (see page 152) reveals some rocky origins of what are today regarded as the greatest compositions ever committed to paper; while 'The Horned Section; or, The Devil in Music' (see page 220) traces the surprisingly long and unsurprisingly insidious history of the tradition known as the *Diabolus in musica* ('the Devil in music'), featuring among others a composition that Leonard Bernstein considered the first piece of psychedelic music (see page 231).

OPPOSITE: *A herald blowing a horn leads the Triumphal Procession of Holy Roman Emperor Maximilian I, a series of engravings, 54m (177ft) long, featuring musicians, soldiers and mythical animals that Maximilian commissioned to celebrate his own magnificence.*

A Tibetan musical score used in Buddhist monastic rituals, with the notation for voice, drums, trumpets, horns and cymbals.

12 *Madman's Orchestra*

One of the great delights in slowly putting together a book such as this is coming across largely forgotten stories that simply seem too strange to be true, and having the happy experience of confirming their unlikely veracity. See, for example, the story of Charlie and His Orchestra, an American swing band heard on British and American public radios during the Second World War that was actually a covert Nazi brainwashing operation; or the tale of how the opening theme of Beethoven's Fifth Symphony was used by the Allies to stoke the resistance in occupied Europe (see 'Cryptographic Music', page 132, which also reveals how to summon dark angels with music to do one's bidding).

From visible music glimpsed by the psychically inclined, through the symphony designed to bring about the Apocalypse, to the seventeenth-century German scholar convinced of the virtuoso singing ability of the American sloth, the intention here is for each story to add context of such intriguing oddness that it has you reflexively reaching for the record player. To aid you in this, each chapter features a playlist allowing the option of listening to the pieces while reading about them.

'Music is liquid architecture; architecture is frozen music', Johann Wolfgang von Goethe (1749-1832) once wrote. I hope the following provides an entertaining tour through a soundscape of some of the most curious musical constructions of human imagination.

OPPOSITE: *The magnificently sturdy 1.9m (6ft 4in), 150kg (330lb) figure of basso Luigi Lablache (1794-1858), who once performed the role of an emaciated prisoner languishing in a dungeon. When he mournfully sang the opening words: 'I'm starving…', the audience laughed so hard that a short intermission had to be held for order to be restored.*

A composition by Frederick Ouseley (1825-89), written when he was three years and three months old. The music was noted down by his sister Mary Jane, as he hadn't yet learnt to read or write at the time. By the age of eight, Ouseley had written an entire opera.

SOME UNUSUAL MUSICAL TERMS

Appoggiatura From the Italian verb *appoggiare* ('to lean upon'), this refers to a non-chord note in a melody on a strong beat (usually the first or third beats of the measure, in 4/4 time) that delays the appearance of the main expected chord note. Often used to create a sense of yearning: see, for example, the appoggiaturas emboldened here in 'Yesterday' by The Beatles: **Yes** – *ter* – *day, all my troubles seemed so* **far** *away. Now it looks as though they're* **here** *to stay…*

Barcarolle From Italian *barca* ('boat'), a traditional folk song sung by Venetian gondoliers, or a piece of music composed in that style (such as Frédéric Chopin's Barcarolle in F sharp major for solo piano). The rhythm mimics the gondolier's stroke, at 6/8 metre in a moderate tempo.

Bisbigliando ('very light and murmuring') A term used as a direction for a rapid but quiet fingered tremolo on the harp.

Cheese paradiddle A hybrid drum rudiment (sticking pattern). Others include side flamadiddle, grandmas and alternated pataflafla.

Chicharra A percussive sound effect made by violinists, cellists and violists in tango orchestras using their bow on the 'wrong side' of the bridge, just below where they usually bow the strings. Named for its similarity to the noise made by the *chicharra* ('cicada').

Chicken pickin' A slang term from American country music of the 1960s and 70s for a particular style of playing on the Fender Telecaster guitar, or similar, by alternating short and longer notes in the manner of the clucking and squawking of a barnyard chicken.

Durchkomponert ('through-music') Through-composed music is a continuous, non-sectional, non-repetitive piece of music with constant introduction of new material.

Duende A term for the hypnotic effect of watching a compelling flamenco performance.

Klangfarbenmelodie ('sound-colour melody') A musical technique of dividing one instrument's musical line or melody between several instruments, rather than assigning it to just one instrument or one set of instruments, to add timbre and texture.

Melisma Singing melismatically is to sing a single syllable of text with several different notes in succession.

Pesantissimo ('very heavy') A term invented by British musicologist Philip Tagg to describe the music of Metallica.

Piangendo ('crying') A term used in Liszt's 'La Lugubre Gondola No. 2'.

Plop A term used in jazz to refer to a note that slides to an indefinite pitch chromatically downwards.

Proslambanomenos The lowest note in Ancient Greek music.

Smite Not just a verb for the strike of an angry god, but also once used to describe plucking or strumming instruments like harps and violins.

Stripper ending A style of ending that comes after a recapitulation of the chorus and draws on a *ritardando* triplet figure, slowing the tempo to half time: exemplified by the final sections of Elvis Presley's 'Winter Wonderland' and Buddy Rich's 'Channel One' Suite.

Tessitura ('texture') The most comfortable vocal range for a singer, that best exhibits their timbre.

Tirade A baroque musical flourish consisting of a rapid run of musical scale between two notes of a melody.

Woodshedding A term that originated in 1936 for practising a musical instrument intensely in private for a short period, after which a musician has dramatically improved their technique.

Some Unusual Musical Terms

MUSIC OF THE UNIVERSE

The universe began with music, and she sings still. As we understand it today, there was absolute silence at the very moment of the Big Bang, but then soundwaves rose with the expansion of the superhot and dense universe until the volume of all creation peaked at a level of just under 120 decibels,♪ which is about the same as that of the rock band Deep Purple's legendarily loud 1972 show at London's Rainbow Theatre. This universal crescendo is slightly harder to tap your foot along to than 'Smoke on the Water', however. Human ears can only detect soundwaves with lengths of up to 17m (55ft) – the Big Bang broadcast wavelengths of about 200,000 light years.

We know these soundwaves existed because we can 'hear' them today. In 2001 a high-altitude balloon with the 'Boomerang' telescope suspended beneath it was released at the South Pole to hover 3,650m (120,000ft) above Antarctica, where atmospheric interruption is minimal. From this vantage point, the international team of thirty-six scientists were able to study the cosmic microwave background, the remnant radiation emitted by the Big Bang that fills all space in the observable universe. The Boomerang team deciphered structures within the microwave radiation and discovered that they formed a harmonic series of angular scales, like a musical score. Amid the jaggedness of these notes, matter coalesced under the sway of gravity into larger structures, and stars and galaxies eventually formed.♫

Beneath this primordial melody, the universal orchestra continues to play with its variety of instruments. Since 2003, for example, scientists at NASA's Chandra X-ray Observatory found that they could listen in on the deep song of a black hole (which we might think of as the octobass of the cosmic theatre's orchestra pit). They detected pressure waves pulsing from black holes that cause ripples in the hot gases that surround them. By assigning frequencies to these wavelengths, they translated them into musical notes and found that black holes hum their bass line in B flat at fifty-seven octaves lower

A depiction of the infinite pretemporal nothingness before the light of Creation, shown here by the physician, occultist and music theorist Robert Fludd in his Utriusque cosmi… *(1617-26).*

♪ As calculated by the English cosmologist and theoretical astrophysicist Peter Coles (b.1963).

♫ One choral piece that reflects the scale of these cosmic mechanics is a composition that Stephen Hawking acclaimed as having 'captured the vastness of space' and helped him to understand the universe's existence. Cheryl Frances-Hoad's 'Beyond the Night Sky' (2017) was commissioned for Hawking's seventy-fifth birthday celebrations at Gonville and Caius College, Cambridge, and was performed again in 2018, at his funeral.

LEFT: *An illustration from Gioseffo Zarlino's (1517-90) 1558 treatise* Le Istitutioni Harmoniche, *one of the greatest works in the history of music theory. The octave* (diapason) *and its divisions into a fifth* (diapente) *and a fourth* (diatessaron) *are linked to the astrological signs for the days of the week and the names of the Muses. (The interval names appear at the bottom, printed upside down.)*

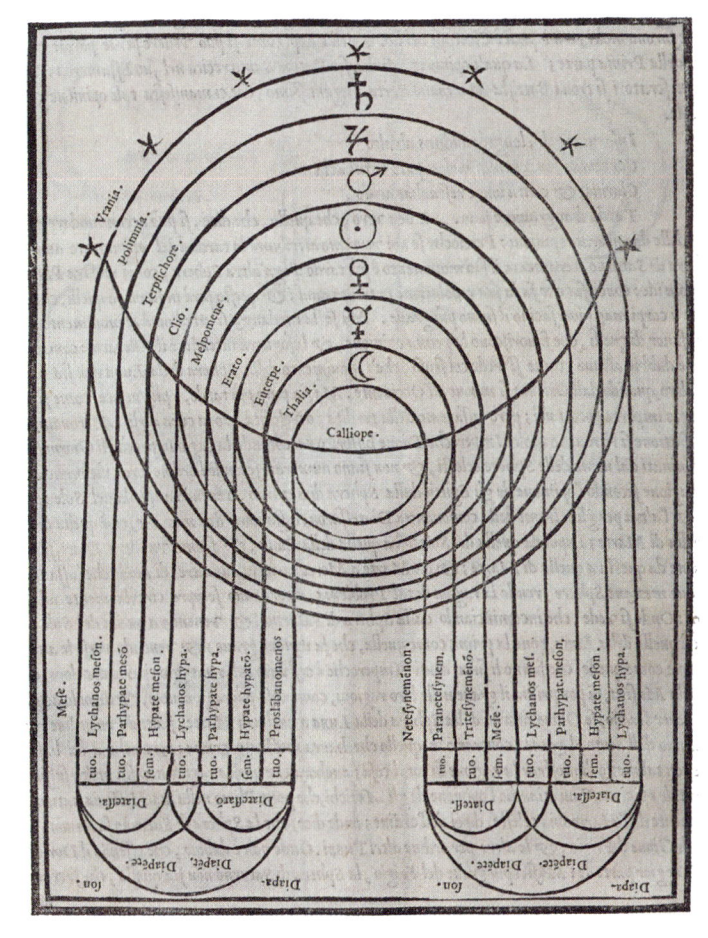

BELOW: *Eric Chappell of the Montreal Symphony Orchestra plays the orchestra's octobass in 2017. The enormous and rare instrument, first built c.1850 in Paris by the French luthier Jean-Baptiste Vuillaume (1798-1875), typically plays one octave below the double bass. The octobassist relies on a series of levers and pedals to play the extra-thick strings.*

than middle C, performing the deepest note in the cosmos. (To hit this note on a piano, you'd need a keyboard 15m/50ft long.) ♪

Music and the fabric of the cosmos have been interwoven in mankind's thinking since we first discovered our voice. The *Rig Veda*, for example, one of the four sacred canonical Hindu texts and one of the oldest extant texts in any Indo-European language, is a collection of hymns that have been sung and transmitted since the second millennium BC. Through the hymns describing the dark, watery and ultimately unknowable state of the beginnings of the cosmos, the material of reality is said to be transformed into musical melody and rhythm. In 'The Creation of the Sacrifice', for example, 'the Man stretches the warp and draws the weft; the Man has spread it out upon

---

♪ So far, the largest performance piano ever created is the model by the Polish architect Daniel Czapiewski (1968-2013) in December 2010. With a keyboard of 2.5m (5ft) in width, it has 156 keys, nearly twice the standard number of 88, and stands 1.92m (6ft 3in) tall, so that the pianist can run from side to side while playing at shoulder height.

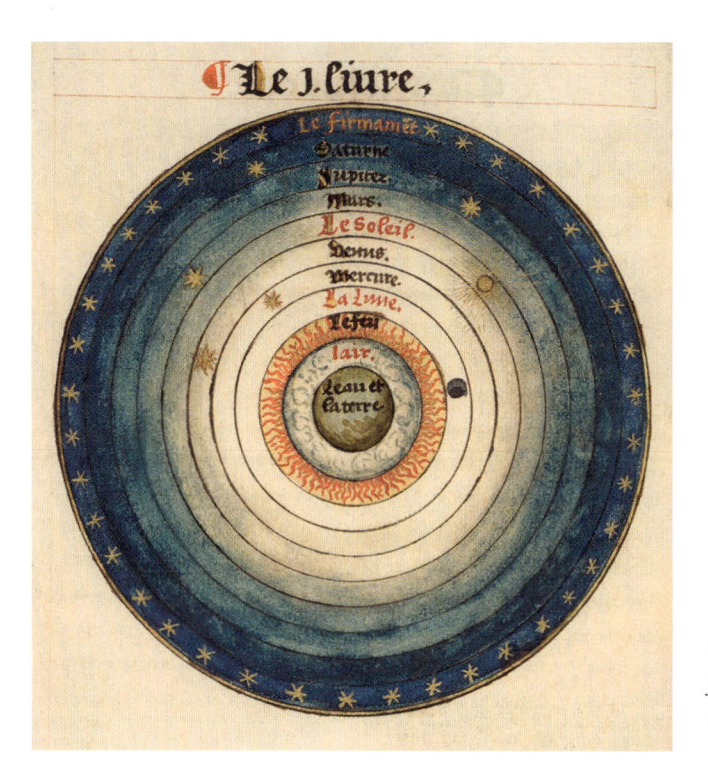

The Greek vision of the cosmos, from Le Sphere du Monde, *1549, by Oronce Fine (1494-1555).*

this dome of the sky. These are the pegs, that are fastened in place; they made the melodies into the shuttles for weaving…' (*Rig Veda*, 1981: 31).

Nearly four millennia after the Hindu faithful first chanted of the chaotic nothingness of the Beginning, the composer Joseph Haydn (1732-1809) also attempted to capture the same sense of primordial mayhem with music, informed by his 1792 visit to the home of British astronomer William Herschel (1738-1822) and his newly built 12m (40ft) telescope. With 'The Representation of Chaos', the prelude to his oratorio *The Creation*, we have perhaps the best melodic representation of the first formlessness of what existed before the moment of Creation with orchestral ideas, before the monumental choral presentations of the following piece that signal the creation of light on the First Day as related in the Book of Genesis.♪ In the key of C minor, the themes of the prelude are vague and drift in unfinished fragments. Harmonies are ambiguous, expected climaxes fail to materialise and wind scales dance unpredictably. As Haydn himself explains in a letter to the Swedish composer Fredrik Silverstolpe (1769-1851): 'You have certainly noticed how

---

♪ Alternatively, intersperse a listen of *The Creation* at this point with Carl Nielsen's *Helios Overture*, op. 17 (1903), written to portray the Sun rising over the Aegean Sea, for a similarly glorious celestial welcome.

I avoided the resolutions that you would most readily expect. The reason is that there is no form in anything [in the universe] yet.' *The Creation* premiered in 1798 in Vienna, conducted by Haydn and featuring Antonio Salieri at the fortepiano. (Its Paris premiere on Christmas Eve 1800 suffered a slight delay of ten minutes after a bomb was detonated beside the coaches ferrying First Consul Napoleon Bonaparte and Joséphine to the theatre.)

If contemporary astronomy did indeed help formulate Haydn's musical interpretation of the universe, it would have been an example of the ancient relationship between the two subjects of learning. For the ancient Greeks and Romans, and on through the centuries to Galileo's (1564-1642) time♪ and beyond, music and astronomy were twinned as complementary sciences, both falling under the umbrella of mathematics.

Cosmographer Andreas Cellarius's (1596-1665) 1660 attempt to give dimension to the orbits of the planets, which the Greeks believed to be physical spheres carrying the celestial bodies. The traditional flat depiction of the Ptolemaic system is in the bottom-left corner, and Tycho Brahe's idea in the bottom right.

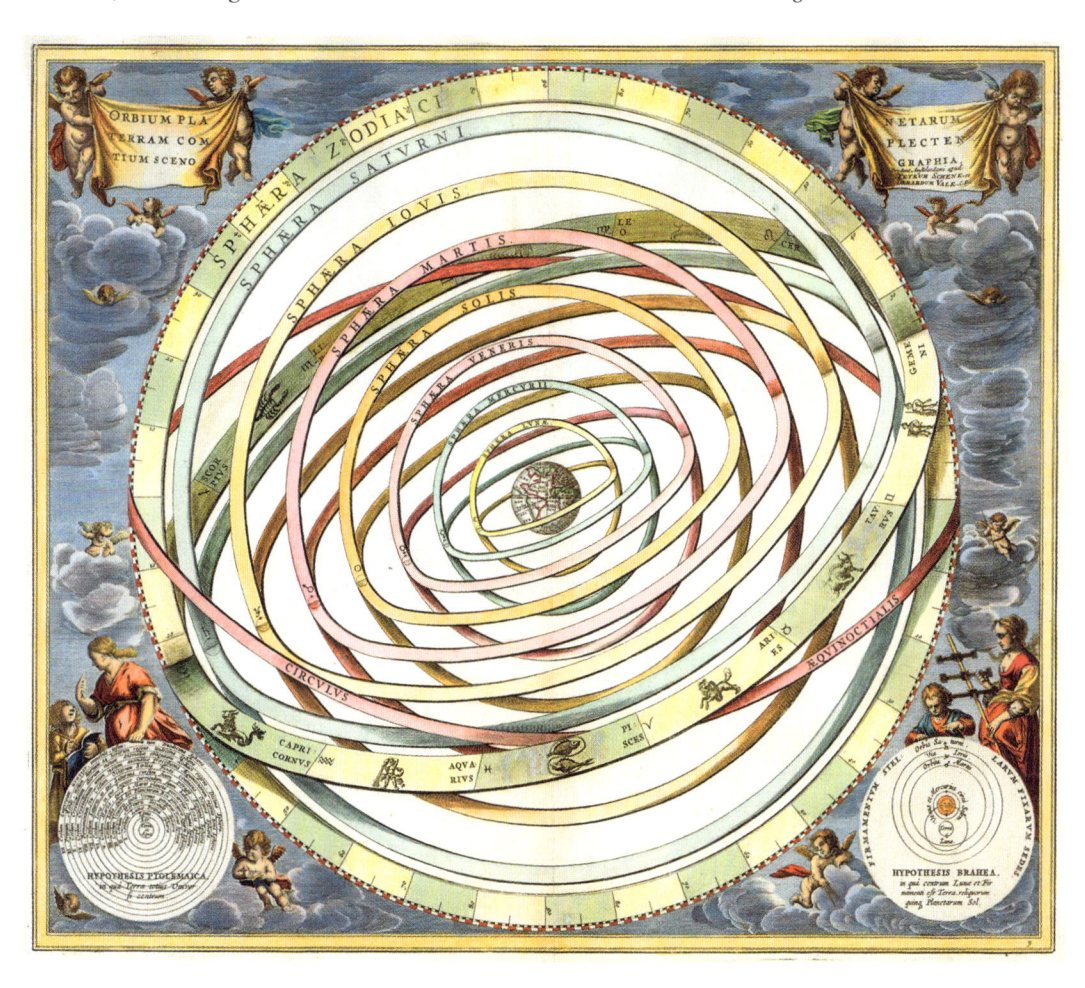

♪ Galileo reportedly found music to be a useful tool in his experiments. With no accurate watches or clocks to rely on, he would time various objects rolling down inclined planes by humming the same tune to himself over and over again.

Music of the Universe

Which brings us to perhaps one of the most enduring, and fascinating, threads of Western music history: the *musica universalis,* also known as 'the music of the spheres'.

Pioneered by Pythagoras (570-495 BC), debated by Aristotle (384-322 BC), championed by the Roman polymath Boethius (480-524 AD), the musica universalis is a natural philosophy of gargantuan scale yet simple reasoning that runs as follows: the moving parts of the cosmos, from the circling planets to the Sun and Moon, all create colossal music with their grinding machinations as they rotate and cross the skies in rhythmic behaviour. So vast is this choir of heavenly bodies that their song is far beyond the capacity of human hearing, but we can *feel* it in our bones and souls as we go about our lives in the light of the singing stars.♪

The idea of these worlds in harmony goes back as far as Pythagoras. Astronomy was essential to revealing the ultimate understanding of music, while music unveiled the workings of astronomy. Only through these, and ultimately mathematics as a whole, could the nature of the universe be known. This was the philosophy of the ancient Pythagoreans, who were the earliest to hold that all of nature is a musical scale.

The story goes that Pythagoras one day passed a blacksmith and noticed that the notes struck by the man's two hammers sounded most pleasing when the ratio between the size of two tools involved two integers, or whole numbers, such as 3:2. This is the origin myth of the 'Pythagorean tuning' in music, in which the ratios of all intervals are based on the 3:2 ratio, also known as the perfect fifth as it is one of the most consonant. (In fact, this is a common misattribution, as this system dates back to ancient Mesopotamia.) The Pythagoreans' obsession with harmonious music led to their focus on the simple numerical ratio of the first four natural numbers derived from the relations of string length: the octave (½), the fifth (⅔) and the fourth (¾). To them, adding these together (1 + 2 + 3 + 4 = 10) was a formula for perfection. The German theoretical physicist Werner Heisenberg (1901-76) declares this as 'among the most powerful advances of human science'.

OPPOSITE: *The planets, Moon, Sun and stars as the tones and modes of the musical scale based on the hermetic tradition of Pythagoreanism, from* Practica musicae, *1496, by Franchinus Gaffurius (1451-1522), choirmaster of the Cathedral of Milan.*

♪ The Latvian composer Ēriks Ešenvalds (b.1977) captures these 'beating hearts of fire' of the night sky in 'Stars' (2011), using a glistening array of tuned wine glasses to accompany a radiant chorale that slowly recedes into the darkness of silence. Pair this with 'Starlight Night' (2011) by the Yorkshire electronica/folk musician Merz, paying his own stellar tribute by singing Gerard Manley Hopkins' poem 'The Starlight Night' (1877) to a gorgeous orchestral composition.

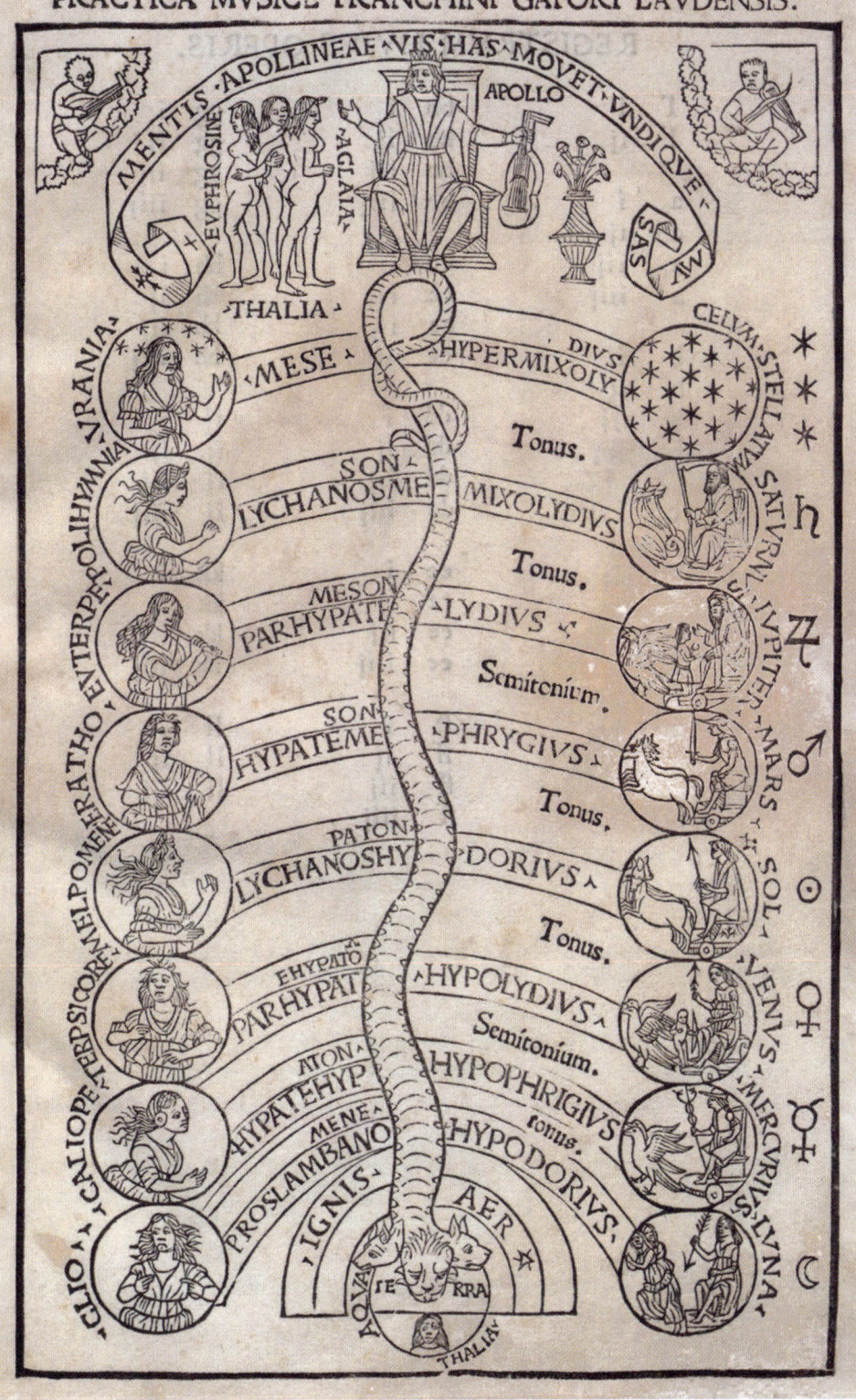

21 *Music of the Universe*

We do know from Aristoxenus of Tarentum (*fl.* fourth century BC), the Greek philosopher and author of the *Elements of Harmonics*, that the Pythagoreans believed musical harmonies – whether it was those sung by the planets or those plucked with simple string instruments – to be the sustenance of the universe. The Pythagoreans treated their soul with music for the same reasons they treated their bodies with medicine. In their philosophy, it was profoundly restorative and soothing to the soul to know that the notes played by their musicians were not only shared by the songs of the spheres, but also existed in the same ratio as the distances of the heavenly bodies from the centre of the Earth. Music *bound them* to the universe.

ABOVE: *The* tetractys *('mystic triad') is a powerful symbol of the Pythagoreans. The four rows add up to ten, in unity of a higher order. The ratios of the rows also function as their musical system.*

OPPOSITE: *Boethius plays a musical instrument, in a twelfth-century manuscript of the work* On the Institution of Music.

Aristotle, however, was not convinced. 'Some thinkers suppose that the motion of bodies of that size must produce a noise', he writes in *On the Heavens* (350 BC), Book 2, Part 9, adding 'they say… how should they not produce a sound immensely great?' He rejected the idea for the simple reason that the noise would simply be *too* audible, to the point of lethality: 'Excessive noises… shatter the solid bodies even of inanimate things' and therefore, he reasoned, the magnitude of the *musica universalis* would obliterate the human body – like an opera singer's high note shattering glass.

Some 800 years later, the idea of universal music is alive in the work of the polymathic Roman senator and philosopher Boethius (480-524), who in his work *On the Institution of Music* (520-524), describes there being three classes of music: *musica mundana* (also referred to as musica universalis); *musica humana* ('music of the human body'); and *musica quae in quibusdam constituta est instrumentis* ('sounds made by singers and instrumentalists'). Only via the intellect could musica mundana be experienced, he writes – but, in keeping with Christian theology, universal music and earthbound audible music both evinced the symmetrical perfection of God.

Along with Nicolaus Copernicus (1473-1543), Tycho Brahe (1546-1601) and the other astronomers battling to develop a more accurate cosmovision in the second half of the sixteenth and first half of the seventeenth centuries, several figures possessed of wildly eccentric ideas also tangled with the musica universalis concept.

22 | *Madman's Orchestra*

discrimina　p̄ monochordū

BOETIVS

Consul & genus scrutator phylosophiæ. Vt iudex vocum　　Iudicat aure sonum. p̄ currentē indice neruum.

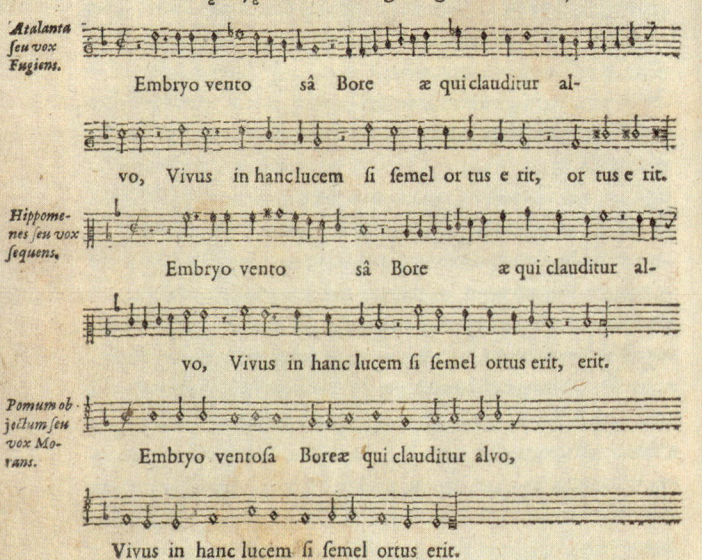

This chapter opened with a striking image of the infinite nothingness before the universe existed, from Robert Fludd's *Utriusque Cosmi...*, 1617-26, a remarkable universal work that begins with an illustrated description of the creation of the cosmos and from there only increases in ambition. Fludd (1574-1637) was an English physician and occultist, who in *Utriusque Cosmi...* brings his alternative approach not just to cosmology and the divine but also to musicology and harmonics. At the core of his beliefs was the hermetic principle of correspondences between man (the microcosm) and the universe (the macrocosm), and how the two were related in proportion and harmony – 'as above, so below'. Pythagorean philosophy formed the basis of his claim to the existence of the musica mundana that permeated and underpinned every creation in the universe. This he supported with magnificent geometric and alchemical illustrations that ripple with flames and crackle

Renaissance alchemists often expressed their ideas through music. This example of the music of alchemy is from Michael Maier's (1568-1622) Atalanta Fugiens, *1617. Each of the fifty discourses in the alchemist's collection are accompanied by a fugue for three voices, as well as prose, poetry and an emblematic illustration, which makes it an early example of multimedia.*

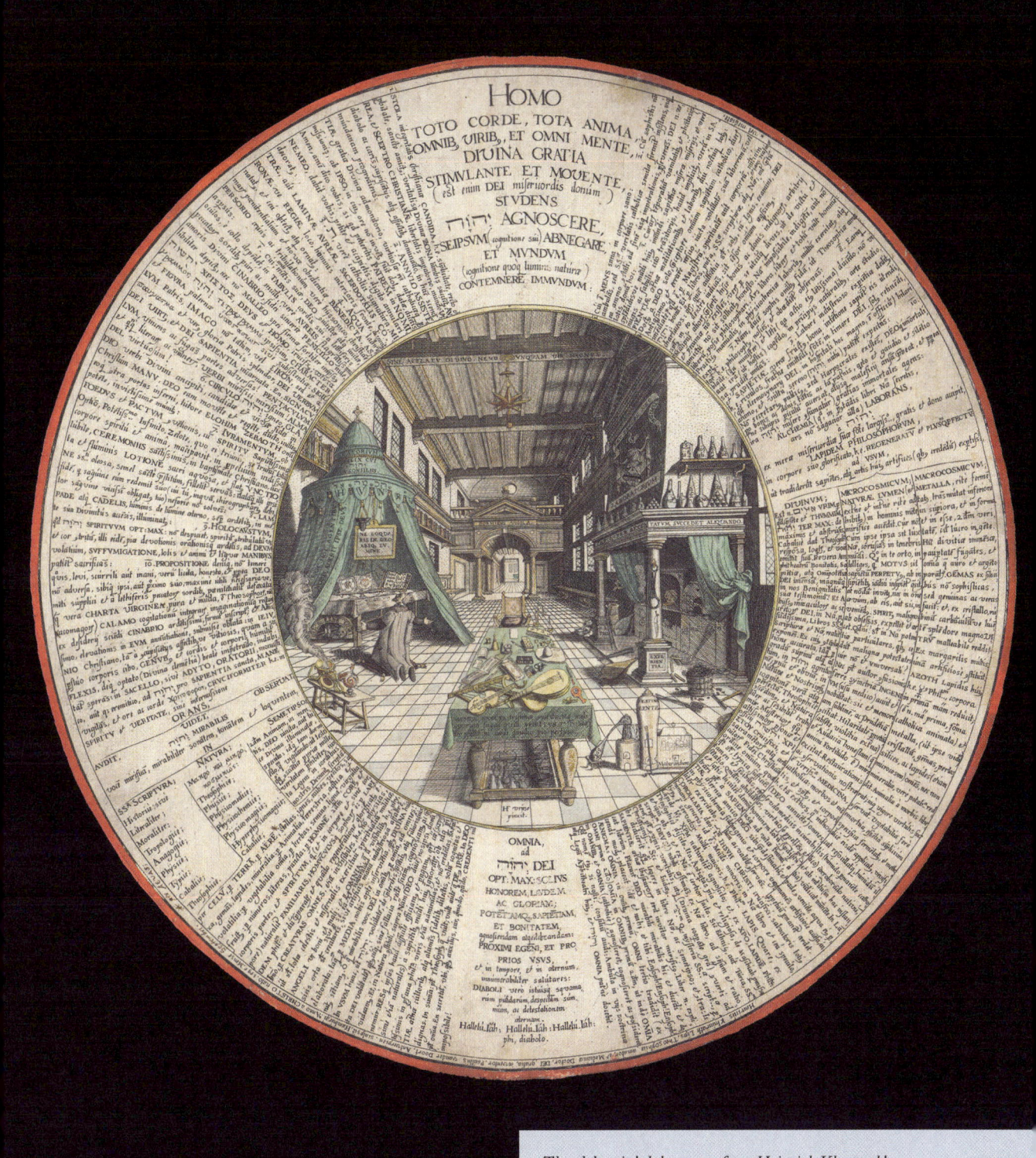

The alchemist's laboratory, from Heinrich Khunrath's Amphitheatre of Eternal Wisdom, *1595. The table inscription reads: 'Sacred music disperses sadness and malignant spirits.'*

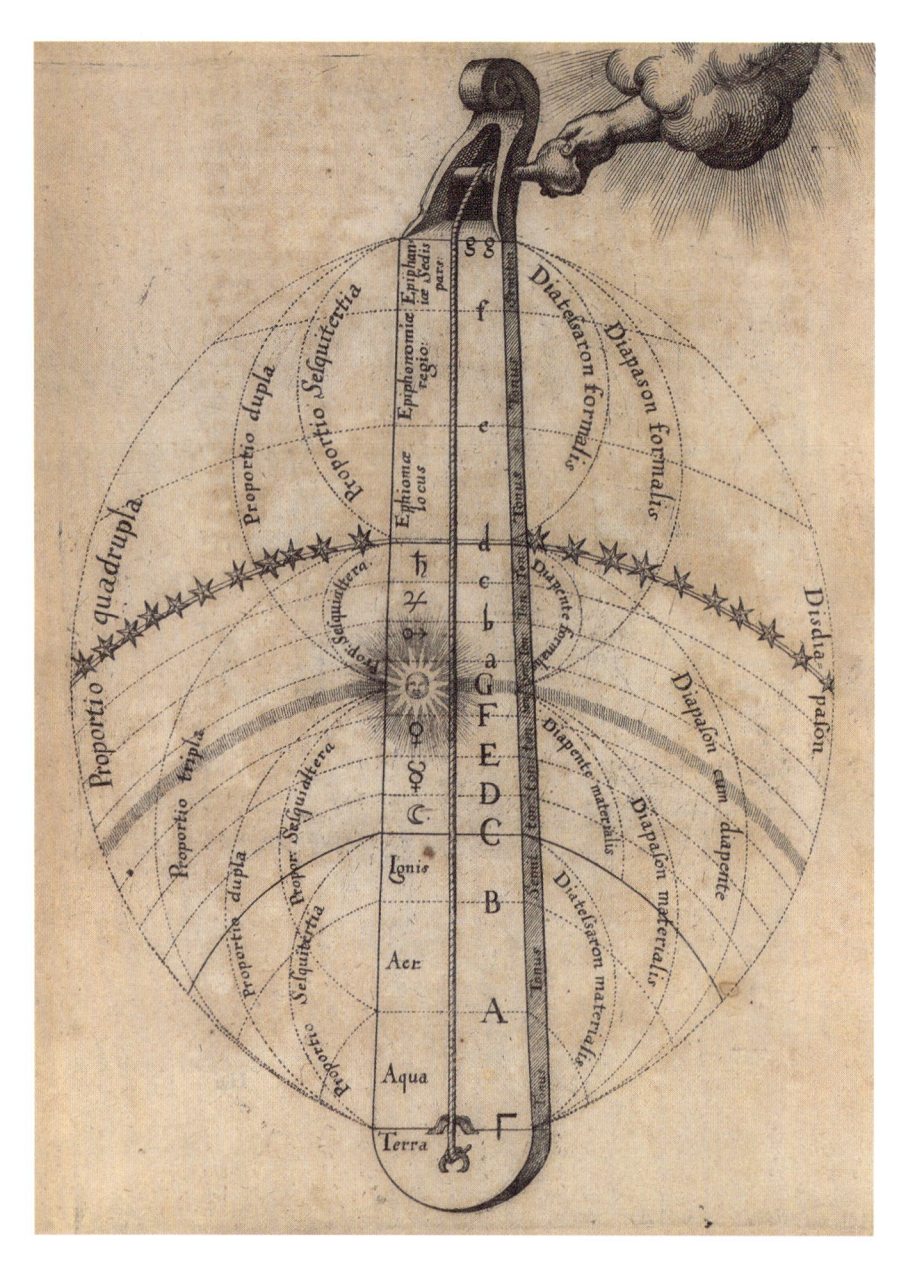

with cosmic power, commissioned from the artists Matthäus Merian (1593-1650) and Johann Theodor de Bry (1561-1623). See, for example, the accompanying image of a 'cosmic lyre' or 'mono-cord', a single-stringed instrument annotated with the proportions of consonances and cosmic harmonies of Pythagorean philosophy. The octaves of the string are a metaphor for the universe, with a scale that runs from Earth up through the spheres, the elements, light, angelic hierarchies to God, with a celestial hand usefully emerging from the cloud at the top to fine-tune the instrument's string.

The cosmic lyre, or Pythagorean mono-cord, from Robert Fludd's Utriusque Cosmi….

26 | *Madman's Orchestra*

Even more magnificent is Fludd's design for a Temple of Music, a gigantic palatial monument to musical theory. Scales and musical symbols and divisions of the Pythagorean scale decorate its pillared walls, while little vignettes reward the eagle-eyed reader: in one alcove, for example, the muse Thalia conducts a music lesson with a baton, pointing out notes of a three-part composition (referred to by scholars as 'Dr Fludd's Dream'), thought to have been composed by Fludd. In a ground-floor room, Pythagoras (or perhaps Fludd?) stands in the doorway and listens to the blacksmith hammering an anvil musically, as per the legend. In the upper-left section, Apollo strums his lyre, symbolising harmony; while above him, perched on an hourglass balanced on the clocktower with a scythe in his hand, stands Saturn, representing both rhythm and the finite quantity of mortality. Forming the principal tower of the Temple are the circles of the spheres and a spiral of air motion, above two open doors resembling keyholes that look like human ears. The diagram serves as a mnemonic to aid the reader's memorisation of the key themes.♪

Fludd's reliance on the Kabbala, astrology, alchemy and traditions of the occult meant he was dismissed by contemporaries as a magician, especially after he published a defence of the Rosicrucian Order (who, among their claims, boasted of possessing a singing technique that could conjure precious jewels into being and control the world's monarchs). In his defence of the order, Fludd confirms the existence of 'wonderful music of true and mysterious power in every creature both animate and inanimate'.

Chief among Fludd's critics was the German astronomer Johannes Kepler (1571-1630), who devotes an appendix in his great work *Harmonices Mundi* ('Harmony of the World'), 1619, to lambasting Fludd and his 'absurd' ideas. A former Lutheran minister, Kepler found little merit in the weirder occult influences in Fludd's work, instead championing his own purely mathematical world system also founded in Pythagorean theories of harmony. At the same time, Kepler takes a firm grip on the idea of a musical universe and develops the idea farther, even

---

♪ Interestingly *Utriusque Cosmi...* was released at around the same time as the posthumous publication of Francis Bacon's (1561-1626) incomplete utopian work *New Atlantis,* 1626, which features structures similar to Fludd's Temple of Music. In a world in which technology is used for the benefit of humanity, 'Sound houses' are built by the state to explore the workings of the universe, housing an array of imaginary instruments that can imitate every sound of the natural world.

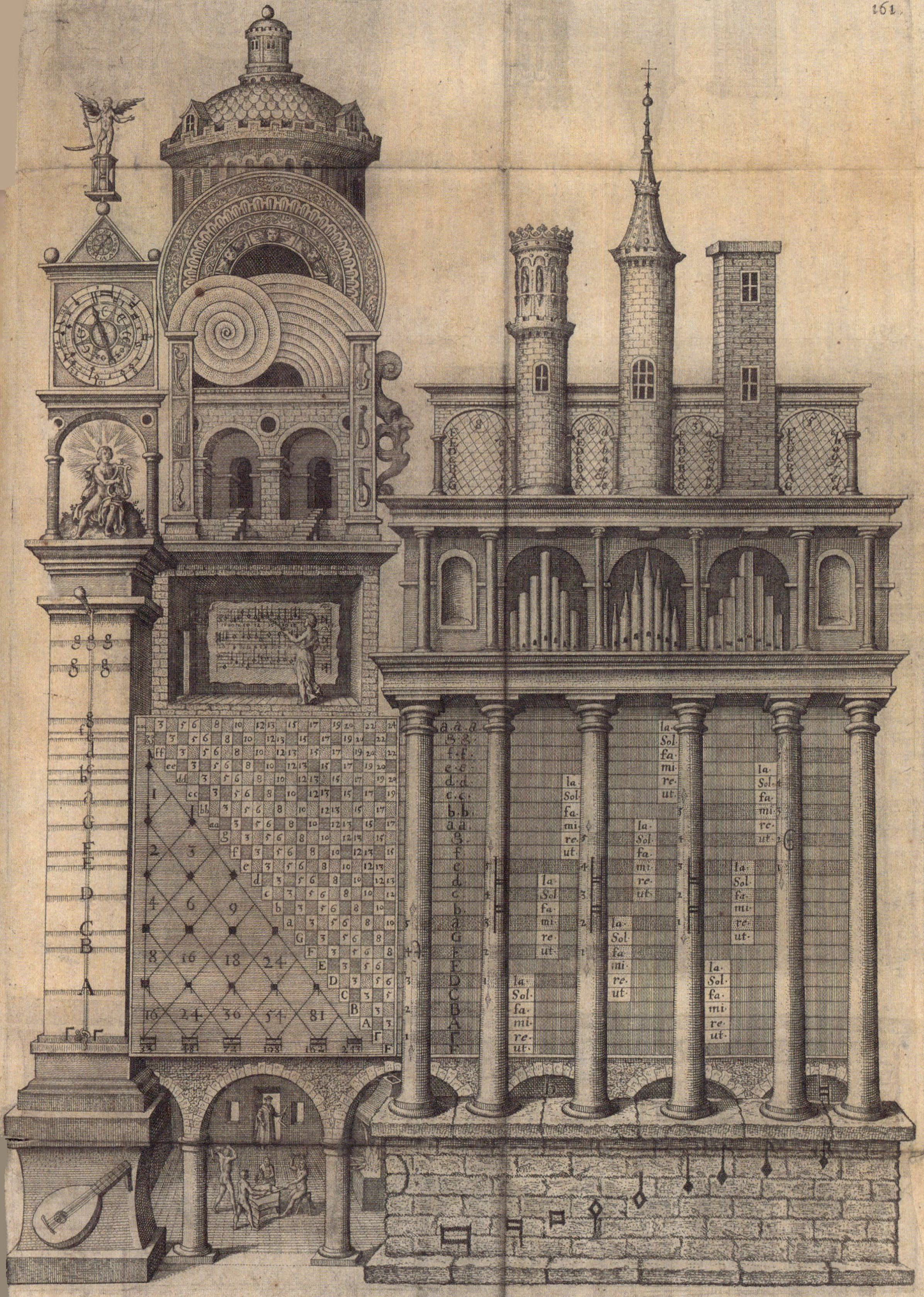
la
Sol
fa
mi
re
ut
G
F
E
D
C
B
A
16
24
36
54
81

OPPOSITE AND P30: *The Temple of Music in Robert Fludd's* Utriusque Cosmii, *1617-26.*

LEFT-TOP: *Inset of p28. The muse Thalia gives a music lesson in an alcove, pointing out a three-part piece of music notation (referred to by scholars today as 'Dr Fludd's Dream'), tucked into an alcove of the* Temple of Music *engraving, and thought to have been composed by Robert Fludd.*

LEFT-BOTTOM: *A page from Kepler's* Harmonices Mundi *('Harmony of the World'), 1619, showing the ratios of each of the six known planets and the Moon transcribed into musical scales.*

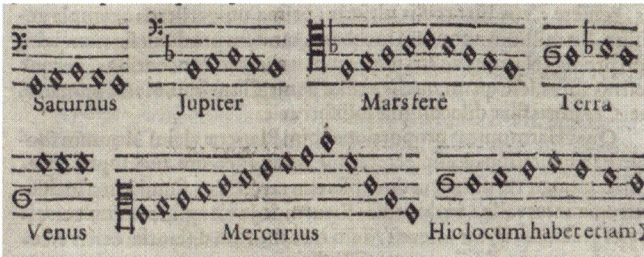

though most of his contemporaries, and even most medieval predecessors, had come to speak of the idea as metaphor.

Kepler found physical harmony and proportion everywhere in the universe. The six known planets moved in musical intervals, he claimed, and generated harmonies that couldn't be heard but instilled in mankind a 'very agreeable feeling of bliss, afforded him by this music in the imitation of God'. He describes these patterns using the language of music: the maximum and minimum angular speeds of Venus he measured from the Sun varied by just a 25:24 interval, the same ratio as the small musical interval called a *diesis*. With its huge elliptical orbit, Mercury has the largest interval between the maximum and minimum speeds of its orbit and produces more notes, in a ratio of 12:5, a minor tenth. The Earth's speed varies with the difference of a semitone (a ratio of 16:15), from *mi* to *fa*. 'The Earth sings Mi, Fa, Mi', he writes, 'you may infer even from the syllables that in this our home, misery and famine hold sway.'

From these musical characteristics of the planets, Kepler built a choir from the planets (an idea perfectly soundtracked

Music of the Universe

VIDEAMINI
1604
COLLEGIVM FRATERNITATIS
16
18
VIDEAMINI
S S
FA MA
ad fratres
Fratri
Nostro T.S.
IVVA PATER
CAVETE!
IESVS NOBIS OMNIA
C.R.F.
Iul. de Campi
AGNOSCO
Per multa discrimina rerum
VENITE DIGNI
SI DIIS PLACET
IGNORANTIAM MEAM
MOVEAMVR
OPINIONVM
OCCIDENS.

by Gustav Holst's (1874-1934) *The Planets*, 1914-17, op. 32): Mars (tenor),♪ Saturn and Jupiter (bass), Mercury (soprano), Venus and Earth (alto). In *Harmonices Mundi*, he writes: 'The heavenly motions are nothing but a continuous song for several voices, to be perceived by the intellect, not by the ear; a music which, through discordant tensions, through syncopations and cadenzas as it were, progresses toward certain pre-designed six-voiced cadences, and thereby sets landmarks in the immeasurable flow of time.' Only once, he writes, had the solar system sung in 'perfect concord' – at the moment of Creation; but it could occur again. Kepler was certain of the divine link between musical and celestial harmonies, that this was the inspiration for the terrestrial music of man.♫

As we build this library of celestial music theory, an essential volume to include is the magnificently eccentric work of musical theory, *Musurgia Universalis…* ('The Universal Musical Art…'), of 1650. This encyclopaedic volume was compiled by Athanasius Kircher (1602-80), a German Jesuit scholar who rivals Fludd for both his unusual ideas and eye-catching engravings.

Kircher's *Musurgia* is a wild read for musicologists. Describing it as 'encyclopaedic' is almost an understatement. Every aspect of music and sound in the universe and natural world is covered, from the structure of the inner ear and the science of echoes to his own composition of 'a canon which may be sung by twelve million two hundred thousand voices', and bizarre theoretical instruments and musical machines of his own invention, which often draw on ancient ideas. Kircher was writing at an interesting time, as music was transitioning from the sacred polyphony of the Renaissance to the secular work of the baroque composers. He makes the first published reference to the 'doctrine of the affections' of baroque, which states that music is ideally analogous to human emotions. In fact, we are only aware of many lost compositions by Giralomo Frescobaldi

---

♪ An interesting auditory discovery made about Mars in 2022 was that, unlike on Earth, the 'red planet' has two speeds of sound. Before the landing of the Perserverance rover, the acoustic environment of Mars was unknown; but then it was discovered that in the thinner atmosphere, the higher-pitched sounds made by the rover travelled slightly faster than its low hums. Theoretically, this means that if ever you were to stage an 'open-air' Martian opera, you'd likely have to ensure the *bassi profundi* began singing slightly ahead of the *soprani* for the music to reach the ears of the audience in synch.

♫ This output is all the more remarkable when one considers that between 1615 and 1621, Kepler was simultaneously battling an accusation of witchcraft made against his mother, Katharina. With the help of friends, Kepler himself defended her against the witch-hunters at her trial, and took her to Linz to be safe. However, she was arrested in 1620 and imprisoned for fourteen months, during which time she was frequently threatened with torture, but refused to confess. She was released in 1621, and died just six months later.

OPPOSITE: The Temple of the Rose Cross*, a depiction of Rosicrucianism in the form of a wheeled fortress with trumpet blaring, from* The Mirror of Wisdom of the Rosicrucians, 1618, *by Daniel Mögling (1596-1635), under the pseudonym Teophilus Schweighardt Constantiens.*

An engraving from Kircher's Musurgia Universalis *showing musical notation of bird songs: first the nightingale's song, then the cockerel, the call of the hen to her chicks as she lays eggs, the cuckoo, the quail and the parrot.*

(1583-1643), Johann Jakob Froberger (1616-1667) and other baroque masters because of Kircher's extensive transcriptions and reproductions of their music in the *Musurgia*. Kircher also looks back into the ancient past, theorising on the music of early civilisations, and reproduces a melody that he claims to have copied from an ancient Greek manuscript he inspected in Sicily. If this is true (and with Kircher one is *never* quite sure), it would be the oldest surviving example of musical notation.

Kircher also evangelises the *musica universalis* idea, stating the mathematical correspondences between musical harmonies and the human body, the heavens and the natural world, and discusses the unheard music not just of the planets in motion but also of the nine angelic choirs and the Holy Trinity. The chorus of the Earth's fauna is also examined in terms of its part in the universal orchestra, with Kircher transcribing birdsong into musical scales,♪ and even reporting on the beautiful singing voice of the American sloth, which he confidently declares as

---

♪ Kircher was not the first, nor the last, to explore the influence of birdsong on the music of mankind, of course. The idea goes back at least as far as Lucretius (99-55 BC), the Roman poet and philosopher, who believed that man's first notation was copied from the birds. In composition, 'Spring', the first concerto in Vivaldi's *The Four Seasons*, 1718-20, is one famous example of birdsong incorporated, while Beethoven in his *Symphony No. 6 'Pastoral'*, 1808, imitates the song of the nightingale, quail and cuckoo with woodwind. Olivier Messiaen (1908-92) was fascinated by birdsong and incorporated into a number of pieces, most notably 'Réveil des oiseaux' ('Awakening of the Birds'), 1953. For the most evocative aural morning, though, there is Maurice Ravel's (1875-1937) 'Daphnis and Chloé (Sunrise)', 1912, which magically evokes a dawn of bursting sunlight, cool breezes and birds singing in treetops purely through music.

'The Harmony of the Birth of the World' – *The creation of the universe, played into existence with a gigantic cosmic organ, from Kircher's* Musurgia Universalis...*, represented by a cosmic organ with six registers corresponding to the days of creation. The firmament, land, waters, animals and plants all emerge from different pipes.*

being able to sing in perfect hexachords: 'It perfectly intones the first elements of music, *Ut, re, mi, fa, sol, la; la, sol, fa, mi, re, ut* in such a way that the Spanish, from the moment they first possessed those shores and heard by night the distinct calling of this kind, thought that they were hearing human beings trained in the rules of our art of music.'

While the theme of the music of the spheres continued in music, it was more as metaphorical and poetical imagery. But the broader idea of cosmic mathematical perfection in music, divine or otherwise, opens up some curious avenues to explore. Certain pieces by Johann Sebastian Bach (1685-1750) are held up as examples drawing on other mathematical patterns like the Fibonacci sequence, a series of numbers wherein each number is added to the last; so 0, 1, 1, 2, 3, 5, 8, 13, 21 and so on.

The farther up the numbers you go, the closer you get to reaching the 'golden ratio', otherwise known as the 'divine proportion' between two numbers that equals approximately 1.618. Bach had no formal training in mathematics, but patterns and structures abound in his prolific output (which the Bach-Werke-Verzeichnis/BWV catalogue lists as 1,128 compositions, more than any other classical composer). In 2010, two researchers named Loic Sylvestre and Marco Costa published a lengthy analysis of Bach's *The Art of Fugue* (BWV 1080), tabulating the number of bars in each of the nineteen movements, and then breaking down the groupings of the movements. They found mathematical patterns. For example, the total number of bars for counterpoint movements one through seven is 602. Of these, 372 are in counterpoint movements one through four and 230 in counterpoint movements five through seven. Both 602/372 and 372/230 equate to the golden ratio of 1.61. 'We report a mathematical architecture of *The Art of Fugue*', conclude Sylvestre and Costa, 'based on bar counts, which shows that the whole work was conceived on the basis of the Fibonacci series and the golden ratio.'

The golden ratio has also been found in the works of Mozart, like his Piano Sonata No. 1 in C major, for example. In his piano sonatas, Mozart would arrange it so that the number of bars in the 'development and recapitulation' part of the sonata, when divided by the number of bars in the 'exposition' part, would equal approximately 1.618. We find this ratio also in the work of the great instrument-maker Antonio Stradivari (1644-1737), who appears to have applied this system of perfection to his violins (though not to his cellos, violas and stringed bass). The neck, pegbox and scroll to the body (upper bout, waist and lower bout) of a Stradivarius violin all have proportions of 1.6.

We can find the ratio in modern music composition too, with examples in both rock and pop. The American metal band Tool released a song in 2002 called 'Lateralus' with complicated structures that follow the Fibonacci sequence – the syllable count of the verses adheres to the numbers of the sequence, while the chorus has three changes in time signatures, from 9/8 to 8/8 to 7/8 (987 being the sixteenth number of the sequence). Pop star Lady Gaga also appears to be a fan of the divine proportion. In her song 'Perfect Illusion', 2016, the Juilliard-trained pianist arranges a noticeably satisfying key change at 111 seconds into the 179-second track. Divide 179 by 111, and you get 1.61.

A 1722 autograph manuscript leaf of Bach's 'Prelude in C major' (BWV 846/1), the opening piece of his The Well-Tempered Clavier *collection of preludes and fugues. The prelude is structured in accordance with the golden ratio, and is often held up as an example of a perfect composition.*

So far we have looked at the music that the universe broadcasts to us, and how the systems and patterns of the universe are integral to music – but what of the music we're sending *out* into the universe? For a fortuitously timed example, just one week before I write this, the first hip-hop song to be broadcast to space was transmitted by NASA to the planet Venus. 'YOOO this is crazy!' announced the US rapper Missy Elliot on X (formerly Twitter). 'We just went #OutOfThisWorld with @NASA and sent the FIRST hip-hop song into space.' In partnership with NASA's Jet Propulsion Laboratory, her song 'The Rain (Supa Dupa Fly)' was transmitted across a distance of about 255 million kilometres (158 million miles) to Venus from a radio dish antenna outside Barstow, California.

('Both space exploration and Missy Elliot's art have been about pushing boundaries', explained NASA spokeswoman Brittany Brown.♪)

Russian cosmonaut Yuri Gagarin performed the first music in space in 1961, singing Dmitri Shostakovich's 'The Motherland Hears, the Motherland Knows' across the radio link from his craft during his re-entry to Earth's atmosphere on his first space mission. This was shortly followed by the second song to be performed in space, a Ukrainian one called 'I Am Watching the Sky and Thinking a Thought', sung on 12 August 1962 by Soviet astronaut Pavlo Popovych aboard the *Vostok 4* spacecraft.♪ (The song was received a lot better than Popovych's next transmission reporting observations of thunderstorms in the Gulf of Mexico – he apparently forgot that 'observations of thunderstorms' was a pre-agreed code phrase denoting severe astronaut health decline. The mission was swiftly brought to a close two days prematurely by ground control.) Fifty-five years after this event, on 12 August 2017, the annual Ukrainian Song Day was introduced to commemorate this first performance of a Ukrainian song in space.

A curious story told of Guglielmo Marconi (1874-1937), the credited inventor of radio, is that he reportedly believed that sound never actually died, it merely grew quieter. Perhaps, he hoped, it would be possible to build a receiver so sensitive that it could detect these wandering, eternal frequencies from the past. From his piazza in Rome, he planned to tune in to hear Jesus of Nazareth giving the Sermon on the Mount. I mention this idea of endlessly wandering sound to lead into the curious fact that the farthest man-made object from Earth carries a musical record.

Alone on its journey across the vast sea of interstellar space, having left behind our solar system in August 2012, is the probe *Voyager 1*. Launched with its sister spacecraft *Voyager 2*

ABOVE: *The* Sounds of Earth, *otherwise known as the* Golden Record, *holding the story of Earth, created by NASA's Voyager Interstellar Message Project, headed by Carl Sagan and Ann Druyan, for the* Voyager *spacecraft.*

BELOW: *The gold aluminium cover is designed to protect the* Sounds of Earth *gold-plated records from micrometeorite bombardment, as well as carry a diagrammatic key explaining how to play the record.*

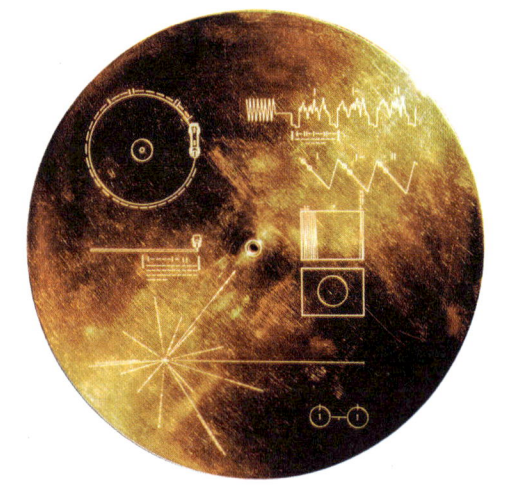

♪ On a related note, a playlist of space curiosities with 'The Rain (Supa Dupa Fly)' should also include 'Transmitting Live from Mars', an interlude from De La Soul's debut *3 Feet High and Rising* (1989). The original concept for the landmark hip-hop album was that the samples used were signals picked up from Mars, and this track is outstandingly weird, drawing on French language snippets that translate as: 'What time is it? It is midday. It is lunchtime. What is there to eat? There is sausage, no doubt.'

♪ Fast-forward forty-nine years, to 11 July 2011, and we find this musical poignancy juxtaposed with the fact that the NASA crew of the thirty-third and final Space Shuttle mission are jolted awake with the sounds of 'Tubthumping' by the British band Chumbawamba as their morning alarm.

Madman's Orchestra

The Voyager 1 Golden Record *is prepared for installation on the spacecraft, 1977.*

in 1977, at the time of writing *Voyager 1* is approximately 23,790,226,634 kilometres (15,532,654,000 miles) from Earth, speeding through the Ophiuchus (Serpent Bearer) Constellation. Composed of equipment to collect and transmit data of the wonders it explores, both craft also carry a 'message in a bottle': a golden record holding audio recordings and photographs representative of life on Earth.

The creation of the golden records was apportioned just $25,000 of the *Voyager* project's budget of $865 million. The creative director of NASA's Voyager Interstellar Message Project, Ann Druyan, worked closely with the astronomer Carl Sagan to produce their interstellar 'mixtape', compiling recordings of Bach's *Brandenburg Concerto No. 2 in F*, 'First Movement'; Mozart's 'Queen of the Night aria, no. 14' from *The Magic Flute*; a 2,500-year-old traditional Chinese piece called 'Flowing Streams'; Senegalese percussion; panpipe music from the Solomon Islands; and Chuck Berry's 1959 rock and roll hit 'Johnny B Goode', among others (for the full playlist, see page 39). Out across the universe sail the golden, long-playing records (LPs), carrying the finest music of the Earth, strapped to the sides of spacecraft expected to still be travelling among the stars long after the human race has come to its end – perhaps even for all eternity.

Engineers secure the cover over Voyager 1's *Golden Record.*

Music of the Universe

▶ PLAYLIST: MUSIC OF THE UNIVERSE

Prelude and Fugue in D major (BWV 532.2), 1710,
JOHANN SEBASTIAN BACH

'Beyond the Night Sky', 2017,
CHERYL FRANCES-HOAD

'Daphnis and Chloé (Sunrise)', 1912,
MAURICE RAVEL

'Die Harmonie der Welt' Symphony' 1951,
PAUL HINDEMITH

'Duetto buffo di due gatti' ('Humorous Duet for Two Cats'), 1825,
G. BERTHOLD

'Harmony of the Spheres', 1979,
NEIL ARDLEY

'Helios Overture', op. 17, 1903,
CARL NIELSEN

'Highway Star', *Deep Purple – Live at the Rainbow* 1972,
DEEP PURPLE

'I Am Watching the Sky and Thinking a Thought', 1903,
LYUDMILA ALEXANDROVA, MYKHAILO PETRENKO

'Il mondo della luna' ('The World on the Moon'), 1777,
JOSEPH HAYDN AND CARLO GOLDONI

'Lateralus', 2002,
TOOL

'Music of the Spheres', (BVN 128), 1916-18,
RUED LANGGAARD

Music of the Spheres, 2008,
MIKE OLDFIELD

'Perfect Illusion', 2016,
LADY GAGA

Prelude and Fugue in C major (BWV 846), 1722,
JOHANN SEBASTIAN BACH

'Réveil des oiseaux' ('Awakening of the Birds'), 1953,
OLIVIER MESSIAEN

Piano Sonata No. 1 in C major (K. 279), 1774,
WOLFGANG AMADEUS MOZART

'Sonnenaufgang' ('Sunrise'); 'Also sprach Zarathustra', op. 30, 1896,
RICHARD STRAUSS

Space Oddity, 1969,
DAVID BOWIE

'Spring', *The Four Seasons*, 1718-20,
ANTONIO VIVALDI

'Stars', 2011,
ĒRIKS EŠENVALDS

Symphony No. 6 'Pastoral', 1808,
LUDWIG VAN BEETHOVEN

The Art of Fugue (BWV 1080), 1751,
JOHANN SEBASTIAN BACH

'The Motherland Hears, the Motherland Knows', 1951,
DMITRI SHOSTAKOVICH

'The Musical Offering', BWV 1079, 1747,
JOHANN SEBASTIAN BACH

The Planets, op. 32, 1918,
GUSTAV HOLST

'The Rain (Supa Dupa Fly)', 1997,
MISSY ELLIOT

'The Representation of Chaos', *The Creation*, 1798,
JOSEPH HAYDN

'Tubthumping', 1997,
CHUMBAWAMBA

Madman's Orchestra

MUSIC INCLUDED ON VOYAGER 1's GOLDEN RECORD

Australia, Aborigine songs 'Morning Star' and 'Devil Bird,' recorded by Sandra LeBrun Holmes

Azerbaijan SSR, bagpipes, recorded by Radio Moscow

Bach, 'Gavotte en rondeaux' from the *Partita No. 3* in E major for violin, performed by Arthur Grumiaux

Bach, Brandenburg Concerto No. 2 in F. First Movement, performed by Munich Bach Orchestra, Karl Richter, conductor

Bach, *The Well-Tempered Clavier*, Book 2, Prelude and Fugue in C, No.1, performed by Glenn Gould, piano

Beethoven, *String Quartet No. 13* in B flat, op. 130, Cavatina, performed by Budapest String Quartet

Beethoven, *Symphony No. 5*, First Movement, Philharmonia Orchestra, Otto Klemperer, conductor

Bulgaria, 'Izlel je Delyo Hagdutin', sung by Valya Balkanska

China, 'Ch'in' ('Flowing Streams'), performed by Kuan P'ing-hu

'Dark Was the Night', written and performed by Blind Willie Johnson

Georgian SSR, chorus, 'Tchakrulo', collected by Radio Moscow

Holborne, Paueans, Galliards, Almains and Other Short Aeirs, 'The Fairie Round', performed by David Munrow and the Early Music Consort of London

India, raga, 'Jaat Kahan Ho,' sung by Surshri Kesar Bai Kerkar

Japan, shakuhachi, 'Tsuru No Sugomori' ('Crane's Nest'), performed by Goro Yamaguchi

Java – Court Gamelan, 'Kinds of Flowers', recorded by Robert Brown

'Johnny B Goode', written and performed by Chuck Berry

'Melancholy Blues', performed by Louis Armstrong and his Hot Seven

Mexico, 'El Cascabel', performed by Lorenzo Barcelata and the Mariachi México

Mozart, *The Magic Flute*, 'Queen of the Night' aria, no. 14, performed by Edda Moser, soprano. Bavarian State Opera, Munich, Wolfgang Sawallisch, conductor

Navajo Indians, night chant, recorded by Willard Rhodes

New Guinea, men's house song, recorded by Robert MacLennan

Peru, panpipes and drum, collected by Casa de la Cultura, Lima

Peru, wedding song, recorded by John Cohen

Senegal, percussion, recorded by Charles Duvelle

Solomon Islands, panpipes, collected by the Solomon Islands Broadcasting Service

Stravinsky, *Rite of Spring*, 'Sacrificial Dance', performed by Columbia Symphony Orchestra, Igor Stravinsky, conductor

Zaire, Pygmy girls' initiation song, recorded by Colin Turnbull

CURIOUS INSTRUMENTS

'Behold', reads the Latin inscription on the oldest surviving keyboard instrument, 'how everything contained in air, heaven, earth and sea is drawn out by the sweet melody of its voice.' The Italian harpsichord is dated to 1521 and signed by its creator, Jerome of Bologna, and is just one of a number of extraordinary harpsichords in the collection of London's Victoria and Albert Museum. Jerome's inscription articulates the wonder and pride of the instrument-maker in being able to channel the music of the cosmos through their own creation. This sensation dates back much earlier than one might expect.

The earliest musical instrument is, of course, the human voice, and while we can have no idea as to when it was first employed to express the first melody, recent research has made fascinating discoveries as to the music of prehistory. Iegor Reznikoff at the University of Paris caused a sensation in 2008 when he published a study of the French Palaeolithic caves bearing ancient paintings on their walls, like the Chauvet-Pont-d'Arc Cave in southeastern France, and concludes there to be a 'sound dimension' to these caves.♪ The areas with a higher frequency of artworks correlate with the areas of greater resonance, suggesting that early man congregated in these areas because of their sonic properties to sing or chant in community. It's also thought that this music had a practical use, too, acting like sonar that allowed others to find their way through the darkness of the cave network.

OPPOSITE AND ABOVE: *The paintings in the Chauvet caves date back 31,000 years, and are today thought to highlight areas of greatest musical resonance.*

♪ Reznikoff, Iegor, 'Sound resonance in prehistoric times: A study of Paleolithic painted caves and rocks', *The Journal of the Acoustical Society of America*, 2008.

41 *Curious Instruments*

Support for the idea that these caves were the first concert halls comes in the form of recent startling finds made by archaeologists at such locations. The Divje Babe flute, for example, was found in the Divje Babe Cave near Cerkno in northwestern Slovenia. Carved from the femur of a cave bear and pierced with evenly spaced holes sometime in the Middle Palaeolithic era (approx. 50,000-60,000 years ago), it was hailed by its discoverers, Ivan Turk and Janez Dirjec, in 1995 as a Neanderthal musical instrument – which, if true, would make it the only evidence of Neanderthal music behaviour known to exist.

LEFT: *The Divje Babe flute, fashioned from a cave bear femur, unearthed in 1995 in a Slovenian cave.*

BELOW: *A prehistoric bird-bone flute found at the Geissenklösterle Cave.*

At the Geissenklösterle Cave, southern Germany, where early modern humans left artwork between 43,000 and 30,000 years ago, a wealth of carved figurines of Ice Age animals and perforated teeth were discovered, along with two flutes carved from the bones of birds and mammoth ivory that were capable of producing distinct melodies for religious ritual, or maybe simply for entertainment. (It is a particularly rich site: in the same cave system was found the oldest known depiction of a human form, the Venus of Hohle Fels, dating from 35,000 years ago.) Birds were also the source material for the oldest playable flute, a bone instrument discovered at Jiahu, China, in 1999, which is dated to 9,000 years ago. The 218mm (8.6in) instrument has seven holes, and was made from the leg of a red-crowned crane. It was unearthed with several others, but when archaeologists attempted to play them, they emitted a terrible cracking sound, and so, fearing damage, replicas were hastily fashioned instead.

Sometimes caves – and their naturally formed rocks – are the instruments themselves. The acoustic properties of the Luray Caverns and their stalactites, for example, in the US state of Virginia, were well known from 1878; but in 1956, an electronics engineer and Pentagon employee named Leland W. Sprinkle implemented a design to convert the entire 1.4-hectare (3.5-acre) area into the world's largest musical instrument. The idea supposedly came to him after his young son fell and hit his head on a stalactite, which rang out with a musical tone. After three years of work, the Great Stalacpipe Organ was born – an electrically actuated lithophone comprising a console controlling solenoid-actuated rubber mallets that each strike one of thirty-seven specially selected ancient stalactites to produce different musical notes. This means the 'organ' is actually a percussive instrument – its name comes from the visual resemblance the natural stalactite array has to a traditional pipe organ. The operator of the organ console can employ pedals and draw-knobs, and the music can be heard throughout the wider, 26-hectare (64-acre) network of caverns. For the next thirty years, Sprinkle sold vinyl recordings of his playing in the Luray Caverns gift shop. Today, over 400,000 tourists a year visit the caverns in order to hear the organ's music.

Lithophones (instruments that produce notes by striking stone) like the Great Stalacpipe Organ have been in use since prehistory, as the ancestor of the glockenspiel, vibraphone, xylophone and marimba. Recent research into the inner circle of bluestones in the Stonehenge monument,♪ which was

Antonio Roca Várez, a native of Maó, Minorca, playing his invented lithophone towards the end of the nineteenth century.

♪ Stonehenge, incidentally, is not technically a henge. This is defined as earthworks consisting of a circular banked enclosure with an internal ditch – Stonehenge's bank is inside its ditch.

Curious Instruments

set up through several phases between 350 BC and 1600 BC, has suggested an alternative function – that the inner circle stones were chosen for their acoustic properties when struck with rocks, which might explain why local stones were disregarded, in favour of hauling the bluestones into place from Pembrokeshire, more than 290 kilometres (180 miles) away, or from the Orcadian Basin in northeast Scotland, where a study published in *Nature* in August 2024♪ revealed the central Altar Stone to have originated from. Interestingly, near the Pembrokeshire source point, the church of the Welsh village of Maenclochog is said to have used bluestone bells into the eighteenth century for their especial resonance.

This lithophone function might also have been the purpose behind the design of the Mayan pyramids, according to Jorge Cruz of the Professional School of Mechanical and Electrical

A magazine engraving from 1886 of the thirty-seven naturally formed stalactites resembling a pipe array of an organ in the Luray Caverns, Virginia, US, that can be played to produce a musical scale.

♪ See 'A Scottish provenance for the Altar Stone of Stonehenge', *Nature*, 14 August 2024.

The Great Stalacpipe Organ booth at Luray Caverns, Virginia, US.

Engineering in Mexico City. In 2009, Cruz published research with Nico Declercq♪ showing how the Moon Pyramid at Teotihuacán in central Mexico and the El Castillo pyramid in Chichen Itza both produce 'raindrop' notes from the footsteps of those climbing the steps of their exterior, as the soundwaves travel through the stone and are diffracted by a corrugated surface. Masks of the rain god Chaac have been found at the peak of both pyramids, and so Cruz hypothesised that the pyramids were devices for believers to pay homage with the god's preferred music of raindrops. 'The Mexican pyramids', suggests Cruz, 'with some imagination, can be considered musical instruments dating back to the Mayan civilisation.'

♪ 'The Acoustic Raindrop Effect at Mexican Pyramids: The Architects' Homage to the rain god Chac?' Cruz Calleja, Jorge Antonio; Declercq, Nico F., *Acta Acustica united with Acustica,* September-October 2009.

ABOVE: *Pyramid of the Moon, Teotihuacán, Mexico.*

OPPOSITE: *Tutankhamun's cursed trumpets.*

In a pyramid on another continent, a 3,000-year-old musical secret came to light when excavators led by the British Egyptologist Howard Carter (1874-1939) excavated the tomb of King Tutankhamun in 1922. Among the treasures of the burial chamber were some particularly unusual items, including 145 undergarments for the pharaoh to employ in the afterlife; a collection of boomerangs (used by the ancient Egyptians for hunting waterfowl); the earliest known example of a folding 'Z-bed'; and a dagger made from iron, which was rarer and more valuable than gold at the time, and which was only recently confirmed as having been sourced from a crashed meteorite. As well as these delights, the tomb-raiders found Tutankhamun's two trumpets, the oldest operational trumpets in the world, with one made from bronze, the other silver. Having once been used to rouse the boy king and call his troops to battle, the trumpets had lain silent for over 3,000 years until 16 April 1939, when 150 million listeners around the world tuned into an international British Broadcasting Corporation (BBC) broadcast to hear bandsman James Tappern of Prince Albert's Own 11th Royal Hussars regiment play them live on air.

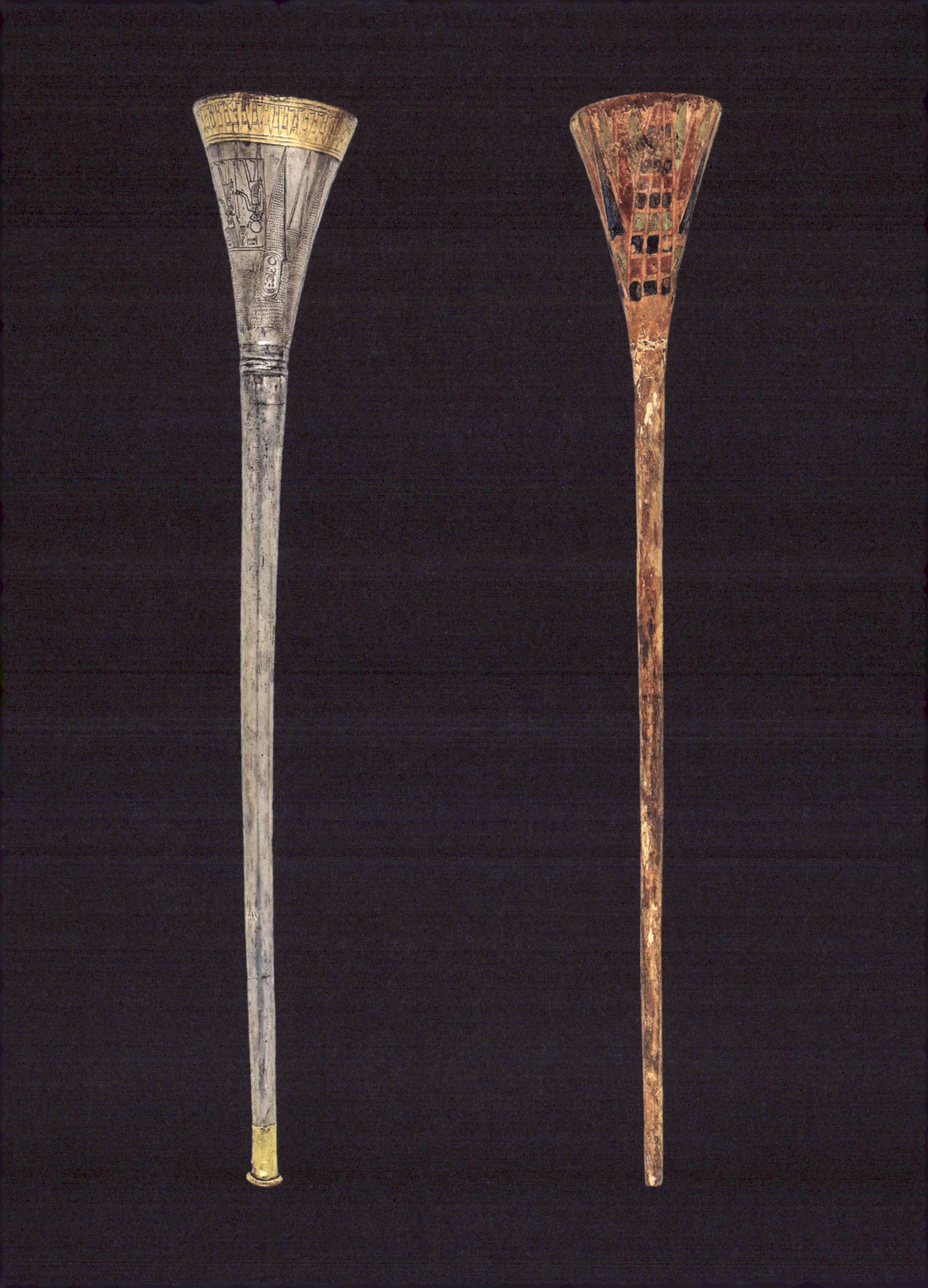

This performance was fraught with risk, and not merely because when the silver trumpet had been tested in rehearsal it had shattered into pieces, which so distressed Alfred Lucas, a member of Carter's team who had restored the pieces, that he had to be briefly hospitalised. Like everything else taken from the tomb, the instruments were said to be cursed. After the bronze trumpet was stolen from the Egyptian Museum in Cairo during the Egyptian looting and riots of 2011, and then nervously returned anonymously several weeks later, its curator Hala Hassan expressed relief because the instrument held 'magical powers' and that 'whenever someone blows into it, a war occurs'. A colleague had blown into it a week before the riots had started, and the same thing had happened just before the 1967 war and the 1991 gulf war. (Seeing as the Second World War broke out shortly after the 1939 BBC broadcast, perhaps we can all agree to not operate haunted instruments as a general rule of thumb.)

A pair of Egyptian hippopotamus tusk clappers, carved into the shape of human hands c.1353-1336 BC. The percussion instruments were used to keep time during dances, or as part of a musical ensemble. These particular examples were discovered in a miniature coffin at Amarna, apparently as a musical offering to the gods.

As well as being sealed underground, it's also thanks to the dry North African heat that the trumpets and so many of Tutankhamun's other treasures survive. Sadly, ancient instruments of considerably wetter climes have not been as fortunate. This is especially true of instruments designed to *be* wet. We can trace the earliest concept of mechanical music back to the third century BC, and the Hellenistic engineer Ctesibius of Alexandria (before 285-222 BC), who is credited with inventing the hydraulis, an early form of pipe organ powered by the dynamic energy of water. The hydraulis is the first keyboard instrument, played by hand with just a gentle touch needed to operate the perfectly balanced keys. This we know from a Latin poem by Claudian (370-404 AD), who writes of the hydraulis player: 'Let him thunder forth as he presses out mighty roarings with a light touch.' Plato (427-348 BC) designed his own water organ, which would play music when the flow of water reached a certain weight, after exactly one hour, although there's no evidence that he ever constructed this musical clock/organ.

In Rome, surviving artwork shows the water-organ player facing the audience, with his back to the pipes. When operating, the musician relied on a team of assistants to work the long-handled pumps either side to maintain the water pressure in a tank that forced air up into the pipes. There is even artwork showing the instrument being played at gladiator fights. Today, you can visit a restored water organ at the Quirinal Palace, Rome, where the water runs from a hilltop spring, once a powerful flow, but now only a stream that can power the organ for about 30 minutes of playing at a time. The water runs down through the palace and into a stabilising chamber, which is about 18m (60ft) above the *camera aeolis* ('wind chamber') in the organ grotto. The water dropping from this height generates sufficient wind to power the restored six-stop instrument.♪

Like the trumpets of Tutankhamun, the ancient carnyx was a bronze wind instrument used by the Iron Age Celts between 200 BC and AD 200 to incite troops to battle, and to terrify the enemy. At the head of its elongated S shape, the bell was usually in the form of a snarling creature, emitting its roar from high above the ranks of fighters.

♪ A perfect soundtrack to reading about water music is the Alaskan composer John Luther Adams's (b.1953) consuming 2014 orchestral work 'Become Ocean', which was commissioned by the Seattle Symphony Orchestra and won the 2014 Pulitzer Prize for Music. Alex Ross of *The New Yorker* describes it as 'the loveliest apocalypse in musical history.' After hearing a performance, the singer-songwriter Taylor Swift was moved to donate US$50,000 to the Seattle Symphony Orchestra.

ABOVE: *Hydraulist and composer Ryan Janzen plays a portable hydraulophone at the University of Toronto's Great Hall in 2007. The instrument has also been used as a sensory exploration device for low-vision individuals.*

LEFT: *The magnificent Fontana dell'Organo, a hydraulic organ at the Quirinal Palace, Rome.*

BELOW: *A Roman bronze medallion of fourth-fifth century AD showing a hydraulis ('water organ').*

50 Madman's Orchestra

In the aquatic section of a musical curiosity cabinet, we should also add the cruder instrument popular in Europe known as the *Glasspiel* or verrillon, which was made by filling beer glasses with different amounts of water. The glasses were hit with wooden mallets shaped like spoons to produce a musical medley. It was from watching a Glasspiel performance during a visit to London in 1757 that Benjamin Franklin was inspired to build his own equivalent, the glass armonica, in 1761. This is a series of glass bowls or goblets half submerged in water that increase in size, mounted on a spindle spun by a foot treadle. As the bowls spin, they produce different musical tones by means of friction from the player's fingertips, making it a close relative also of the glass harp, in which the rims of wine glasses holding water are rubbed to produce sound.

A balnaphone (from the Greek balnea *meaning 'bath') in the snow, 5 February 2011. The hydraulist is immersed in the same fluid used by the instrument, keeping warm while playing.*

ABOVE: *A glass armonica and its operator, Dean Shostak, in 2007.*

OPPOSITE: *The manuscript score of 'Aquarium', the seventh movement of Camille Saint-Saens' The Carnival of the Animals – the top stave is a part for glass armonica.*

Marie Antoinette (1755-93) took lessons in playing the glass armonica. Franz Mesmer (1734-1815) entranced his patients by playing with its soothing voice, which also inspired the Swiss composer Franz Xaver Joseph Peter Schnyder von Wartensee (1786-1868) to write 'Der durch Musik *überwun-dene* Wüterich' ('The Angry Man Calmed by Music'), 1830, in which the glass armonica calms the volatile temper of the pianoforte. Ludwig van Beethoven (1770-1827), Gaetano Donizetti (1797-1848) and Richard Strauss (1864-1949) all composed for it, as did Camille Saint-Saëns (1835-1921), who wrote a part for the water music of the glass armonica in 'Aquarium', the seventh movement of his humorous musical suite *The Carnival of the Animals*. By this point, the instrument was more of an obscure curiosity, however, having fallen out of popularity in the nineteenth century owing to changing music tastes, but also because of the baseless rumour popularised by the German music critic Johann Rochlitz that touching its glass caused lead poisoning and drove its players insane.

Lead poisoning is of little concern to the Norwegian musician Terje Isungset (b.1964) – a greater threat is frostbite. Hailed by CNN as the 'first and only ice musician in the world', Isungset leads an orchestra of instruments made entirely from ice, from the trumpet he plays himself while wearing thick mittens, to a xylophone of bars cut from a Norwegian lake with a chainsaw. He has credited the idea to being commissioned to compose and play in a frozen waterfall for the Lillehammer winter festival of 1999, and today performs around fifty indoor ice concerts each

AQVARIVM

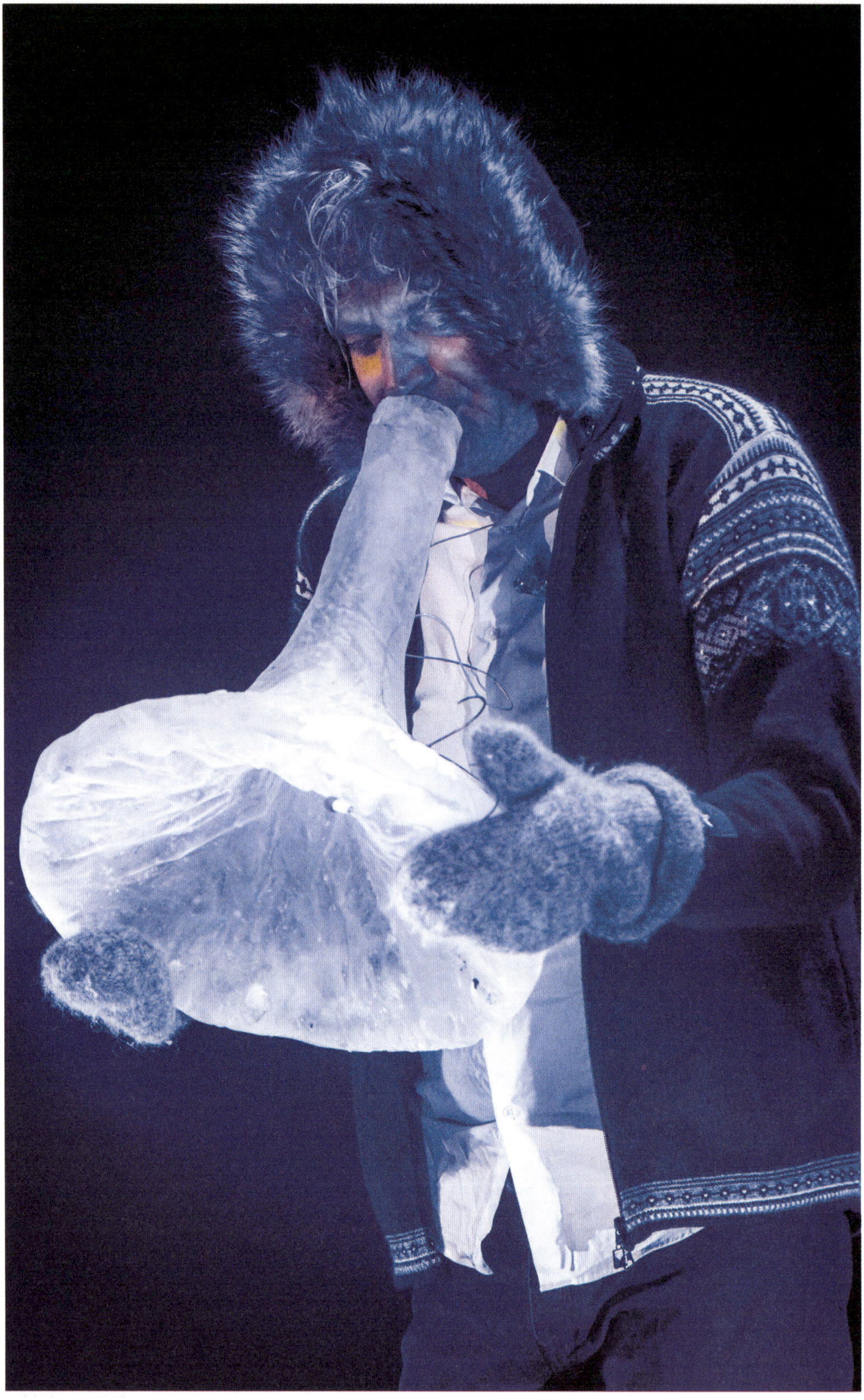

year. In 2006, Isungset founded the Ice Music Festival Norway, where visitors come from around the world to witness performances of the ice kantele, ice didgeridoo, ice harp, ice udu, ice drum, ice balafon, ice hardanger fiddle, tub ice, ice leik, ice bass, ice ofon, ice trumpet, ice horn and ice percussion.

Isungset has referred to his frozen instruments as 'the only instruments you can drink after you've finished playing,' which isn't *quite* accurate, as the Vienna Vegetable Orchestra can attest when blending their instruments into soup for the audience to enjoy as an encore at their performances. Founded in 1998, the ten members of the Vegetable Orchestra play an array of instruments constructed entirely from fresh carrots, celery, peppers, squash, courgette and other raw vegetables an hour before each show. More than 150 types of instruments have been incorporated in their repertoire, including carrot xylophones, radish bass flutes, pumpkin drums, leek violins and onion maracas. The group perform around thirty shows a year, and hold the Guinness World Record for 'Most Concerts by a Vegetable Orchestra'. There is some precedent to this. Sudanese drums, for example, are often made out of baobab fruit. In 1975,

ABOVE: *The Vienna Vegetable Orchestra perform with instruments made of vegetables, during Turkey's first international ecology festival, ECOFEST, in June 2012.*

OPPOSITE: *Terje Isungset playing his ice trumpet at the Apex, Bury St Edmunds, UK, on 7 November 2023.*

55 *Curious Instruments*

John Cage (1912-92) composed 'Child of Tree', and 'Branches' in 1976, both of which call for 'amplified plant materials'. This was memorably brought to life in a 2007 performance by Jason Treuting of So Percussion, who played an amplified cactus by running his hand over the plant's spikes, which ivien Schweitzer of *The New York Times* reported sounded like 'a babbling brook'.

What pairs well with musical vegetables, one might wonder – how about musical cutlery? Notation knives are a rare kind of dining blade originating in the sixteenth century, with only a few examples surviving in the collections of the Victoria and Albert Museum, London; and the Musée national de la Renaissance at Château d'Ecouen in France. While there is no contemporary documentation as to how they were used, the long spatula blades are etched with music notation for singing, while the sharp edge suggests they were also used to cut meat, with their broadness being useful for serving that meat to diners. The blessing on one side and a grace on the other suggests one was sung together before the meal, and the other after. Each blade carries the notation of a different vocal part – a complete set produces a harmonious chorus, giving us a wonderfully boisterous image of a Renaissance-era dinner party.

As musical *aides-mémoire* go, though, there is perhaps none more striking than the Guidonian hand, a device popularly misattributed to Guido d'Arezzo (990-1050), the Italian Benedictine monk credited with the invention of modern stave notation. Its illustrated form started appearing in manuscripts of the twelfth century, long after Guido's death, based on his reported teaching system of using different portions of the hand to represent each note within his hexachord system – the famous *ut* (today sometimes replaced with *do*), *re*, *mi*, *fa*, *sol* and *la* scale of tones. These six words come from the first syllable of each half-verse of the first stanza of the eighth-century Vesper hymn: Ut *queant laxis* re*sonare fibris* / Mi*ra gestorum* fa*muli tuorum* / Sol*ve polluti* la*bii reatum…*, the relative pitches of which singers had well memorised. The nineteen points of the hand were each assigned a note, spanning nearly three octaves.

A notation knife created in Italy in the first half of the sixteenth century.

For any medieval German musician failing in such studies and found to have inflicted an unacceptably poor level of performance ability on the public, there was said to be punishment readily available in a more painful form than boos, jeers and the odd tossed cabbage. The *Schandflöte*, which literally translates as 'shame flute', was reportedly an instrument of torture specifically designed for the torturous musician. Taking the form of a clarinet-like body ending with a trumpet-like

ABOVE: *A simplified diagram of the Guidonian hand to show the locations of the notes. The colours indicate the three modes of the hexachord:* durum *(hard, G major),* naturale *(natural, C major) and* molle *(soft, F major).*

LEFT: *A Guidonian hand, together with a ladder diagram of the musical gamut (the full range of pitches). Both are teaching instruments erroneously said to have been employed by eleventh-century musical theorist Guido d'Arezzo.*

57   Curious Instruments

bell, in place of a mouthpiece was a collar that locked around the offender's neck, while his or her fingers were clamped to the body of the instrument to fix them in a pose of perpetual performance. They were then put on public display, to feel shame of an intensity equal to the awfulness of their (in)ability. Examples can be found in the Medieval Crime Museum in Rothenburg, and the Torture Museum in Amsterdam, although these do appear to be of later manufacture, and just as with that old myth of the chastity belt one can't help but wonder whether the shame flute might have been concocted up by a mischievous eighteenth- or nineteenth-century imagination, apparently with a particular dislike of musicians.

The medieval torture device for inept musicians known as the Schandflöte ('shame flute').

For the greatest imaginative concoctions, we can always turn to the notebooks of Leonardo da Vinci (1452-1519), and indeed there are two inventions in particular that have fascinated musicians and inventors for over 500 years. Despite its fantastically imposing name, the Great Continuous Organ exists in just three sketches on folio 76r of the Leonardo notebook collection known today as *Codex Madrid II*. Having become intrigued by the use of organs at theatrical events and court festivals, Leonardo turned his intellect towards the problem of air supply interruption halting the flow of the performance. Other master organ-makers at the time had come up with their own solutions as to how to prevent the bellows reaching a standstill, like using a backup tank of air like an emergency lung, but the problem persisted. The Great Continuous Organ was Leonardo's solution, an organ with a double-bellows system that, remarkably, didn't require an assistant to help pump the air. Instead, the organist could produce an uninterrupted air flow using their feet to activate the double bellows either side of the organ, while playing with their hands. 'When bellows *n* opens, bellows *m* closes and vice versa. The wind will thus be continuous', notes Leonardo. On 24 June 2019, the Great Continuous Organ was played for the first time in history at a presentation co-organised by the City of Milan in the Palazzina Liberty, using a reconstruction built by the Leonardo3 Research Centre of Milan, based on the notebook designs.

Leonardo da Vinci's sketch of the Great Continuous Organ, the last of three organ sketches.

Leonardo would no doubt be delighted to learn that the other examples of his most complex theoretical musical instruments have also enjoyed modern reproductions.

58 | *Madman's Orchestra*

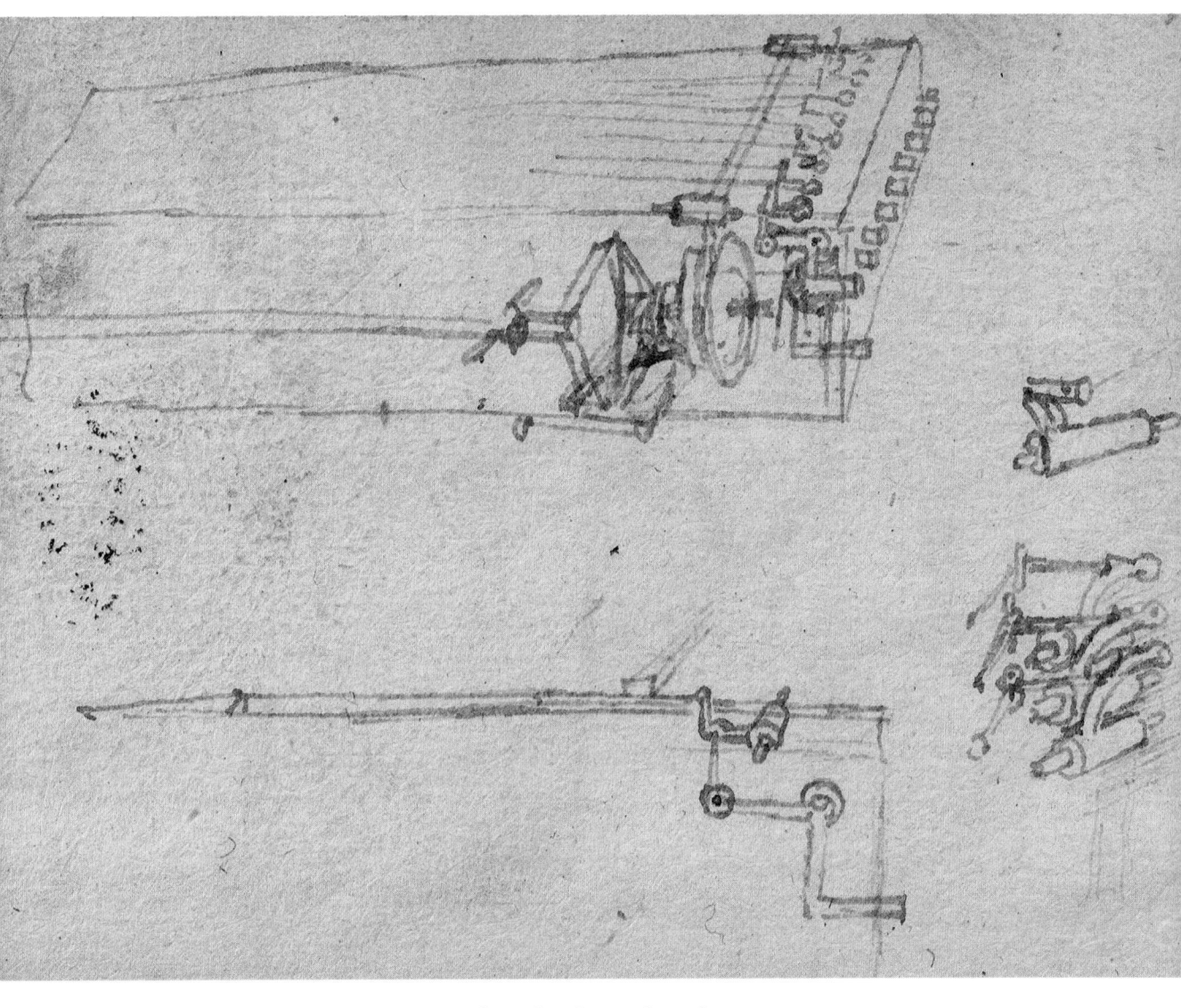

The experimental *viola organista* is the earliest known bowed keyboard instrument, preserved in the notebook collection known as the *Codex Atlanticus*. His idea was to use continuously spinning wheels to each pull a looping bow, similar to a fan belt in a car engine, across individual strings, like a mechanical violin, with the strings activated by pressing a key on the keyboard. No contemporary example has ever been found, but in 2013, the Polish musician Sławomir Zubrzycki (b.1963) completed a four-year project to build a viola organista, debuting it at the Academy of Music in Kraków and taking it on tour around Europe. One way to hear its voice is to listen to the song 'Black Lake' on the album *Vulnicura Strings* by the Icelandic musician Björk, on which Zubrzycki plays the instrument.

Leonardo da Vinci's original sketch for the viola organista, from the collection of his notebooks known as the Codex Atlanticus, *at the Bibliothèque de l'Institut de France.*

Curious Instruments

A modern working recreation of Leonardo's Great Continuous Organ.

For wilder inventions, and reports of ludicrously impossible instruments, we can revisit the German scholar Athanasius Kircher (1602-80) and his designs for theoretical instruments in his *Musurgia Universalis*, 1650. These include harps that can be played by the wind, an early hearing aid, musical automata and devices to channel public street chatter up through pipes, to emerge from the mouths of indoor statues and make them appear to be talking. There is also the first device in history for algorithmically composing music. The remarkable *Arca musarithmica* ('musical ark') was Kircher's answer to the question posed by a contemporary French scholar, Marin Mersenne (1588-1648) in his *Harmonie universelle*, 1636, as to how to compose the perfect melody. Mersenne's suggestion was to lay out every option by considering all 720 possible permutations of the six notes of the hexachord *ut-re-mi-fa-sol-la*. Kircher took this farther and proposed a 'mechanical' composing tool that would allow even a musical amateur to write four-part liturgical hymns.

The box was filled with wooden plates covered with *toni* (akin to modern musical keys) and other staves, each one linked to a different *strophe* (like a musical bar) of different syllables in length. The user could mix and match these different plates in whimsical combinations to produce an original composition of a unique series of musical notes. With its combinatory function, this primitive computer could also be used to write cryptic messages in cipher, calculate the date of Easter in any given year and 'design fortifications'. A limited number of the devices were made and gifted to European noblemen, including the English diarist Samuel Pepys (1633-1703). The composer Johann Jakob Froberger (1616-67) delivered one of the arks to Ferdinand III (1608-57) of the Holy Roman Empire, who was said to have had a terrific time creating compositions with it.

In Book 6, Part 4, Chapter 1 of his *Musurgia Universalis*, Kircher makes the first recorded mention of a legendary instrument – the cartoonish *Katzenorgel* ('cat organ') –

Kircher's design for his musical ark, an automatic composing tool proposed in the second volume of his Musurgia Universalis, *1650.*

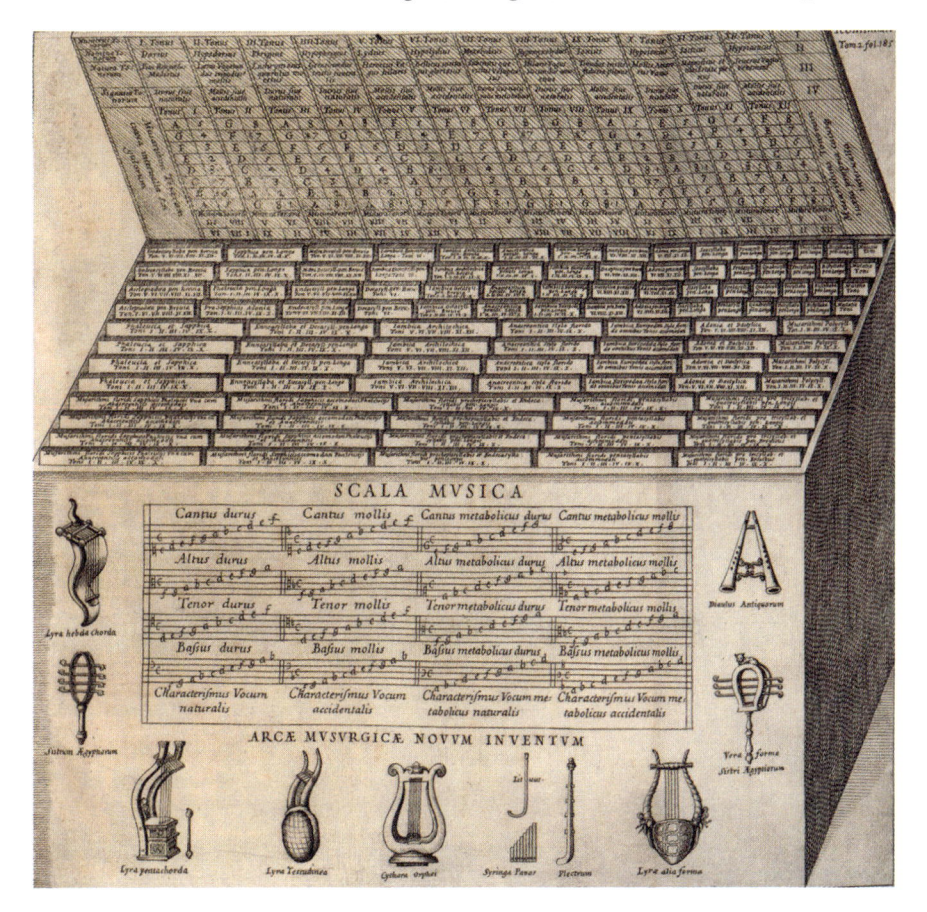

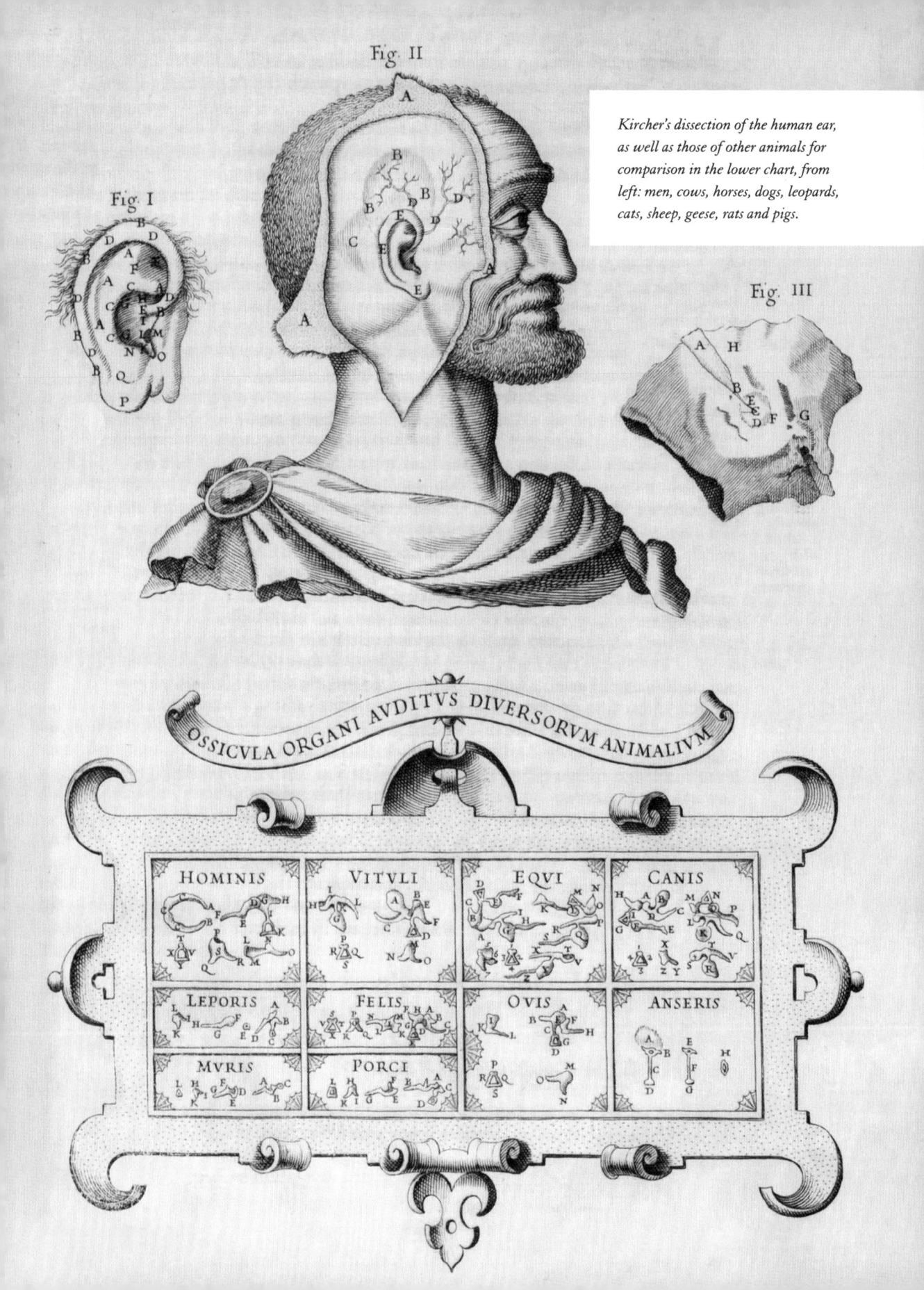

Kircher's dissection of the human ear, as well as those of other animals for comparison in the lower chart, from left: men, cows, horses, dogs, leopards, cats, sheep, geese, rats and pigs.

Fig. I

Fig. II

Fig. III

OSSICVLA ORGANI AVDITVS DIVERSORVM ANIMALIVM

HOMINIS	VITVLI	EQVI	CANIS
LEPORIS	FELIS	OVIS	ANSERIS
MVRIS	PORCI		

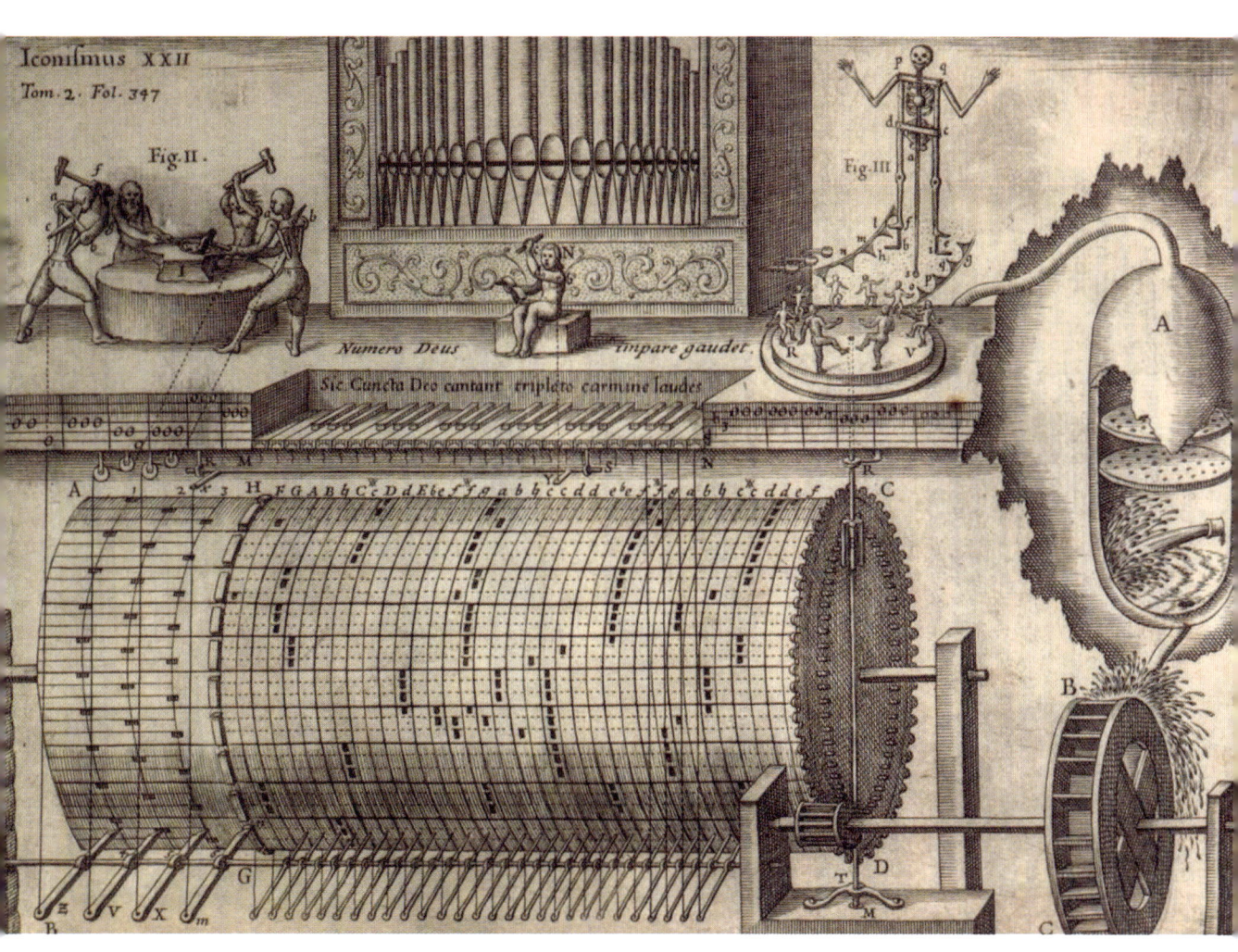

ABOVE: *A hydraulic automata organ, one of Kircher's inventions from his* Musurgia Universalis. *Three automata of Pythagorean blacksmiths hammering in turn are driven by a water-powered organ while it plays music. The motto on the organ translates as 'God rejoices in odd number. Thus, all together they sing praises to God with a triple-meter song.'*

LEFT: *Kircher's design for channelling public conversation from a piazza to emerge from the mouths of statues inside a residence.*

63 Curious Instruments

64 *Madman's Orchestra*

sometimes *Katzenklavier* ('cat piano'). This bizarre instrument, he reports, was built by a talented inventor to lift the melancholy of his prince. Live cats of different sizes (and, therefore, vocal tones) were enclosed in boxes with their tails poking out of holes at the back. Each key on the organ's keyboard corresponded to a hammer that hovered above each cat's tail; when pressed, the hammer swung down and the cat 'sang' its note.

Kircher includes no illustration, and it's believed – mercifully – that the device was never actually built. Nevertheless, the idea has held fascination for centuries. In 1803, for example, the medical theorist Johann Christian Reil (1759-1813) suggested its therapeutic potential in treating the mentally disturbed, with the idea that it could help anchor the attention of those incapable of focusing on reality. The cats would 'be arranged in a row with their tails stretched behind them. And a keyboard fitted out with sharpened nails would be set over them. The struck cats would provide the sound. A fugue played on this instrument – when the ill person is so placed that he cannot miss the expressions on their faces and the play of these animals – must bring Lot's wife herself from her fixed state into conscious awareness.'

The Katzenorgel likely fed into another magnificently weird conjectural instrument known as the *piganino*, aka the hog harmonium, swineway or porko forte, which bears a twisted similarity. Even fewer sources can be found for this instrument's origination, but it is confidently detailed in *The Gentleman's Magazine* of September 1885 by J. Crofts, who writes:

> That brutal monarch, Louis XI of France, is said to have constructed, with the assistance of the Abbé de Baigne, an instrument designated a 'pig organ', for the production of natural sounds. The master of the royal music, having made a very large and varied assortment of swine, embracing specimens of all breeds and ages, these were carefully voiced and placed in order, according to their several tones and semitones, and so arranged that a keyboard communicated with them, severally and individually, by means of rods ending in sharp spikes. In this way a player, by touching any note, could instantly sound a corresponding note in nature, and was enabled to produce at will either natural melody or harmony! The result is said to have been striking, but not very grateful to human ears.

OPPOSITE-TOP: *While the first image of a* Katzenorgel *('cat organ') is commonly said to be that published in Gaspar Schott's* Magia universalis, *1657-59. More than sixty years earlier, Johann Theodor de Bry (1528-98) produced this magnificent illustration of the instrument in his* Emblemata... *of 1596.*

OPPOSITE-BOTTOM: *The* Katzenorgel *drawn in* La Nature, *1883.*

Kircher constructed and collected curiosities of all areas of science and history, displaying them in his museum at the Collegio Romano, Italy, where visitors found 'vomiting statues' standing alongside ghost-conjuring mirrors and an array of musical instruments. We know these details thanks to Filippo Buonanni (1638-1725), Kircher's successor both as Professor of Mathematics and custodian of the museum, publishing a near-800-page catalogue of the museum contents in 1709. Buonanni brought out his own gargantuan work in 1722, *Gabinetto Armonico pieno d'istromenti sonori* ('The Harmonic Cabinet Full of Sonorous Instruments'), which was intended to be the

A musician operates the screaming components of the piganino, or hog harmonium, by pulling the tails of assorted swine while his feet work pedals connected to leads that open and close their mouths, 1805.

66 | Madman's Orchestra

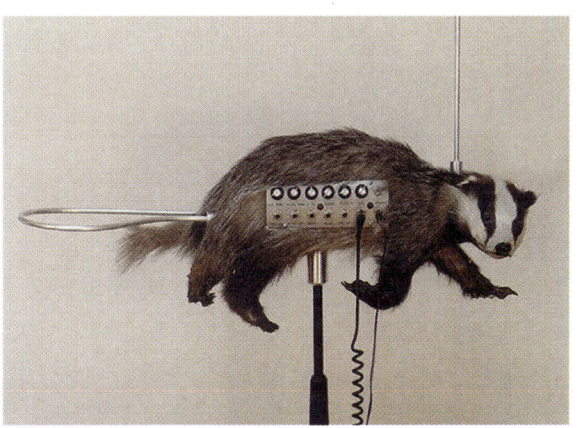

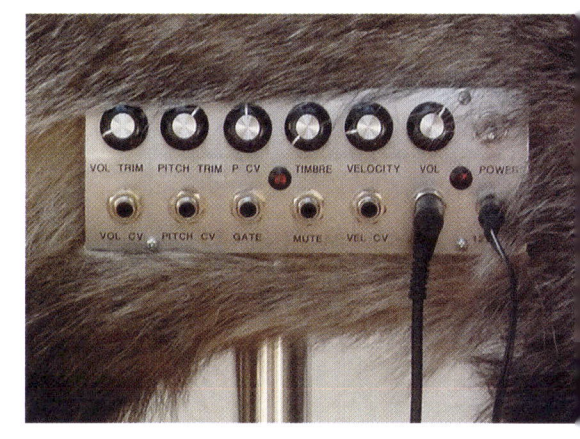

The badgermin, the spiritual descendant of the Katzenorgel and piganino. The customised theremin was made in 2012 by the British inventor David Cranmer, who has also built a programmable musical pig, a phonograph controlled by space debris, and a ticklish car.

67 *Curious Instruments*

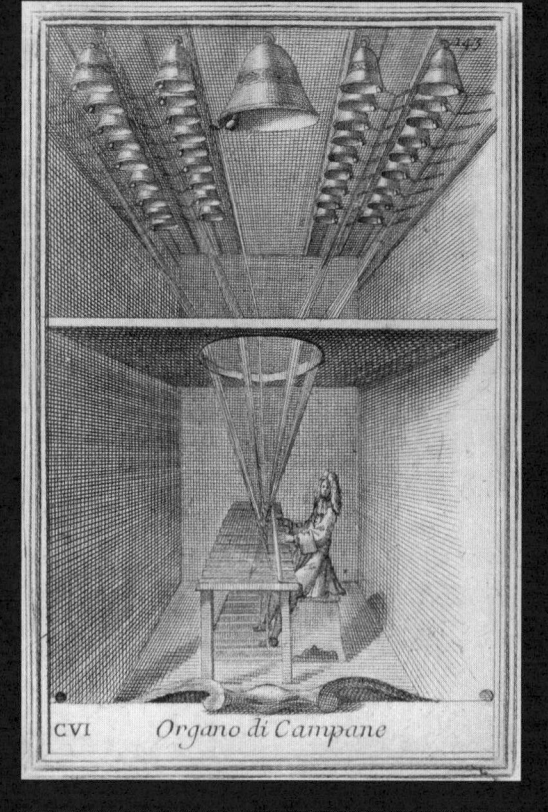

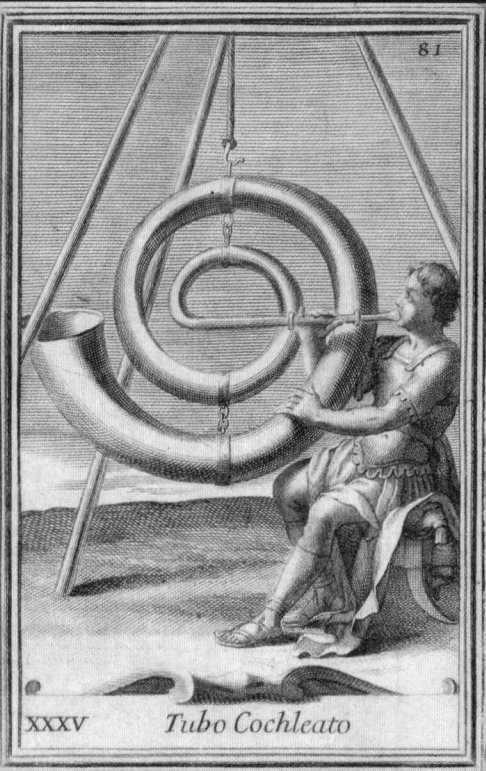

CVI *Organo di Campane*	LXXX *Tubo Timpanite*
XXXV *Tubo Cochleato*	VIII *Altra Tromba piegata antica*

XLVII. *Arcileuto*	CXV. *Rota Fiammenga*
XXXVI. *Tromba Marina*	XXXVII. *Tubo di Alesandro Magno*

first catalogue of musical instruments of the world throughout history. Like his mentor, Buonanni was nothing if not thorough – he includes the rhythm of the beekeeper banging his tub, the footsteps of shoes on a hard floor, the bell hung around a criminal's neck and the note of a soldier's sword hitting its target. He also features instruments that did not yet exist: the *tubo cochleato* ('spiral tuba') for one, which is also described by Kircher in *Phonurgia Nova*, 1673. Bonanni explains that the spiral curve of the tubo cochleato's body would amplify the voice more effectively than any other shape, as shown in nature by the fact that the ears of hares and other sensitive animals were formed in a spiral. Unfortunately, the technology of his time wasn't able to produce such a shape, and so the instrument was never actually built.

The perfume organ, a concept instrument proposed by Joseph H. Kraus in Science and Invention Magazine *in June 1922. The organist blasts the audience with scents activated by keyboard – the bass notes releasing heavier essences like sandalwood, patchouli and balsam of Peru, while the higher keys trigger notes of rose, tonka bean and violet.*

Madman's Orchestra

Facing no such technical restrictions was the Belgian inventor Adolphe Sax (1814-94), who is most famous for his invention of the saxophone in the early 1840s. This was, in fact, just one in a huge repertoire of experimental musical devices, from tinkering that began with two new flute designs and one for clarinet at the age of fifteen. Sax's saxhorn was an improved form of valved bugle, which impressed Hector Berlioz (1803-69) so much that he composed a piece entirely for saxhorns. Then came the short-lived saxatromba, intended to replace the French horn; the clarinette-bourdon, a revamp of the contrabass clarinet; sopranino to subcontrabass versions of the saxophone; the saxtuba; the four-valve trumpet; the six-valve trombone; and a trumpet with thirteen bells. Sax would continue to make instruments throughout his life, though this often came with protracted legal troubles from rivals suing for patent infringement, which drove him into bankruptcy three times.

Persistence was fundamental to Sax's character, as we can tell from a biography that is filled with an astonishing number of near-death experiences. As an infant, he fell from a three-storey height, landing head-first on stone; at the age of three, he drank a bowl of acidic water and later swallowed a pin. He suffered burns from a gunpowder explosion, and more burns from falling onto a heated cast-iron frying pan. He survived poisoning and asphyxiation from sleeping in a room with wet varnish drying, and almost drowned from falling into a river after being knocked unconscious with a cobblestone. His mother once described him as 'a child condemned to misfortune; he won't live'. His neighbours called him 'little Sax, the ghost'.

Sax's instruments live on, however, and he would doubtless be delighted to learn of the parade of descendants of his experimental spirit that stretches into the modern day. Take the superbone ♪ (also known as the double trombone), for example; it's a hybrid tenor trombone with both a slide *and* a set of valves, patented by Larry Ramirez of Holton Musical Instruments, a division of Steinway, in the 1970s.♫ To hear its versatility in practice, try jazz trumpeter and bandleader Maynard Ferguson's track 'Superbone and the Bad Man' on his *Chameleon*, 1974, album.

♪ The trombone and its variants are a family of strange names. In the Renaissance and baroque eras, the trombone was called the sackbut, or *sagbut*, in English and French, and in the eighteenth century the Italian *trombone* became the dominant label (which incidentally is the word for 'paperclip' in French due to its shape).

♫ 'Never look at the trombones, it only encourages them.' Richard Wagner.

PREVIOUS SPREAD: *Curious ancient instruments of the world, from Buonanni's* Gabinetto Armonico Pieno d'Istromenti Sonori *('The Harmonic Cabinet Full of Sonorous Instruments') of 1722, including the non-existent* tubo cochleato *('spiral tuba') and the* organo di campane *('bell organ').*

Three of Adolphe Sax's inventions

Trumpet with four valves.

Trombone with six valves.

Trumpet with thirteen bells.

72 *Madman's Orchestra*

Adolphe Sax's tenor valve trombone, c.1863, featuring six independent valves, useful for when space in the orchestra was too limited for a slide trombone.

One of only two surviving examples of the enormous saxtuba, inspired by the Roman cornu, as depicted on Trajan's Column. This bass in E flat was the second largest size at nearly 1.5m (5ft) in height.

Curious Instruments

Adjacent to the superbone we can hang the goofus, the easier-to-pronounce nickname for the couesnophone, an instrument that resembles a saxophone but produces a sound like a harmonica. The free-reed goofus has a two-octave range, with twenty-five valves arranged chromatically in two long columns like a piano keyboard. Produced by the couesnophone factory in 1924, the goofus can be held vertically like a saxophone, or horizontally like a melodica, with the rubber mouthpiece allowing both positions. The keys are arranged similarly to the first Hohner melodicas. The goofus was introduced to jazz by saxophonist and vibraphonist Adrian Rollini (1903-56), who even named his group the Goofus Five. (You can hear it featured on their 1924-25 songs 'Everybody Loves My Baby' and 'Oh! How I Love My Darling'.)

The klaxophone should also be added to this musical *Wunderkammer* – a musical instrument made of twelve car horns mounted on a table and powered by a car battery, created by the American composer Henry Fillmore (1881-1956) for his march 'The Klaxon: March of the Automobiles', which was commissioned for the 1930 Cincinnati Automobile Show.

And, finally, this collection is suitably completed by the 'junkstrument' instruments made by the modern builder Iner Souster (b.1971), who, like the inventor David Cranmer (creator of the aforementioned badgermin shown on page 67), produces experimental musical instruments of unexpected form. In his studio in Toronto, Ontario, Canada, Souster creates most of his instruments from discarded rubbish and salvaged materials that one would ordinarily not consider to have much musical potential.

The couesnophone, also known as the goofus.

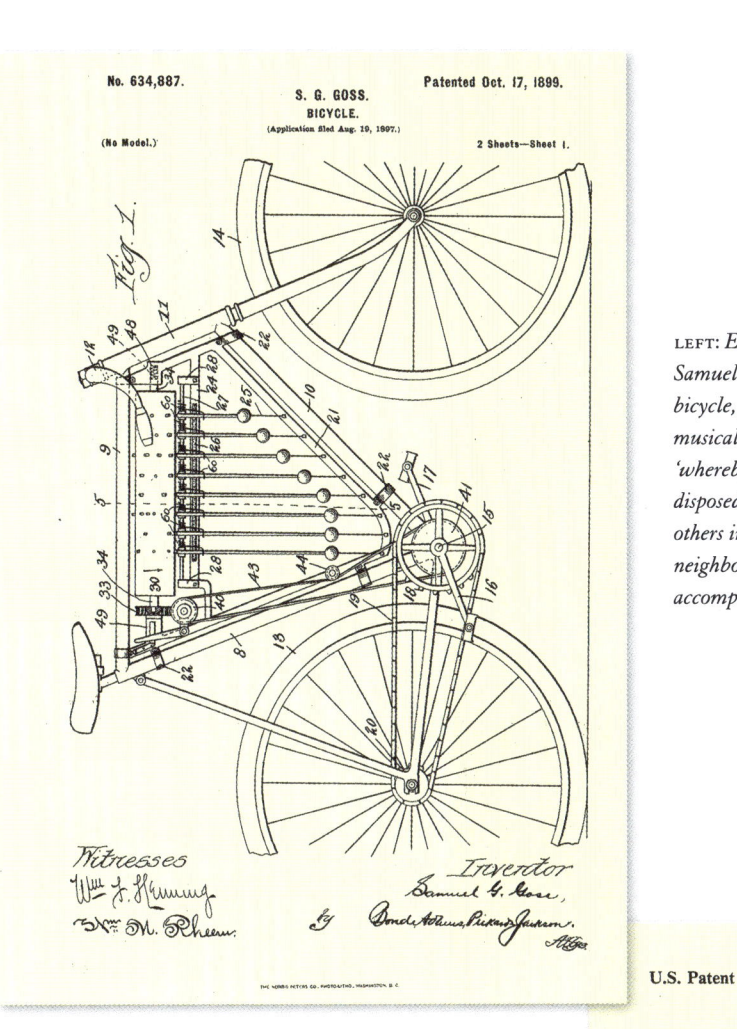

LEFT: *Even goofier than the goofus: Samuel Goss's design for a musical bicycle, patented in 1899, with a musical box driven by the pedals 'whereby the rider when so disposed may treat himself and others in his immediate neighbourhood to a musical accompaniment as he rides along.'*

RIGHT: *US Patent No. 5,163,447 issued to Paul Luons for his design for a musical 'force-sensitive, sound-playing' condom in 1993. 'Even if I made a million dollars off it, I probably wouldn't want to go around telling everyone I've succeeded in this area', he told a reporter for the* Seattle Times*. 'It's enough just for me to know it.'*

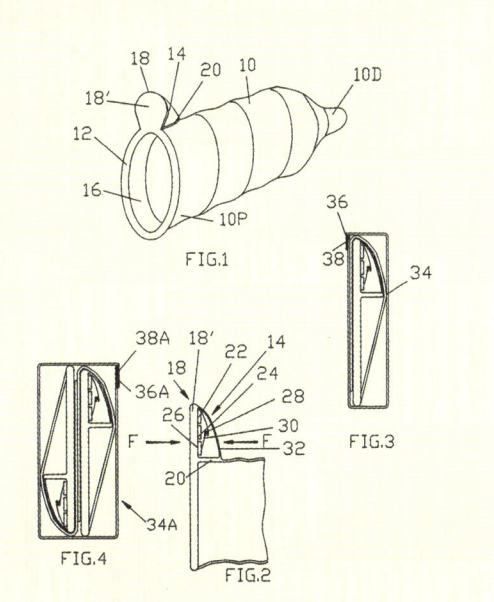

75 *Curious Instruments*

Iner Souster and his bowafridgeaphone.

There is the banjo-ukelele hybrid called the banjolele; the little noise wheel, made from his nephew's bicycle and a brass candy dish; and an Underwood typewriter with keys attached to an array of miniature bells. Most notable is his bowafridgeaphone (bow a fridge a phone), built both from the eponymous components as well as an old broken speaker, a Bundt cake tin, a metal salad bowl and other scrap metal, with thirty-six strings stretched along its body for resonance, which went through several iterations after the springs snapped the instrument apart with the tension of a bear trap. Finally, 'it all came together with amazingly fantabulous speed', writes Souster in his construction diary, before neatly summing up the spirit of the musical inventor in his last sentence: 'Let me tell you, the idea of adding strings to this thing again scared the heck out of me, but I did it anyway because that's just the way I am.'

▶ PLAYLIST: CURIOUS INSTRUMENTS

'Adagio and Rondo for glass harmonica, flute, oboe, viola and cello, K. 617', 1791,
WOLFGANG AMADEUS MOZART

'Aquarium', *The Carnival of the Animals*, 1922,
CAMILLE SAINT-SAËNS

'Black Lake – viola organista version', *Vulnicura Strings*, 2015,
BJÖRK

'Branches', 1976,
JOHN CAGE

'Broken and Blue', *Small Town Murder Scene*, 2003,
FEMBOTS (INER SOUSTER)

'Child of Tree', 1975,
JOHN CAGE

'Dance of Herne', *Dragon Voices: The Giant Celtic Horns of Ancient Europe*, 2016,
JOHN KENNY

Der durch Musik überwun-dene Wüterich ('The Angry Man Calmed by Music'), 2025,
FRANZ XAVER JOSEPH PETER SCHNYDER VON WARTENSEE

'Do-Re-Mi', *The Sound of Music of Music* (Original Soundtrack Recording), 1965,
RODGERS & HAMMERSTEIN, JULIE ANDREWS

'Everybody Loves My Baby', 1924,
THE GOOFUS FIVE, ADRIAN ROLLINI

'Forest Camp', *Dragon Voices: The Giant Celtic Horns of Ancient Europe*, 2016,
JOHN KENNY

Il castello di Kenilworth, 1829,
GAETANO DONIZETTI

'Largo for Glass Armonica in G minor', *The Glass Armonica*, 2004,
DEAN SHOSTAK

'Leonardo3 – The Great Continuous Organ', 2019,
LEONARDO3 MUSEUM AND EXHIBITIONS

'Leonore Prohaska, WoO 96: IV. Funeral March', 1815,
LUDWIG VAN BEETHOVEN

'Liadain and Cuirithir', *Dragon Voices: The Giant Celtic Horns of Ancient Europe*, 2016,
JOHN KENNY

Lithophone, picancala, 2011,
THE TRILOGY TAPES

'Oh! How I Love My Darling', 1924,
THE GOOFUS FIVE, ADRIAN ROLLINI

Onionoise (2010),
THE VEGETABLE ORCHESTRA

'Stonehenge', 1984,
SPINAL TAP

'Superbone Meets the Bad Man', *Chameleon*, 1974,
MAYNARD FERGUSON

'The Great Stalacpipe Organ', presented by Luray Caverns (date unknown),
LELAND W. SPRINKLE, SR

Togo – Orchestres et lithophones Kabiyé, 2007,
VARIOUS ARTISTS

World of Glass, 2014,
TERJE ISUNGSET, ARVE HENRIKSEN

COMPOSERS ON COMPOSERS

'He composes by splashing ink over his manuscript paper; the result is as chance wills it.' *Berlioz on Chopin*

'Rossini would have been a great composer if his teacher had spanked him enough on the backside.' *Beethoven*

'A composer for one right hand.' *Wagner about Chopin*

'I like your opera – I think I will set it to music.' *Beethoven to another composer*

'Wagner has lovely moments but awful quarters of an hour.' Rossini, who went on to say: 'One can't judge Wagner's opera *Lohengrin* after a first hearing, and I certainly don't intend hearing it a second time.'

'One ought to wash one's hands after dealing with one of his scores.' *Mendelssohn on Berlioz*

'I've been to the theatre a few times and heard Wagner's *Walküre*, from which I carried away memories of two or three glorious minutes and a whole ocean of boredom and utter emptiness.' *Tchaikovsky on Wagner*

'What a good thing it isn't music.' *Rossini on Berlioz's 'Symphonie fantastique'*

'A regular freak, without a vestige of talent.' *Mendelssohn on Berlioz again*

'Such an astounding lack of talent has never before been united to such pretentiousness.' *Tchaikovsky on Strauss*

'A tub of pork and beer.' *Berlioz about Handel*

'I played over the music of that scoundrel Brahms. What a talentless bastard! It annoys me that his self-inflated mediocrity is hailed as genius.' *Tchaikovsky*

78 Madman's Orchestra

'My fingers itch to do battle, to begin to write anti-Liszt.' *Brahms*

'I despise Liszt to the very depths of my soul.' *German pianist and composer, Clara Schumann*

'Hygienic, but unexciting.' *Liszt on Brahms's music*

On Debussy's *La Mer*: 'The audience… expected the ocean, something colossal, but they were served instead with some agitated water in a saucer.' *Marine band director and music critic Louis Schneider*

'This music leaves an evil impression with its broken rhythms, obscurity and vagueness of form, meaningless repetition of the same short tricks…' *Russian composer and music critic, César Cui, on Rachmaninoff's Symphony No.1, 1897*

'A six-and a half foot scowl.' *Stravinsky about Rachmaninoff*

'All you need to write like him is a large bottle of ink.' *Stravinsky on Messiaen*

'Bach on the wrong notes.' *Prokofiev about Stravinsky*

'I liked the opera very much. Everything but the music.' *Britten on Stravinsky's opera* The Rake's Progress

On John Cage's '4'33"', four and a half minutes of silence: 'I look forward to hearing his longer works.' *Stravinsky*

'Listening to the Fifth Symphony of Ralph Vaughan Williams is like staring at a cow for forty-five minutes.' *Aaron Copland*

'Liam is the angriest man you'll ever meet. He's like a man with a fork in a world of soup.' *Noel Gallagher on his brother and sometimes former, sometimes current, Oasis bandmate*

VISIBLE MUSIC

What is the colour of music? For some of the greatest musicians and artists in history, this is a question that could actually be answered. 'The violins, the deep tones of the basses and especially the wind instruments at that time embodied for me all the power of that prenocturnal hour', writes Wassily Kandinsky (1866-1944) of his visceral reaction to hearing Richard Wagner's (1813-83) *Lohengrin*. 'I saw all my colours in my mind; they stood before my eyes. Wild, almost crazy lines were sketched in front of me.' And when he saw light blue, he heard flutes; deep blue, double basses; dark blue, cellos; and darker blue, a low organ. In his 1912 work *Concerning the Spiritual in Art, Especially in Painting*, the Russian painter writes about the colour of the sound of a trumpet: 'Light warm red… in music, it is a sound of trumpets, strong, harsh and ringing.' Some 222 years earlier, the English philosopher John Locke (1632-1704) mentions in his *Essay Concerning Human Understanding*, 1690, a blind man able to 'see' the colour scarlet in his mind's eye: 'It resembles trumpeting.'

Madman's Orchestra

LEFT AND ABOVE: *Sergei Rachmaninoff (1873-1943) was inspired to compose his 1909 symphonic poem* Isle of the Dead, op. 29, *after being deeply affected by a powerful black-and-white print of the painting of the same name by the Swiss Symbolist artist Arnold Böcklin (1827–1901). When he later saw the painting in the flesh, he said that had he first seen the coloured original, he would not have been moved enough to have written the music.*

The term synaesthesia was coined from the Greek words *syn* (together) and *aisthesis* (sense) as a label for this perceptual phenomenon of an individual receiving a stimulus in one sense modality, but experiencing a sensation in another.♪ 'Coloured hearing', or seeing colours when listening to music, is one of the most commonly reported forms of the ability that, neurologically, remains something of a mystery. While it is, of course, problematic to retrospectively diagnose historical figures with conditions, it's fascinating to examine references made by musicians of history that seem to clearly indicate the presence of synaesthesia because it offers unique access into their universe: we are able to share in the vision of how they literally *saw* music.

Nikolay Rimsky-Korsakov (1844-1908) reported 'seeing' the key of A major as yellow. To Aleksandr Scriabin (1871-1915), the key of F sharp major was violet. The piano part in the second movement of Olivier Messiaen's (1908-92) profoundly moving *Quartet for the End of Time*, written while he was a German prisoner-of-war in 1940-1, carries the instruction to reach for a 'gentle cascade of blue-orange chords'. While he might simply have been employing metaphor, Beethoven once referred to B minor as 'black clef' and D major as 'orange clef'; while Franz Schubert (1797-1828) describes E minor as 'a young lady dressed in white, with a pink and

OPPOSITE: Impression III (Concert). *A painting of music made by Wassily Kandinsky the day after he attended a concert by composer Arnold Schoenberg on 2 January 1911 in Munich. He was fascinated by how his 'colour hearing' (what we term today as synaesthesia) allowed him to 'capture music' with paint.*

♪ A curious fact about the study of colour synaesthesia is that the first documented medical case was of the 'colourful albino', a doctor named Georg Tobias Ludwig Sachs (1786-1814), who in 1812 wrote of his and his albino sister's visualisation of colours evoked by vowels, consonants, musical notes and the sounds of instruments, numbers, dates, days of the week, city names, periods of history and the stages of human life.

Visible Music

red bow on the chest'.♪ In 1855, the German-Swiss composer Joachim Raff (1822-82) writes that the sound of each instrument gave him impressions of different colours: 'The sound of the flute produced the sensation of intense azure blue; of the hautboy, yellow; cornet, green; trumpet, scarlet; the French horn, purple; and the flageolet, grey.' Franz Liszt (1811-86) was said to give musicians instructions in the vocabulary of colour, like his famous plea during one rehearsal: 'Gentlemen, a little bluer, if you please!' According to the *Neue Berliner Musikzeitung*, Liszt also told his orchestra at one point not to go 'so rose', as the music was clearly a 'deep violet'. His compatriot György Ligeti (1923-2006) once revealed that, for him, 'major chords are red or pink, minor chords are somewhere between green and brown'. Each colour association, though, is entirely subjective. For comparison, here are the key-colour associations of the synaesthetic Russian composers Nikolai Rimsky-Korsakov (1844-1908) and Alexander Scriabin (1872-1915), compiled from their writings:

Rimsky-Korsakov	**Scriabin**
C: white	C: red
D flat: darkish, warm	D flat: violet
D: daylight, yellowish	D: yellow
E flat: dark, gloomy, grey-bluish	E flat: steel colour with metallic sheen
E: blue, sapphire, bright	E: whitish-blue
F: green, clear (colour of greenery)	F: red, dark
F sharp: greyish-green	F sharp: blue, bright
G: brownish-gold, light	G: orange-pink
A flat: greyish-violet	A flat: purplish-violet
A: clear, pink	A: green
B flat: darkish	B flat: similar to E flat
B: gloomy, dark blue with steel	B: similar to E

♪ In terms of ostensibly baffling musical descriptions, there is also the author E. T. A. Hoffmann's (1776-1822) description of his character Dr Johannes Kreisler as 'the little man in a coat the colour of C sharp minor with an E major coloured collar', which somehow perfectly sums up the musical genius whose creativity is impeded by an excessive sensibility. The character of Kreisler inspired Robert Schumann's (1810-56) 'Kreisleriana' for piano, op. 16, 1838, and the first movement of György Kurtág's 'Hommage à R. Sch.', op. 15/d (Merkwürdige Pirouetten des Kapellmeisters Johannes Kreisler), 1990, for clarinet, viola and piano.

American composer, pianist and synaesthete Amy Beach.

American composer and piano virtuosa Amy Beach (1867-1944) experienced such vivid synaesthesia that she allowed it to direct her compositions. Minor keys shared the same colour of black to her, most likely linked to the fact in childhood her mother would play songs in minor keys to her as a punishment, and so nearly all her own compositions are in major keys. 'By the Still Waters', op.114, 1925, is written in A flat major, her aquatic-blue key. The second movement of her piano duet for four hands, *Summer Dreams*, 1901, is 'Robin Redbreast', which is written in G major, the key she associated with red. The third movement, 'Twilight', is written in blue – A flat major. In the fifth movement, 'Elfin Tarentelle', she evokes the accompanying Shakespearean incipit, 'Fairies, black, gray, green and white/You moonshine revellers, and shades of night,' by dancing between the keys of A minor (black), C major (white, and therefore creating grey between A minor) and A major (green). And so on.

Synaesthete Duke Ellington referred to his band as his 'palette' and described a performance as like creating a new painting. By all accounts his creative imagination was extremely reactive to stimuli – he read the flight patterns of birds as musical phrases, and interpreted the rumble of approaching

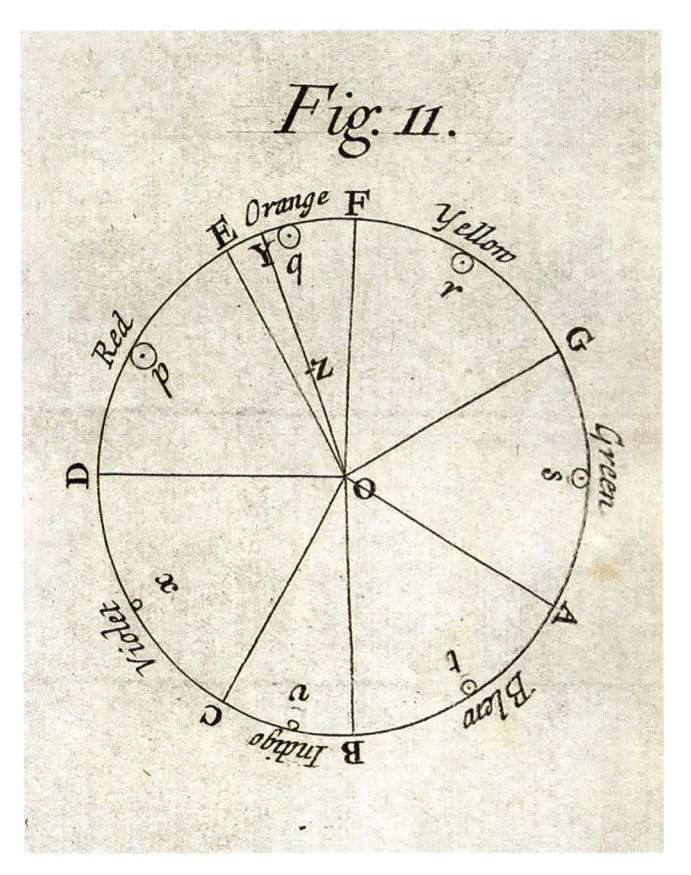

The first colour wheel, published by Isaac Newton in Opticks…, *1704, with musical notes assigned to each colour segment.*

trains as bass lines. For him, the 'D' notes of his baritone saxophonist Harry Carney were of a dark blue hessian; while the 'G' played by Johnny Hodges on his alto sax flashed up as a light blue satin. Such synaesthetes populate music both then and now: Itzhak Perlman, Beyoncé, Jean Sibelius, Billie Eilish, Richard Wagner, Olivia Rodrigo… the list goes on.

Synaesthesia is just one aspect of the meaningful correlation between music and colour discussed since the time of the ancient Greek philosophers, when Pythagoras and later the Greco-Egyptian Claudius Ptolemy (100-170) both shared the intuition to link the musical scale with the rainbow spectrum of colours. Aristotle also theorised a connection between colour and music, and suggested that the effect of colour combinations as perceived by the eye might work by the same numerical proportions as those of musical sounds.

Following his famous 'crucial experiment' in which he split white light using a prism, Isaac Newton (1642-1727) published *Opticks: or, A Treatise of the Reflexions, Refractions, Inflexions and Colours of Light* in 1704. An understated part of this historic study on the fundamental nature of light is that it

OPPOSITE: *The mapping together of colours and musical sounds, from the 1835 edition of George Field's* Chromatics, or, An Essay on the Analogy and Harmony of Colours.

84 Madman's Orchestra

COLOURS AND SOUNDS.

EXAMPLE XXIII.

MODERN DIATONIC.

ANALOGOUS SCALE OF SOUNDS AND COLOURS.

Primary. Secondary. Tertiary.

Enharmonic,   *Chromatic,*   *Diatonic.*

Genus Spissum.

ANCIENT HARMONIC GENERA.

was with musical analogy that he broke down the component colour wavelengths. The seven notes of the musical scale, before returning to the same note in the next octave, were compared to the seven component colours of the rainbow. *Opticks…* contained the first published colour wheel, with each of the seven spectral colours in the circle divided into unequal segments according to the pattern of musical scale. It is this geometric model that laid the foundation for all subsequent theory on colour harmony.

Johannes Wolfgang von Goethe (1749-1832) suggests a similar association between colours and musical keys: 'It would not be unreasonable to compare a painting of powerful effect with a piece of music in a sharp key; a painting of a soft effect with a piece of music in a flat key', he writes in *Theory of Colour*, 1810. 'That a certain relation exists between the two has been always felt.'

David Ramsay Hay (1798-1866), a Scottish artist, not only thought similarly, but also explored farther than one imagines Goethe would have thought possible. Hay produced a staggering fifteen books between 1828 and 1856 on his theories of decoding visual beauty with music. He took colour, geometric shapes, angles and structures, and mapped their construction with notes, scales, chords and pitches. This he considered a continuation of the ancient Greek brilliance in

Scottish artist David Ramsay Hay's colour-mapping on the musical scale, from his The Laws of Harmonious Colouring…, *1838.*

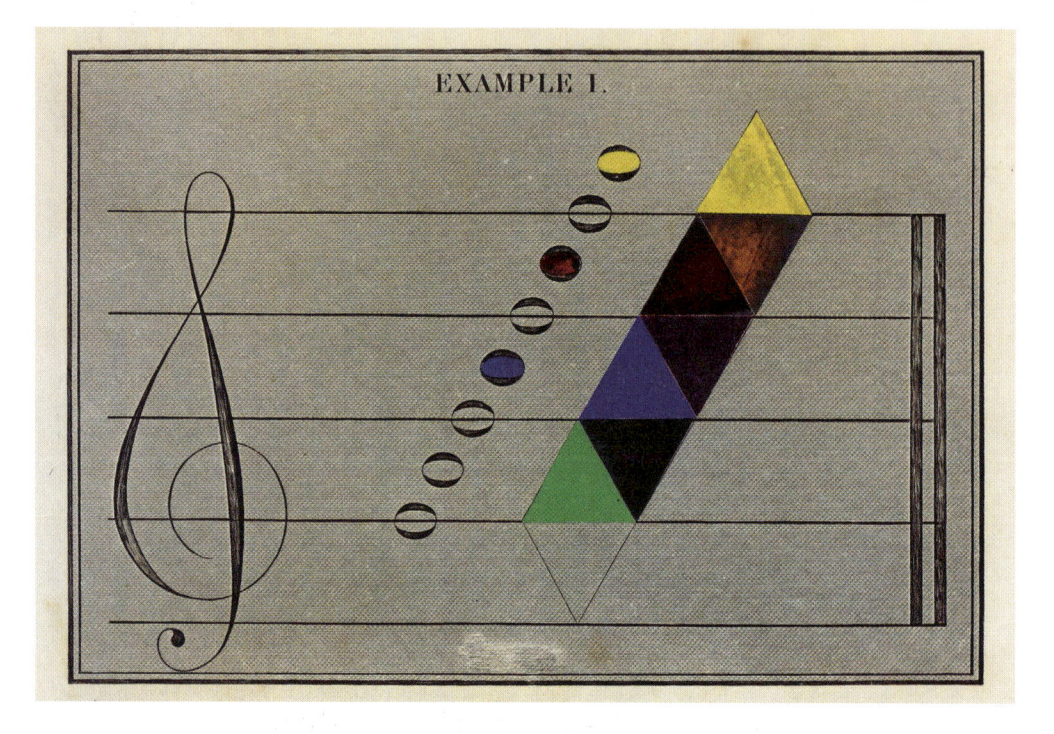

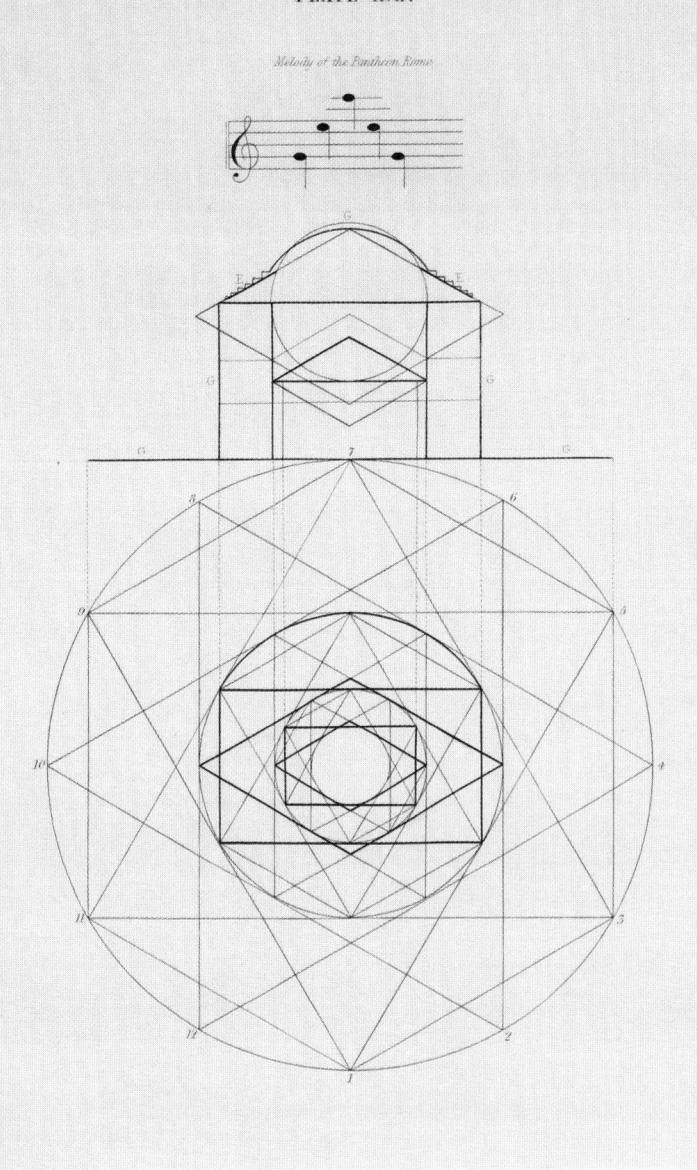

basing their design process of everything from sculptures to buildings on the Pythagorean system of mathematical harmony. In *The Natural Principles and Analogy of the Harmony of Form*, 1842, he draws a direct link from the circle, triangle and square with the tonic, mediant and dominant, which are the first, third and fifth notes of the musical scale. When played together, the basic chord, a triad, is formed. The aesthetic beauty of any object could be broken down the same way into the triad 'notes' of these three shapes, says Hay. Everywhere he looked, he saw that physical beauty in both the natural and man-made world was composed of music.

'Melody of the Pantheon, Rome' – the lower illustration shows each of the building's principal structures superimposed on each other to demonstrate their harmonious proportion. From Hay's *The Natural Principles and Analogy of the Harmony of Form, 1842.*

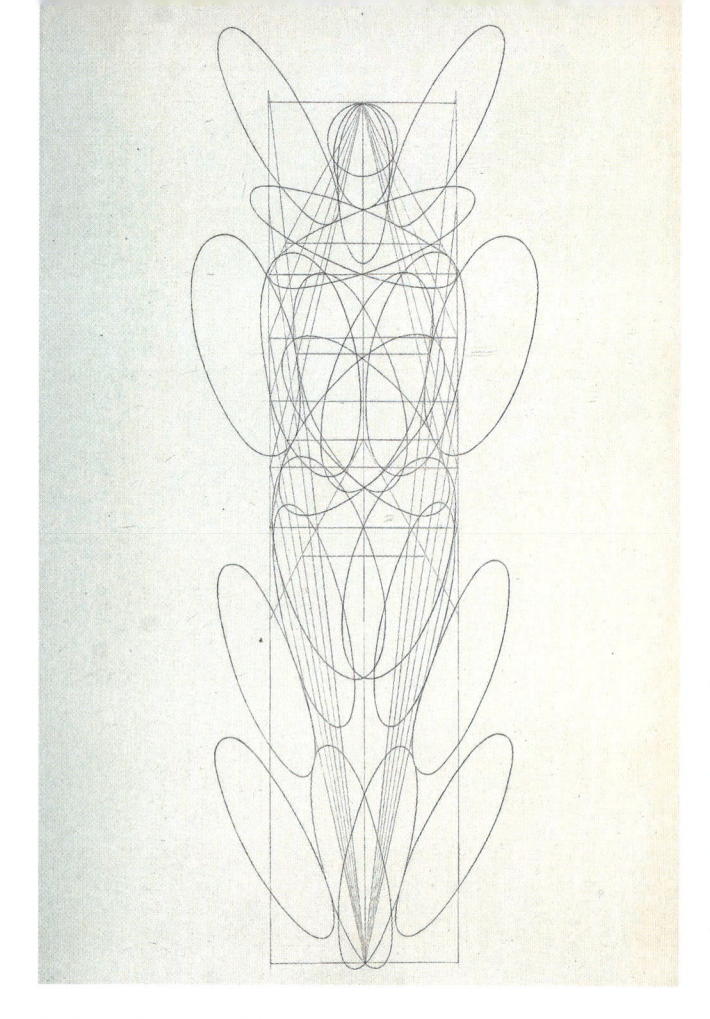

LEFT: *Hay's theories applied to the beauty of the female form.*

OPPOSITE-TOP: *A colour organ from the June 1922 edition of* Science and Invention. *The coloured light bulbs respond to notes sung by the operator.*

OPPOSITE-BOTTOM: *Illustration of Kircher's 'magic lantern', from Willem Jacob Gravesande's* Physices elementa mathematica…, *1742 edition.*

So far, we've walked through the purely theoretical wild side of musical colour theory, but where things become most curious is with the all-but-forgotten attempts to make 'colour music' a reality. Most notably, the dream of conjuring 'light symphonies' with a truly marvellous instrument known as the colour organ.

The idea of painting music with colours can be traced at least as far back as the sixteenth century to the Italian Renaissance artist Giuseppe Arcimboldo (1527-93), who devised entertainments for the Holy Roman emperors in Prague and painted the sounds of live music using notations of colour, live on canvas. Then came the magic lantern, an early type of image projector. One of the earliest adopters of this invention was Athanasius Kircher (see page 60 for more of his work), about whom the anecdote is told that he used the projector to boost church service attendance by frightening parishioners, projecting images of Death and the Devil onto the windows of their farmhouses. As it happens, it was also Kircher who inspired a fellow Jesuit and theoretical musical inventor named Louis-Bertrand Castel (1688-1757).

Madman's Orchestra

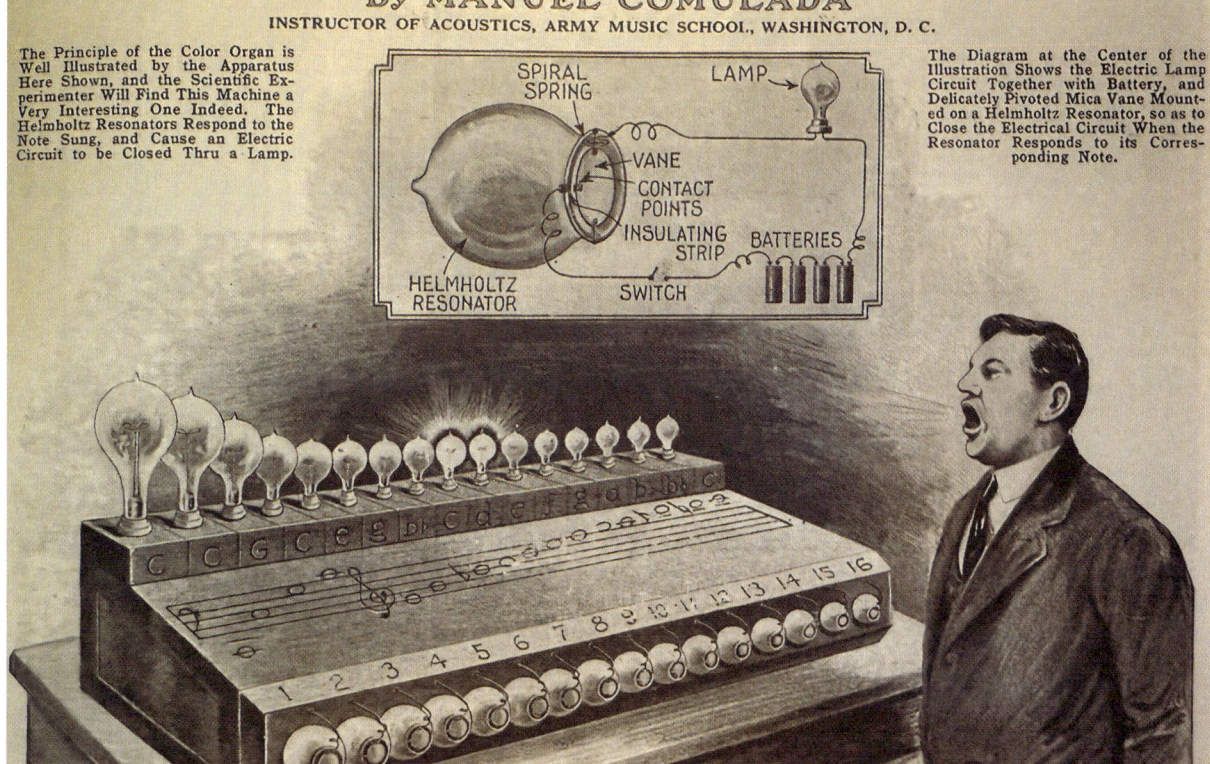

Building a Color Organ

By MANUEL COMULADA
INSTRUCTOR OF ACOUSTICS, ARMY MUSIC SCHOOL., WASHINGTON, D. C.

The Principle of the Color Organ is Well Illustrated by the Apparatus Here Shown, and the Scientific Experimenter Will Find This Machine a Very Interesting One Indeed. The Helmholtz Resonators Respond to the Note Sung, and Cause an Electric Circuit to be Closed Thru a Lamp.

The Diagram at the Center of the Illustration Shows the Electric Lamp Circuit Together with Battery, and Delicately Pivoted Mica Vane Mounted on a Helmholtz Resonator, so as to Close the Electrical Circuit When the Resonator Responds to its Corresponding Note.

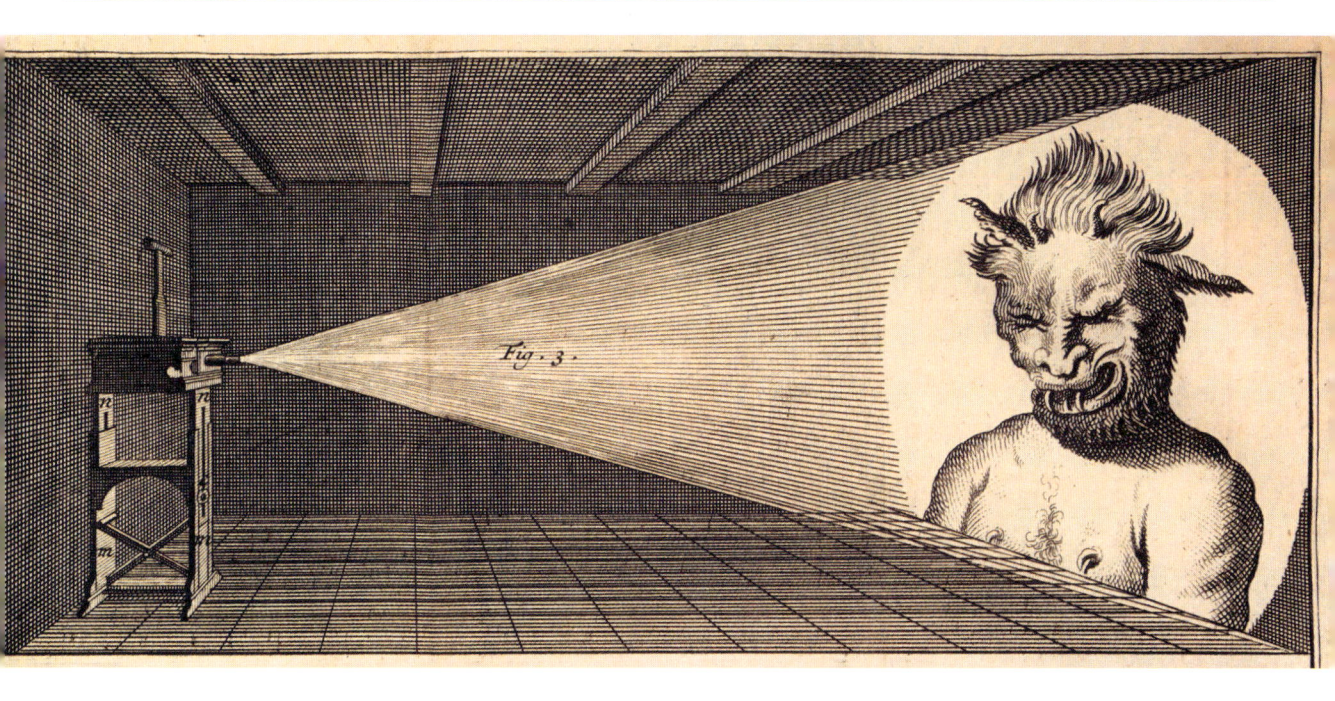

89 *Visible Music*

Castel is the earliest on record to have designed a colour-music instrument, announcing his idea for a *clavecin oculaire* in November 1725 in the *Mercure de France* with a letter entitled 'Harpsichord for the eyes, with the art of painting sounds, and all kinds of pieces of music'. His proposal for achieving this was to adapt a standard harpsichord by adding a mechanism so that 'the pressing of the keys would bring out the colours with their combinations and their chords'. Exactly *how* this would be achieved was not mentioned, because Castel didn't know. He freely admitted to being more of a 'philosopher' than an 'artisan'.

Though he had never intended to build the ocular harpsichord himself, the public interest in the idea was so overwhelming that he embarked on its creation. The composer Georg Philipp Telemann (1681-1767) writes excitedly in a 1739

A sketch of Louis-Bertrand Castel's ocular harpsichord, by Charles Germain de Saint Aubin, believed to be the only surviving illustration of the instrument.

90 | *Madman's Orchestra*

letter of having seen a prototype of Castel's invention while visiting Paris: 'When the key opens the valve to produce the tone, Father Castel has fitted silken threads or iron wires or wooden levers, which by push or pull uncover a coloured box, or a ditto panel, or a painting, or a painted lantern, such that at the same moment when a tone is heard a colour is seen.' Telemann even wrote several pieces specifically for the ocular harpsichord in the hope they would become a foundational part of the new instrument's standard repertoire.

In 1755, Castel announced in the *Mercure de France* that he had completed his ocular harpsichord and performed a colour concert for an audience of fifty (who demanded four encores), and another for 200 people on 1 January 1755. From the reports of the evening, this model of the ocular harpsichord must have been magnificent to behold: it was said to have shone beams of colour via a vast array of glass windows tinted with every hue, illuminated from inside with the blaze of one hundred wax candles. Yet even this iteration, to the perfectionist Castel, was 'not even a sketch, a beginning of it, so far was it from being perfect'. Two years later, a new iteration dwarfed previous models: exhibited in London in 1757, the extended keyboard of this grand ocular harpsichord offered a staggering twelve octaves (a standard grand piano has a mere seven-and-a-quarter octaves). Each one of the 144 keys operated a shutter over its own coloured window, lit by an inferno of candle power. Imagine the supernatural effect this instrument must have had on an eighteenth-century audience in a darkened room, with its starbursts of prismatic colours. But it's possible this model never found an audience – the planned demonstration at the concert rooms in London's Soho Square was cancelled because the giant instrument was deemed too much of a fire risk.

Perhaps with more time and another round of funding the world might have gained a multisensory colour-music machine that we would today find installed in every church, theatre and 'in every home in Paris' as its creator confidently predicted; but sadly, Louis-Bertrand Castel died that year, still refining his masterpiece. No first-hand illustration, plans nor any physical trace of the instrument survives.

The dream, however, did not die. In the nineteenth century, there was a resurgent interest in discovering universal principles of harmony in colour theory, which also resurrected attempts at creating a colour-music instrument. A US inventor named Bainbridge Bishop (1837-1905) secured patent no. 186,298 in

Bainbridge Bishop's colour organ, 1877, from a rare souvenir pamphlet.

THE COLOR-ORGAN.

1877 for 'Attachments for key-board musical instruments', a huge colour organ that featured lights shining through coloured panes, which shifted in lightness and darkness of hue with the rise and fall of the octaves played. 'In practice', writes Bishop in his patent application, 'the instrument is placed before a strong natural light, either direct or deflected, and the colors may be shown upon screens or other suitable surfaces.' In other words, it was 'powered' by sunlight. In a later iteration of the design, and with the progress of technology, Bishop upgraded the sunlight windows to electric lights, and built three of the instruments. The concerns about fire risk that Castel's instrument had caused were well-founded if Bishop's models were anything to go by – all three were destroyed in fires, with one gutting the home of the infamous show promoter P. T. Barnum (1810-91).

Alexander Rimington with his colour organ, 1893.

In 1893, the British painter Alexander Wallace Rimington (1854-1918) unveiled his own invented colour organ to the wonder of visitors including Richard Wagner, and held the first public performance in June 1895 at St James Hall, London.

Rimington's colour organ was a monster: looming 3m (10ft) high with a case of fourteen coloured lamps at its crown, it had a five-octave keyboard like that of a church organ, with a row of 'colour keys' just above it. The instrument used tinted glass discs to project individual colours that moved and merged like chords on large screens, devouring the equivalent electric power of 13,000 candles, and thereby liberating art from the canvas. In a technological leap forward from Castel's design, Rimington's colour organ could also adjust the hue, brightness and saturation of the coloured lamps, with a 'swell pedal' for the operator to brighten colours as they wished. It also came with instructions for the operator: Wagner's trumpet blasts, for example, should be matched with a bright orange,

Chromatic scale in Music and Colour.
Shewing correspondence of intervals when C = lowest spectrum red.

'which palpitates with the harmonic colours corresponding to a subordinate passage on some of the other orchestral instruments. The blast ceases; there is a faint echo of it upon the violins, while the screen pulsates with pale lemon and saffron hardly discernable. Again, comes the blast of trumpets, and once more the screen flames with orange modulations.'

The English journalist Sarah Tooley (1856-1946) remarked that the colour organ would 'flood the most prosaically dull room in London's murky atmosphere with vibrating rainbow hues, which will bring music to the soul of those cultivated

Quotes with each image on this page and opposite come from Alexander Rimington's Colour Music, *1912.*

ABOVE: *'Chromatic scale in music and colour' – the colour-music note mapping of Alexander Rimington, 1895, for the first demonstration of his colour organ in London.*

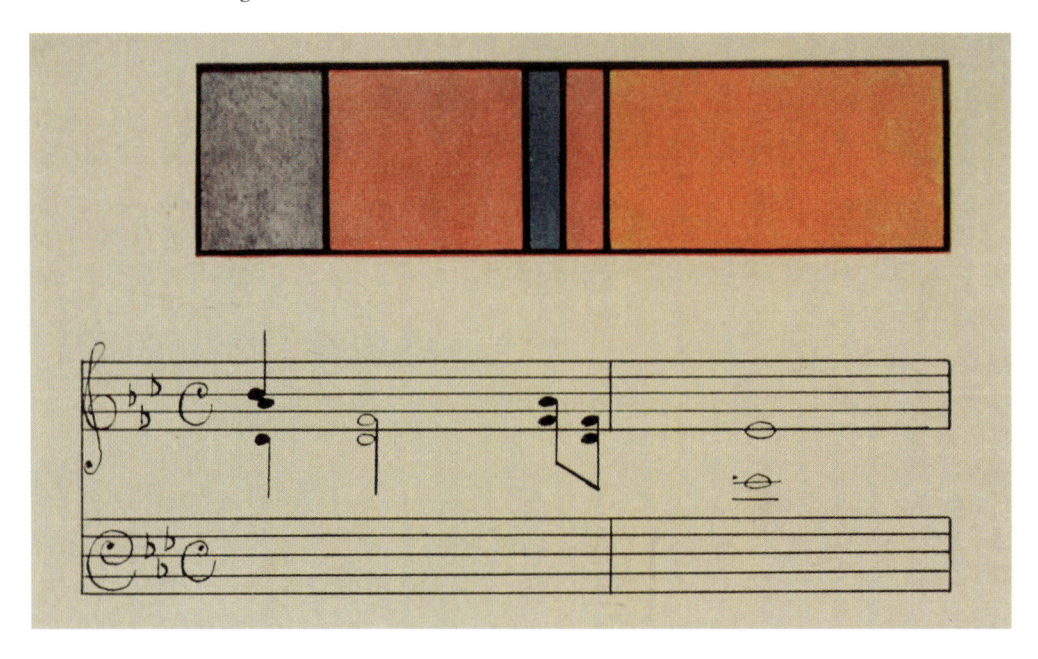

94 *Madman's Orchestra*

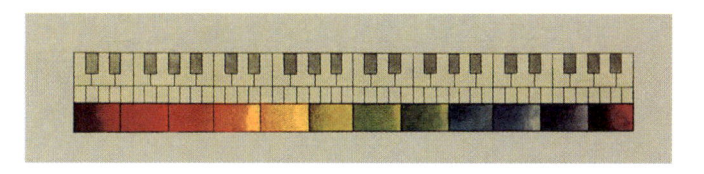

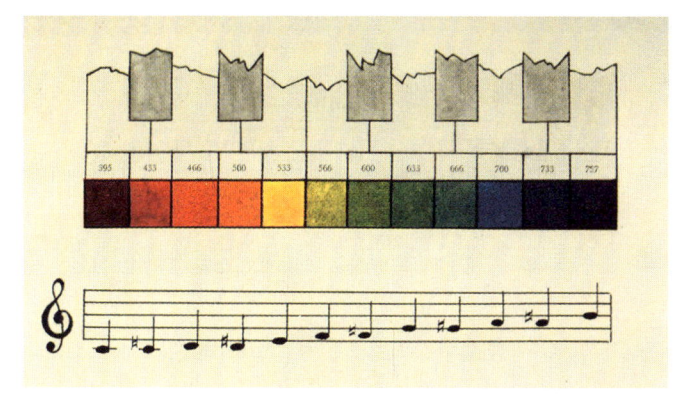

LEFT-TOP: *'To show division of colour scale when the spectrum is extended over the whole length of the keyboard of the colour organ by spectrum stop.'*

LEFT-MIDDLE: *'To show normal division of colour scale upon keyboard of colour organ, colour musical methods of execution are employed. The figures in the spaces above the colour give the approximate frequencies of aether vibration in millions of millions per second. The colours cannot be accurately given in pigments, and of course do not correspond more than roughly to those produced by the instrument.'*

LEFT-BOTTOM: *'Example of a simple colour phrase in correspondence with musical notation. Note: It must be understood that the colours are merely diagrammatic, and give little idea of their purity as actually seen upon the screen.'*

OPPOSITE-BOTTOM: *'Diagram to illustrate introduction of time into colour effects – the duration of the colour chords upon the screen corresponding to the musical notation.'*

to receive these impressions'. Rimington hoped that 'colour music could act as a bridge between the everyday and a sense of enhanced awareness of the world'. However, despite further demonstrations in London and Manchester, public reception towards the sensory overload delivery system failed to catch alight, and regrettably plans for the instrument were taken no farther.

Rimington's failure did little to kill the 'visible music' dream, however. In 1918, American pianist Mary Hallock-Greenewalt (1871-1950) was inspired by the stories of the Jesuit Castel and the early attempts of Bishop to invent her own colour organ, which she called the Sarabet (named after her mother), patenting nine inventions related to the instrument.♪

♪ One of these was for a non-linear variety of rheostat that was then copied by General Electric and other companies. She furiously sued for infringement, and won in 1934. One fascinating fact about Mary Hallock-Greenewalt is that, despite the lack of recognition her name commands, she is credited with producing the earliest hand-painted films known to still exist. These were made for an early version of the Sarabet, which operated like a kinetoscope.

Visible Music

Mary Hallock-Greenewalt, seated at her Sarabet, 1927.

With the Sarabet, Hallock-Greenewalt performed her own form of visual music that she called *nourathar*, formed from the Arabic words *nour* ('light') and *athar* ('essence'). She also patented a system of musical lighting cues to be read like notation in tandem with the notes of a musical performance, using an illuminated Beethoven's 'Moonlight Sonata' to demonstrate. The Sarabet iterations grew ever more vast and complex, and expensive to manufacture. Hallock-Greenewalt toured theatres with her demonstrations, with the consoles demanding a lengthy site-specific installation in order to fill auditoriums with the coloured light bursts.

ABOVE: *Mary Hallock-Greenewalt's patent for a system of notating lighting cues in coordination with musical performance, using Beethoven's 'Moonlight Sonata' as an example.*

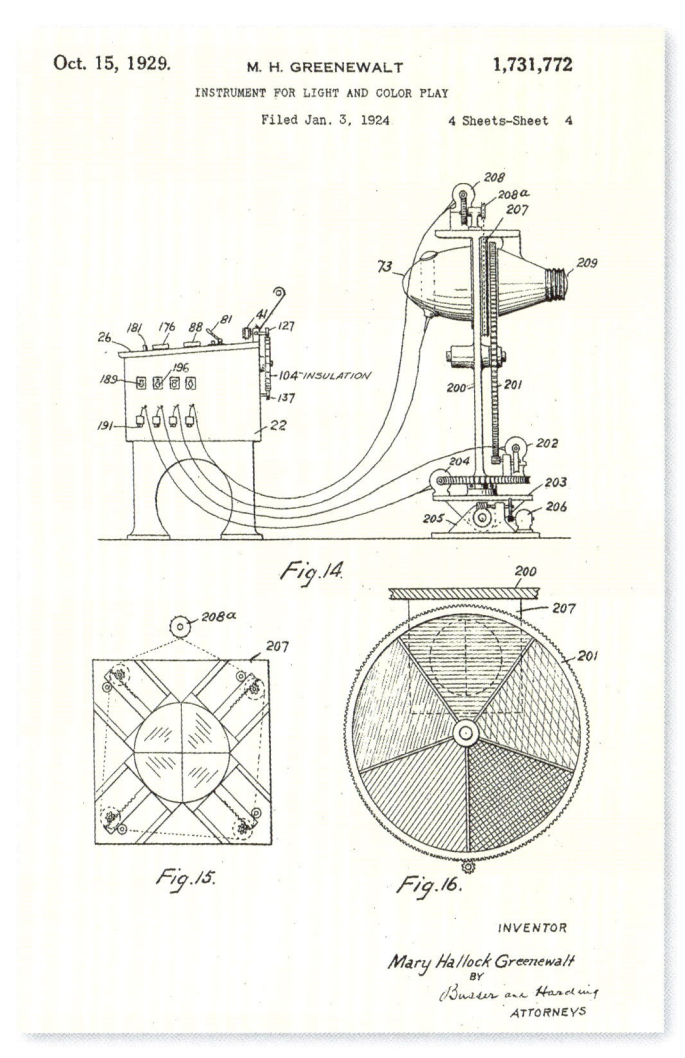

LEFT: *Hallock-Greenewalt's patent design for an 'an instrument of light and color play', filed 3 January 1924.*

All of which brings us back around to the synaesthete Aleksandr Scriabin, who combined his neurological aptitude for colour music with the latest colour-organ technology in 1910 to compose the stunning symphony of sound and light, 'Prometheus: The Poem of Fire'. The music premiered in Moscow on 2 March 1911, but was first played with colour in New York in 1915. Scriabin provides a *luce* ('light score') in two parts on its own stave in treble clef above the standard musical score. One light part changes with the harmony, while the other instructs long sustained notes for several pages at a time, with no explanation of how these should be presented together. Coloured light with a symphony, Scriabin believed, would act as 'a powerful psychological resonator for the listener'. He used his own colour associations with the musical keys (see page 82) as the basis for the instrument's keyboard.

The 1911 cover of 'Prometheus: The Poem of Fire', op. 60, by Aleksandr Scriabin.

For the New York premiere at Carnegie Hall in 1915, the colours beamed from a huge box suspended above the orchestra, and Scriabin requested that everyone in attendance dress all in white, so that the coloured light would reflect off the audience and they would themselves be colour instruments in the multimedia show. However, hopes that 'Prometheus' would finally elevate colour music into qualifying as the Wagnerian idea of the *Gesamtkunstwerk* ('total artwork', i.e. an artwork that synthesised all forms of art) were stalled somewhat by the mixed reviews of the debut performance. The colour symphony would, however, be successfully performed numerous times throughout the next hundred years, with its English debut taking place on 4 May 1972 by the London Symphony Orchestra led by Elyakum Shapirra at the Royal Albert Hall.

Scriabin was fascinated – and heavily influenced – by theosophy, a philosophy of mysticism and spiritualism, which shared an obsession with music and colour. The best illustration of this, and what might have fed into the imagination of the

'Musico-Chromo-Logo Schema', the chart of colour-sound associations used by Scriabin for 'Prometheus: The Poem of Fire'.

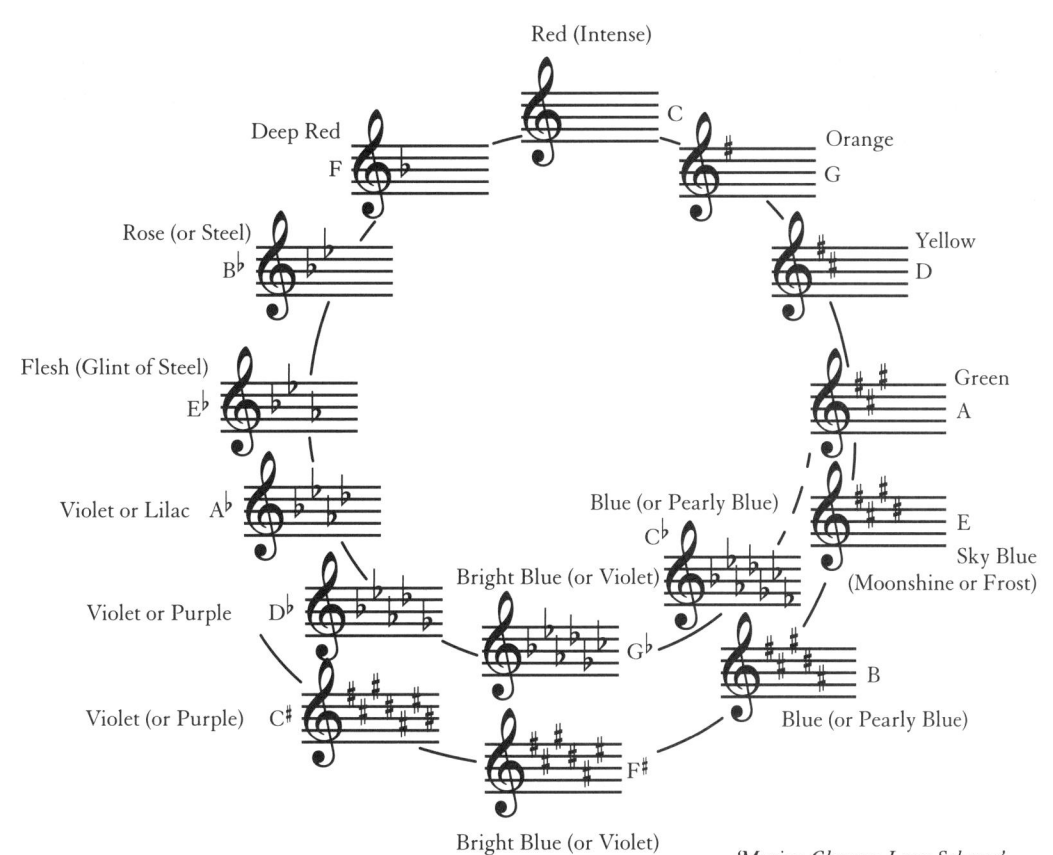

Russian composer, can be found in the book *Thought-Forms: A Record of Clairvoyant Investigation*, 1901, written by two clairvoyant London Theosophical Society members, Annie Besant and Charles Leadbeater. The duo claimed to be able to observe the 'substance of thought' and other invisible things, including music, and provided colourful illustrations as evidence, like those shown on pages 100-101.

While instruments of colour music in their various forms over the centuries dominate this theme of visible music, one other curious instrument of even greater scarcity should be added to this orchestra of the observable. The absence of the pyrophone from modern concert venues and living rooms seems a shame, but also makes perfect sense when one considers that the other names this instrument went by were the fire organ and the explosion organ.

Since 1777, with the discovery by Bryan Higgins (1741-1818) of the 'singing flame', it was known that burning jets of hydrogen in an open-ended glass pipe produced a musical note. The English scientist Michael Faraday (1791-1867) then

A painting of the colour-bubble of Charles Gounod's organ music visibly floating out of a church. From the theosophist work Thought-Forms: A Record of Clairvoyant Investigation, *1901, by Annie Besant and Charles Leadbeater, who claimed they could observe and illustrate the 'substance of thought' and other invisible things.*

attributed these singing tones to very rapid explosions of the hydrogen and oxygen gases, and the physicist John Tyndall (1820-93) found that keeping the flame burning at one-third of the tube length matched the harmonics of the tube, maximising its singing and vibrating. Perhaps, at this point, it was inevitable that a physicist of musical leanings would follow these ideas through. Georges Frédéric Eugène Kastner (1852-82) discovered in 1871 that, with two flames, he could control the note at will. He calls this the 'interference of flames', and devised an 'internal combustion organ' with these glass tubes, operated by a standard keyboard. He filed the patent for the explosive musical instrument on Christmas Eve of 1874.

Hopes were initially high that the instrument's jets of flame would be seen bursting from the orchestra pits of every theatre and concert venue in the world, and composers rushed to include it in new compositions. Charles Gounod (1818-93) attempted to incorporate the pyrophone in his opera *Jeanne d'Arc* in 1873; and Wendelin Weißheimer (1838-1910) composed *Five Sacred Sonnets for Voice, Flute, Oboe, Clarinet, Pyrophone*

ABOVE-LEFT: *The music of Mendelssohn from* Thought-Forms*…, visible to those with psychic sensitivity.*

ABOVE-RIGHT: *The music of Wagner, also from* Thought-Forms*….*

101   *Visible Music*

The pyrophone of Georges Frédéric Eugène Kastner (1852-82).

and Piano in 1880. Theodore Lack (1846-1921) wrote several pieces for the pyrophone, including an arrangement of 'God Save the Queen', which was performed in public. Sadly, Kastner had no time to persevere with his invention – he died soon after, in 1882.

In one sense, sound had been visible as early as 8 July 1680, when Robert Hooke (1635-1703) had covered a glass plate with flour and struck it. The flour rose up the glass. At first,

OPPOSITE: *The German composer Wendelin Weißheimer plays a pyrophone.*

102 | Madman's Orchestra

103   *Visible Music*

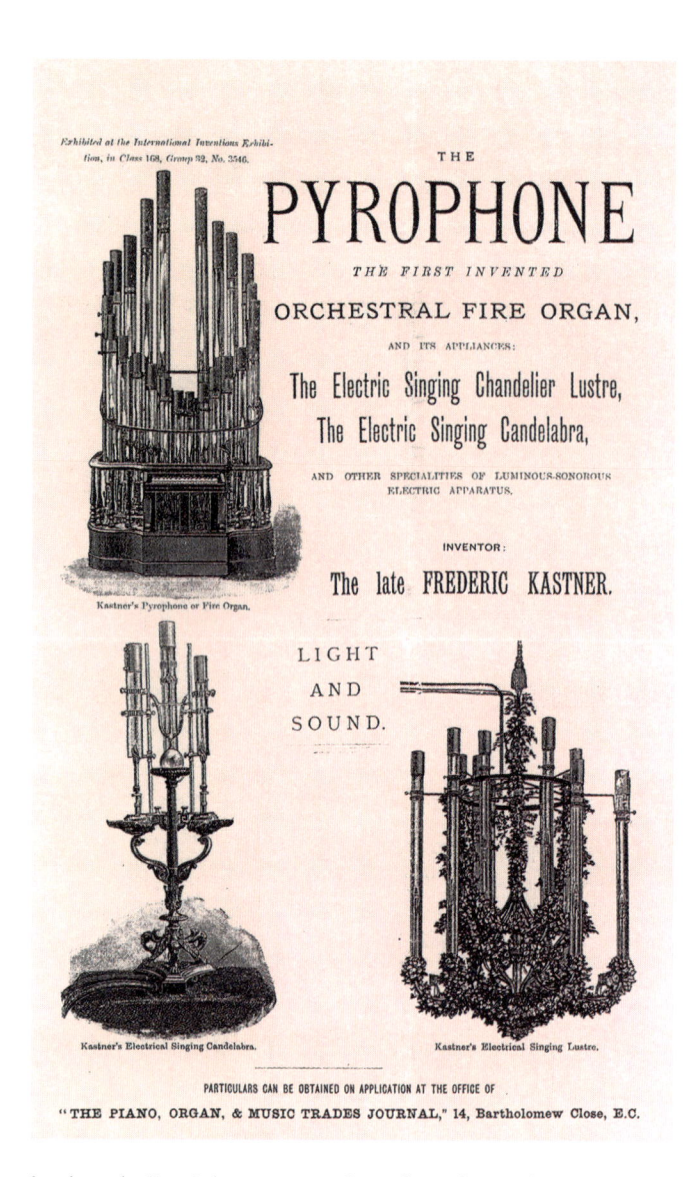

LEFT: *A poster advertising 'The Pyrophone, the First Invented Orchestral Fire Organ', along with sister instruments 'The Electrical Singing Lustre' and 'The Electrical Singing Candelabra'.*

OPPOSITE: *An illustration of the pyrophone from* El Mundo físico…, *1882, by Amadeo Guillemin.*

FOLLOWING SPREAD-LEFT: *Examples of Chladni figures, from a mathematical exhibit at the Institute of Mathematics and Statistics of the University of São Paulo. Ernest Chladni (1756-1827) was a German physicist, musician and foundational figure in the study of acoustics. He is known for the technique of visualising vibrations by running a violin bow along the edge of metal plates covered in sand. When the plate resonates, patterns of nodal lines appear where no vibrations occur. Robert Hooke had first observed this using the same technique on 8 July 1680.*

he thought 'it might suggest an hypothesis for explaining the motion of gravity', but then he discovered that different strokes against a glass bell-jar produced distinct notes, and each one caused a new pattern to form in the flour. Sir Christopher Wren (1632-1723) then suggested Hooke try running a violin bow against the edge of the glass, which resulted in dramatically distinct nodal patterns forming in geometric shapes, which today are known as Chladni figures after the German physicist who made the same observation later in the eighteenth century. The lines of the patterns form in the areas of the struck material where the vibration *doesn't* pass through – and so in the negative space, between these lines, is where one finds the visible shape of the 'music' made.

104 *Madman's Orchestra*

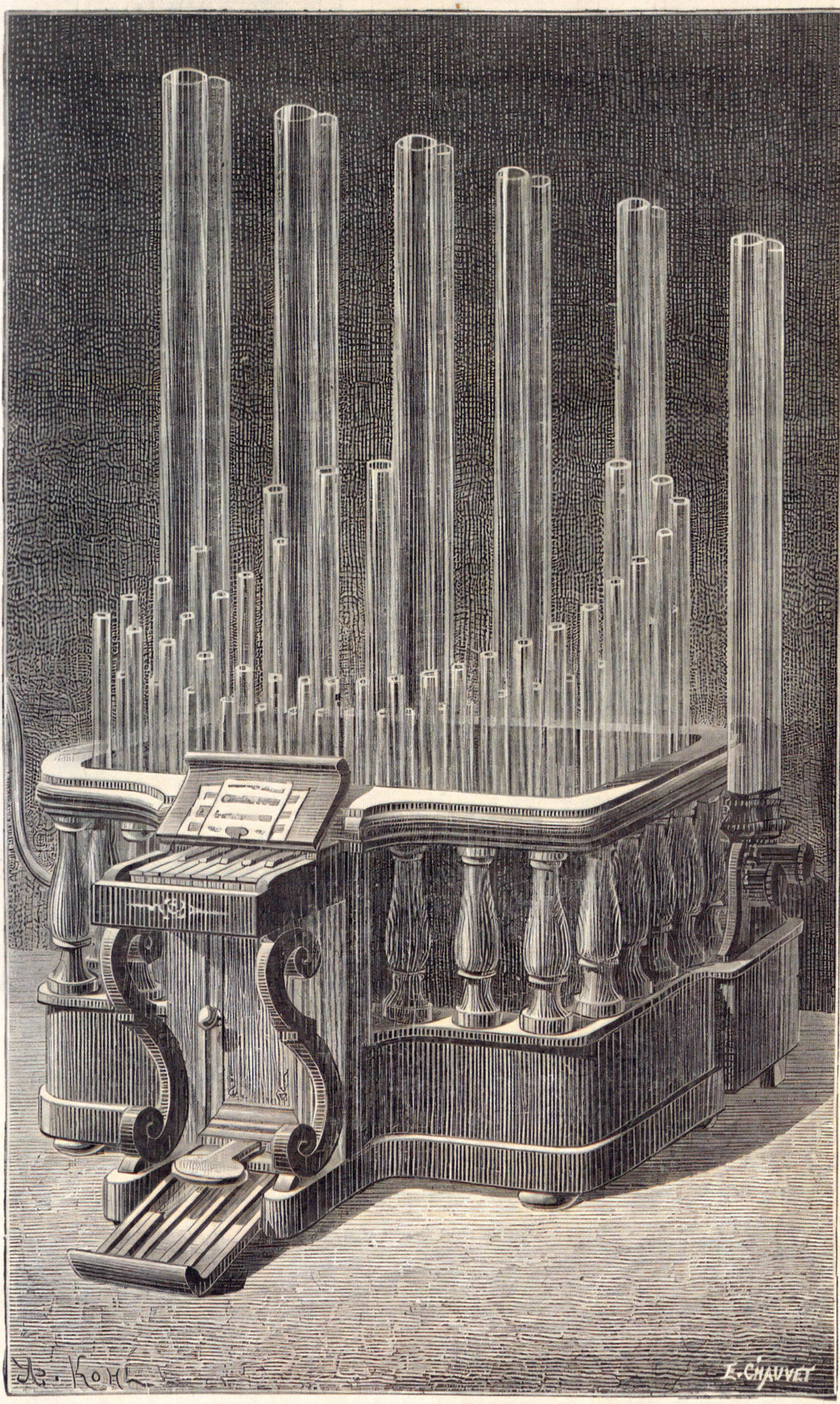
E. CHAUVET

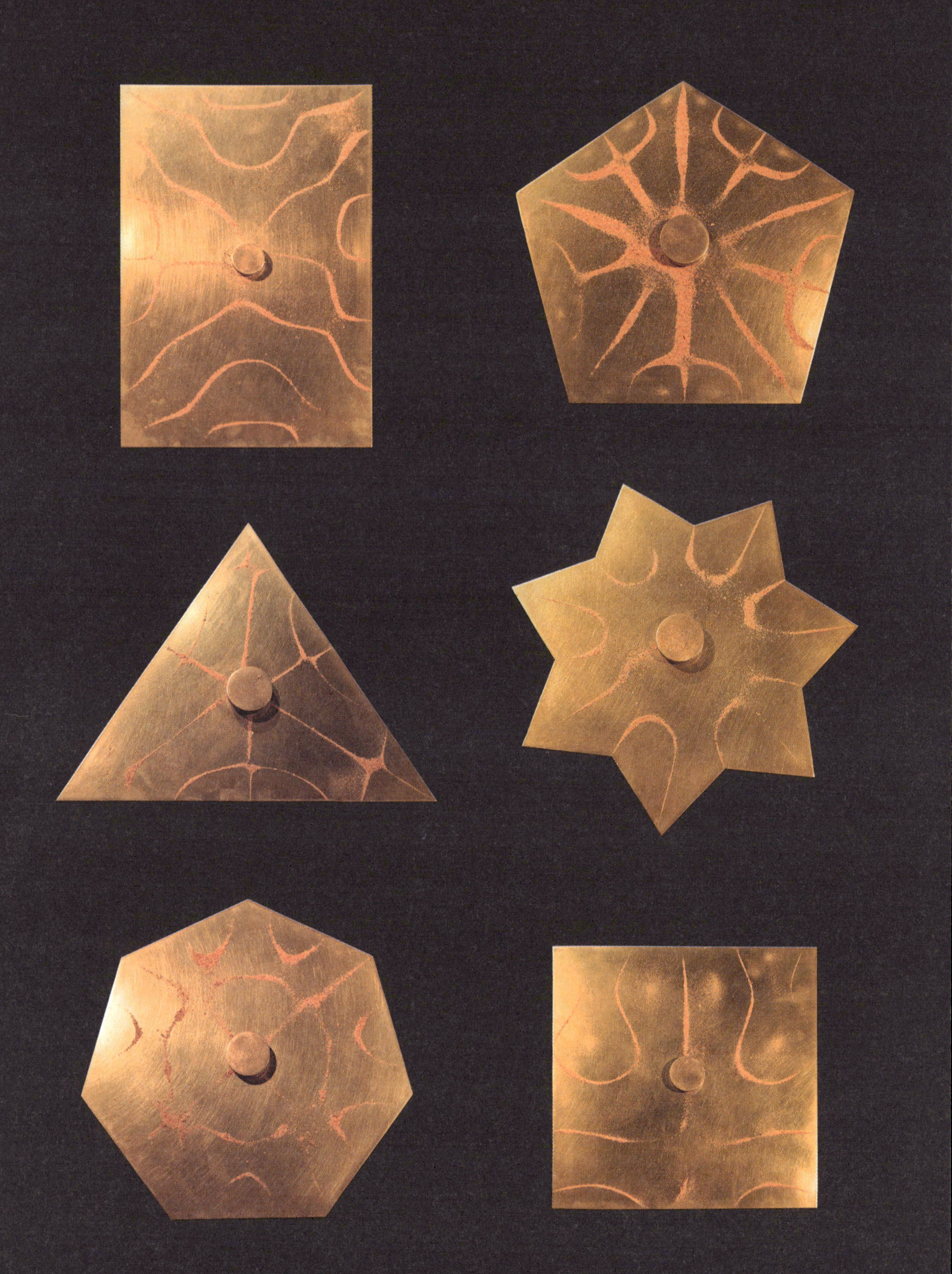

As striking as these Chladni figures are, the best illustrated story with which to bring this chapter to a close is that of Megan (born Margaret) Watts Hughes (1842-1907), a little-known Welsh singer who developed her own technique for creating 'the visible voice'. The eidophone was a device of Watts Hughes's invention, a mouthpiece connected by tube to a larger receiving chamber, over which was stretched a rubber membrane, like a drum. Like Hooke and Chladni before her (of whose work she might well have been unaware), she placed material – sand and lycopodium powder, at first – on the membrane and watched as they formed patterns as she sang loud notes into the device. The shapes would be lost, however, as the seeds scattered, and so she substituted them with various pastes, liquids and paints. When a glass plate was place on top, these formed and bound ever more complex geometric lines of her 'voice-figures', as she called them. As she refined her technique, the geometrics began to give way to more rounded and natural shapes, and she discovered something startling: 'While engaged one day in producing this class of figures', she writes in an article for the May 1891 issue of *The Century Magazine*, 'I observed that exactly in the middle of each of the motion-centres there was a tiny shape like a forget-me-not flower… I was able to observe clearly the remarkable behaviour of these voice-flowers at the instant they spring into shape.'

Here was a technique for both recording and painting the skilfulness of a human voice, capturing music in the form of voice-flowers that were sung into being at the right pitch and resonance, and frozen in time on glass slides. However, as it was not possible to turn these patterns back into sound, like with the etched grooves of vinyl records, nothing more was made of Megan Watts Hughes's eidophone and her voice-flowers. And yet, in the context of this chapter, she achieved what none of the inventors of colour instruments ever managed: to convert and preserve music in a visual power. Here, printed on the pages of this book, is the frozen moment of her song. Her voice will sing for centuries, for as long as there are eyes to hear it.

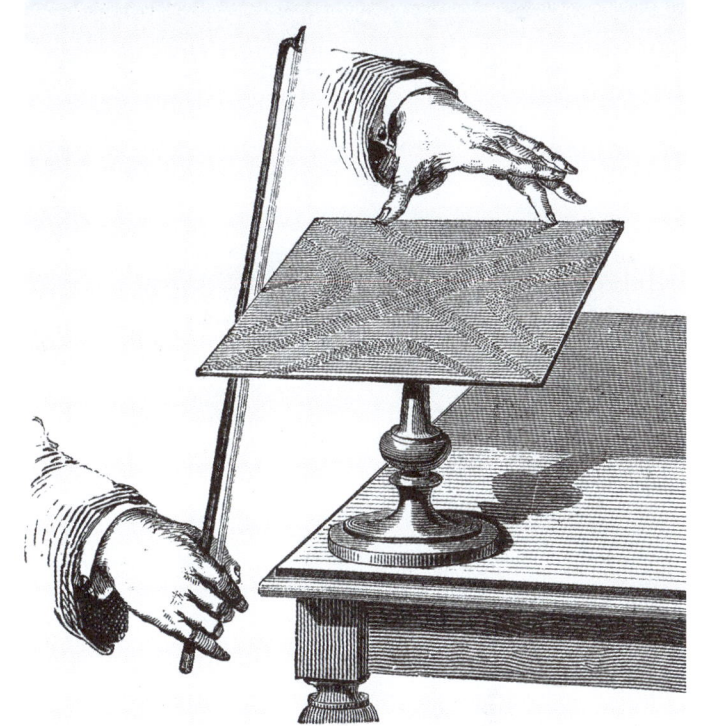

ABOVE: *An illustration from 1879 of the technique used by Ernest Chladni to create figures of vibration on metal plates.*

BELOW: *The various iterations of Megan Watts Hughes's instrument for painting sound – the eidophone.*

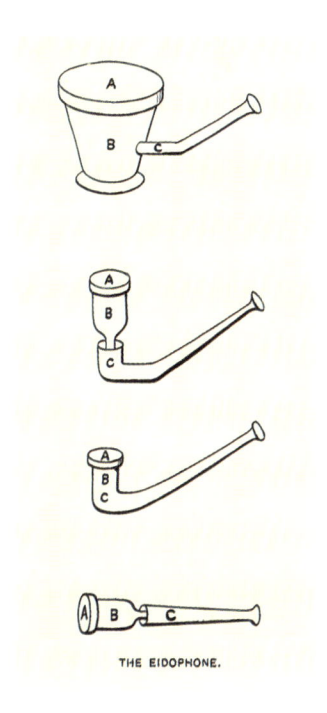

THE EIDOPHONE.

107 *Visible Music*

THIS SPREAD AND THE FOLLOWING PAGE:
'Voice-figures' created by Megan Watts Hughes with her eidophone.

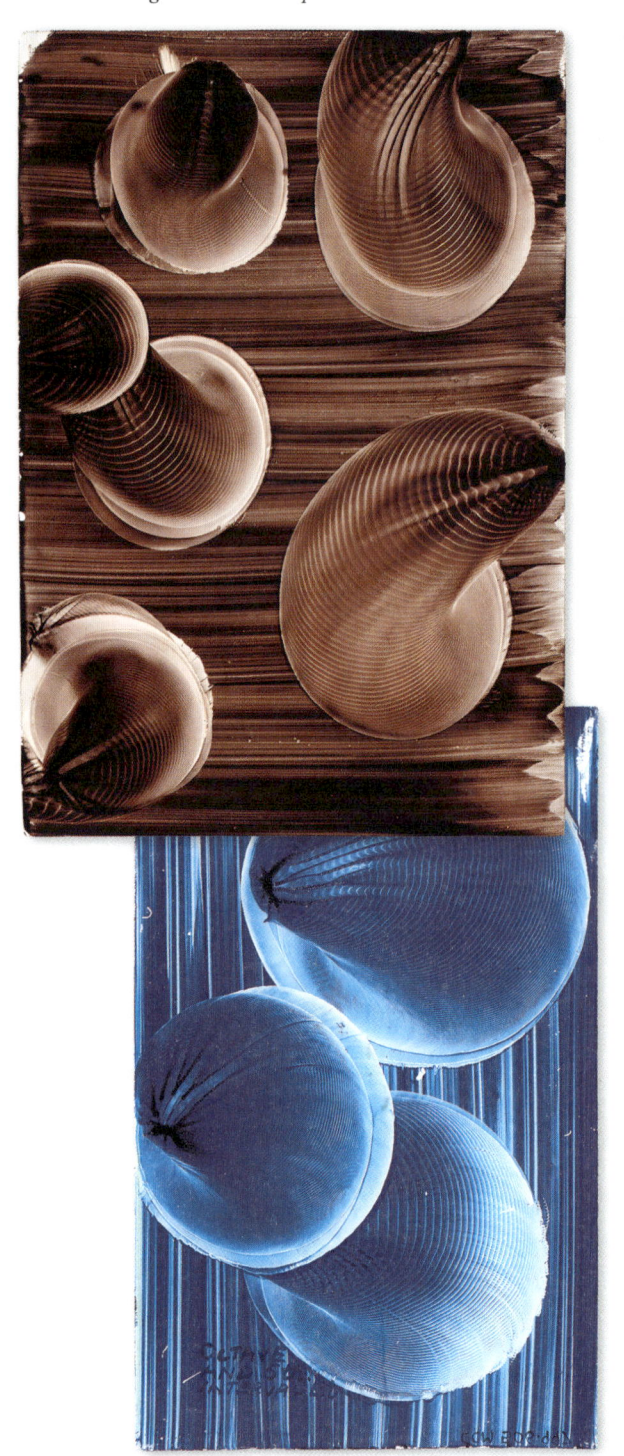

108   *Madman's Orchestra*

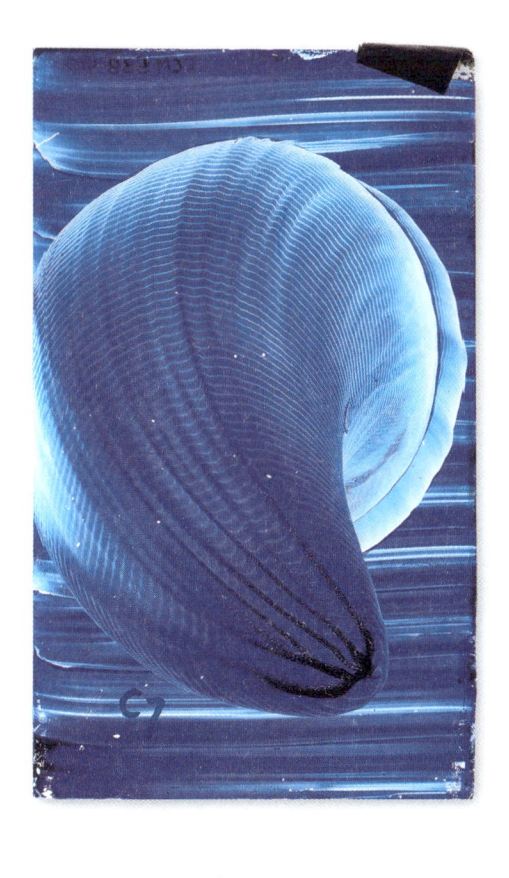

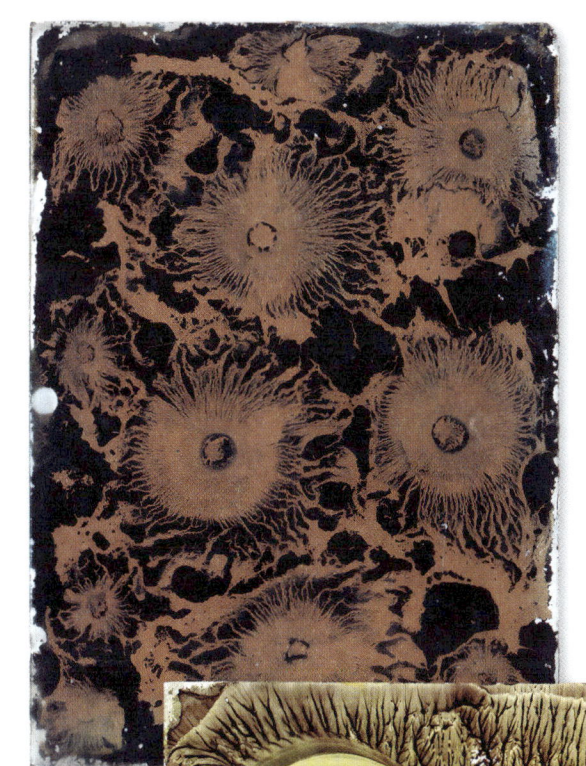

Visible Music

110 *Madman's Orchestra*

▶ PLAYLIST: VISIBLE MUSIC

'V. Louange à l'éternité de Jésus', 1940-41,
Quatuor pour la fin du Temps,
OLIVIER MESSIAEN

Allegretto in B minor, WoO61, 1821,
LUDWIG VAN BEETHOVEN

Ave Maria, CG 89a,
for trumpet and organ, 1852-53,
CHARLES GOUNOD

'Blackbird', *Cowboy Carter,* 2024,
BEYONCÉ

'Blue', 2024,
BILLIE EILISH

'By the Still Waters', op.114, 1925,
AMY BEACH

Preludes in E minor, C minor and
A major, 1839, and Nocturne in G major, 1840,
FRÉDÉRIC CHOPIN
PERFORMED BY MARY HALLOCK GREENEWALT,
COLUMBIA RECORDS 1920

'Diminuendo and Crescendo in Blue', 1937,
DUKE ELLINGTON

Hommage à R. Sch. op. 15/d (merkwürdige
Pirouetten des Kapellmeisters Johannes
Kreisler), 1990, for clarinet, viola and piano,
First movement,
GYÖRGY KURTÁG

'Jealousy, Jealousy', 2021,
OLIVIA RODRIGO

'Kreisleriana' for piano, op. 16, 1838,
ROBERT SCHUMANN

'Liebesträume' ('Dreams of Love')
No. 3 in A flat major, 1850,
FRANZ LISZT

No. 2 'Robin Redbreast',
Summer Dreams, op. 47,
AMY BEACH

No. 3 'Twilight',
Summer Dreams, op. 47, 1887,
AMY BEACH

No. 5 'Elfin Tarentelle',
Summer Dreams, op. 47, 1887,
AMY BEACH

Piano Sonata in E minor, D 566, 1817,
FRANZ SCHUBERT

Piano Sonata in F major, op. 12, 1893,
JEAN SIBELIUS

Piano Sonata No. 4 in F sharp major,
op. 30, 1903,
ALEXANDER SCRIABIN

Prelude to Act 1, *Lohengrin* WWV 75, 1848,
RICHARD WAGNER

'Prometheus: The Poem of Fire', 1910,
ALEXANDER SCRIABIN

Romance in F minor, op. 11, B.39, 1873,
ANTONÍN DVOŘÁK,
PERFORMED BY ITZHAK PERLMAN

Sonatina for Piano 4 Hands II. Andante, 1950,
GYÖRGY LIGETI

String Sextet in A major, 1876,
NIKOLAI RIMSKY-KORSAKOV

Symphony No. 3 in F major,
Im Walde ('In the Forest'), 1869,
JOACHIM RAFF

Violin Concerto in D major, op. 61, 1806,
LUDWIG VAN BEETHOVEN

LOST MUSIC FOUND

Of all the secrets that lie discarded in the folds of time, many are musical. Fragments and full manuscripts of masterpieces have lain – and continue to lie – undiscovered or miscatalogued among the endless paper spires of archives both personal and private. Others are stolen and assumed lost; or submerged with other remnants of their civilisations under deserts, ice sheets or jungle flora; or maybe even trapped inside a nineteenth-century Sicilian postal vessel that was sealed up inside volcanic lava after being caught in an eruption of Mount Etna. The last was reported by the respected opera expert Fred Plotkin in 2012, who announced to the world the extraordinary rediscovery of the long-lost first operatic work by the Italian composer Vincenzo Bellini (1801-35). As part of his application to the Naples Conservatory in 1819 at the age of eighteen, Bellini had wrapped the one copy of his only opera, *Pesci d'Aprile* ('The Fishes of April'), in a leather pouch and dispatched it via postal boat to the Conservatory. The work was never seen again, until archaeologists digging through a lava tomb in a cove near the village of Vambolieri cracked open the rock and found the perfectly preserved garlanded vessel with its contents inside.

This story was confirmed by Riccardo Nasello, a spokesman at the Teatro Bellini in Catania, writes Plotkin; and the arts patron Mercedes Bass was said to be funding the costly process of writing out the orchestral parts of *Pesci d'Aprile*. If this sounds too fantastic to be true, then your radar for a fishy story is stronger than that of nearly everyone else at the time it was published, who bought it hook, line and sinker. Few noticed that the article was published on 1 April; and that both 'Nasello' and 'Bass' are types of fish. *Pesci d'Aprile* is the Italian

The grave of British Army second lieutenant and violinist Hugh Gordon Langton (1885-1917), killed in action in Belgium on 26 October 1917. The phrase of music engraved in his headstone has never been identified and remains a mystery after more than a century.

equivalent of April Fool's Day, named after the traditional prank of attaching a paper fish to the back of an unsuspecting victim. There never was such a manuscript; Plotkin had invented the whole story. It continues to be a most persistent and widely spread hoax. But perhaps the strangest part of this tale occurred one year later, when reality indulged in its habit of out-weirding fiction, and researchers at the National Library of Spain announced their discovery of a never-before-seen autograph manuscript of Bellini that had been hiding among a nineteenth-century sailor's album of landscape drawings of Malta and Sicily. Comprising the scene and duet 'Tu m'apristi in cor ferita' from his opera *Il Pirata*, which premiered at La Scala in Milan on 27 October 1827, the document carries the inscription 'Manuscript of Vincenzo Bellini and his brothers Mario and Carmelo' and features a different score to the piece, offering us fascinating insight into the evolution of Bellini's compositional process.

There would be no Bellini composition, nor Western classical music in its entirety, without the development of polyphony ('many sounds') in the early history of music, in which two or more independent lines or voices of melody are combined simultaneously. From the ninth century, polyphonic

ABOVE: *Portrait of Vincenzo Bellini by an anonymous artist.*

ABOVE-LEFT: *The rediscovered autograph manuscript fragment of the composer Vincenzo Bellini, discovered in a nineteenth-century album of landscape drawings in the collection of the National Library of Spain in 2013.*

BELOW: *This musical inscription was etched on the tomb of Vincenzo Bellini, from the character Amina's last aria in his work* La Sonnambula, *1831: 'Ah! non-credea mirarti / Sì presto estinto, o fiore' ('I did not believe you would fade so soon, oh flower').*

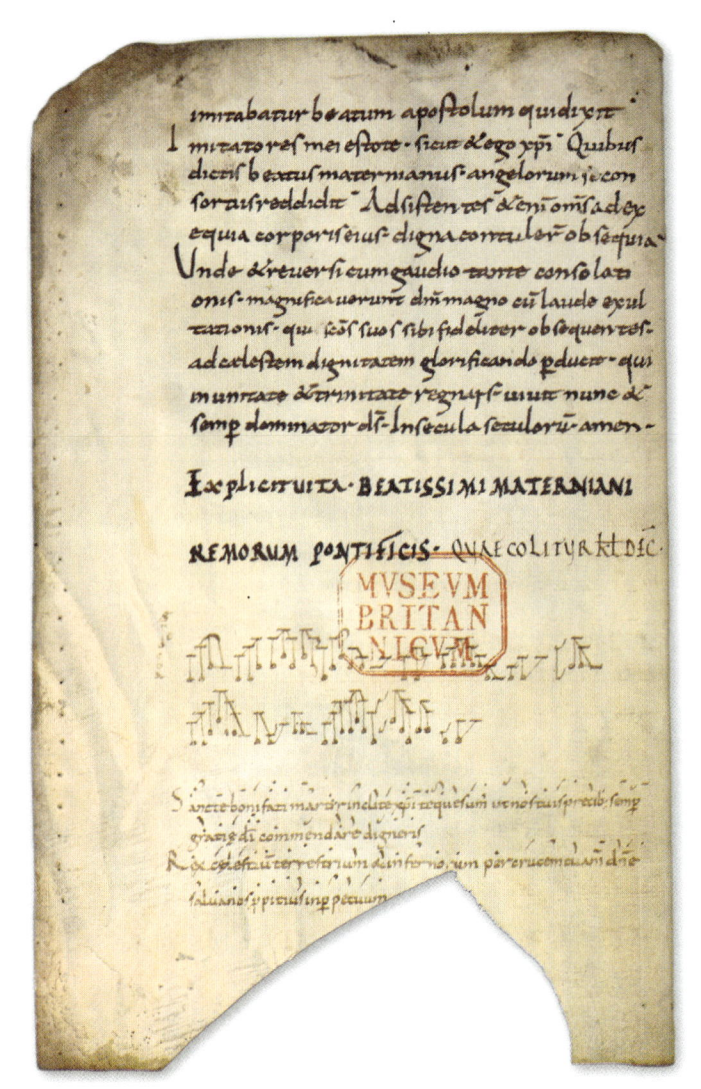

ABOVE: *Detail of the earliest known polyphonic notation, showing two vocal parts, the first indicated by circles at the bottom, the other by the upper horizontal dashes.*

LEFT: *The tenth-century manuscript leaf holding the earliest piece of polyphonic music, discovered in the British Library in 2014.*

OPPOSITE-TOP: *The Seikilos epitaph, in the collection of the National Museum of Denmark.*

OPPOSITE-BOTTOM: *A rough transcription of the Seikilos song into modern musical notation, with the original text and translation.*

music took over from the previous dominant form of music with its single melody line known as plainsong, or plainchant. With polyphony being such a seismically consequential invention in the history of music, one would expect its origins to be well established, but in fact the earliest known written polyphonic composition was only recently discovered by chance, in 2014, by a British Library intern named Giovanni Varelli. Dated to around the year 900 and produced by a scribe working somewhere in northwest Germany, the short 'Dedication to Saint Boniface' was inked into the margin at the end of a manuscript of the life of the fourth-century Bishop Maternianus of Reims, and consists of a short antiphon (a chant used in Christian ritual) with a second voice providing a harmonic accompaniment.

What's so fascinating about this particular piece of music is that in it we can see the inchoate form of music as we know it today. While the scribe uses notation, it's of a kind that appears to break the rules and conventions that we previously believed were set by this time. Predating the invention of the stave, the strange pattern of symbols are arranged with dashes at their heads and dots at their feet. It is only when noticing the consistency of this arrangement that one realises each symbol carries the notes for two different melody lines: the dashes being the upper part, the circles being the lower melody to be sung in accompaniment. Upon even closer inspection, we can see that there is a faint early form of the stave, an invention traditionally credited to Guido d'Arezzo (991-1033) a century later (see page 56), ruled on the parchment with a dry point. All of this went unnoticed in the centuries that followed the manuscript's addition to the Harley Collection (held by the British Museum, now by the British Library) in 1753.

We can go back a further nine centuries or so to find the earliest surviving complete musical composition secreted in time, known as the Seikilos epitaph or Seikilos Stele, which was thought to have been created sometime in the first or second century AD. It was not discovered until 1883, when it was found as part of a pillar at the ancient Hellenic town of Tralleis (in what is now Turkey). Its two poems are written in ancient Greek, with one a *distich* (couplet) and the other a song with musical notation for voice etched above the words. Following its discovery in 1883, it is next documented in 1922, when after the end of the Greco-Turkish war of 1919-22, it turned up in Buca, Smyrna, where the Dutch Consul kept it safe from the fighting. In that intervening period it suffered damage. Sources vary as to the cause of this, and to whether Sir W. M. Ramsay was the first to find it; or if it was Edward Purser, a director of a building firm constructing a railway in the area, who was the

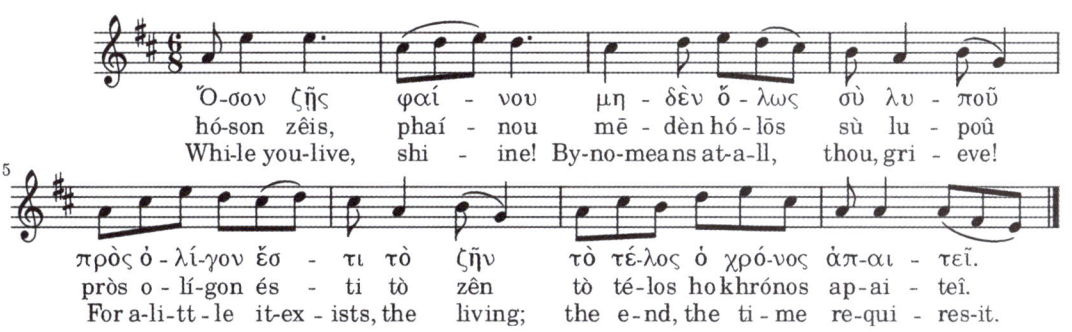

115 | *Lost Music Found*

one to discover it and allowed Ramsay to publish it. Regardless, in the subsequent decades, the Stele had its base sawn off (shoring away one of the lines of text) so that Mrs Purser could use it as a pedestal for her flowerpots.

The song's lyrics have been translated into English as: 'As long as you're alive, shine, don't be sad at all; life is short, time asks for its due.' For a stunning modern arrangement and performance of the Seikilos song, it's worth seeking out the 2019 recording by the artist Jamie Lenman.

Safer from the destructive repurposing of idle Victorian hands was the etched clay tablet known as Hurrian Hymn, or the Hurrian Moonrise, which astonishingly dates back another 1,500 years *before* the Seikilos epitaph. Inscribed *c*.1400 BC in cuneiform, the oldest known writing system, this tablet was discovered during French excavations of the 1950s in the ancient Amorite-Canaanite city of Ugarit, northern Syria. At over 3,200 years old, the Hurrian Hymn is the oldest surviving substantially complete work of notated music in the world. The lyrics, which are on the theme of fertility, are in the Hurrian language, while the music notation is in Akkadian; together, they form a song to the moon goddess Nikkal, referencing offerings left at the feet of her statue. The music instructions are for an open-stringed musical instrument like a harp or lyre, and, while specific notes are of course not given, the relative intervals and modes are specified, which means that if we assign the first string with the note of E like on a modern guitar, then its default starting chord or open tuning would be: E F G A B C D. From here, rather wonderfully we can create a 3,200-year-old chord-book to play with (on a seven-string instrument), as the dichords given are:

kitmu ('close')	E F# G A B C D
embūbu ('reed pipe')	E F# G A B C# D
pītu ('open')	E F# G# A B C# D
nīd qabli ('fall of the middle')	E F# G# A B C# D#
nīš gabrî ('rise of the duplicate')	E F# G # A# B C# D#
qablītu ('middle')	E# F# G# A# B C# D#

Questions abound, of course, as to the exact style of the performance, and so it is up to the modern performer to decide whether the notation is for an instrument, singer or both. Are the dichords played successively, as we construct music today,

LEFT: *The Hurrian Hymn, the earliest known example of music notation.*

BELOW: *The entrance to the Ugarit Palace, where the Hurrian songs were hidden inside.*

or in harmony? Should one pluck the notes or strike/strum the dichord as a whole? As challenges go, it's a pretty fun avenue of investigation with a seven-string guitar.

But as the discovery by Giovanni Varelli shows (see page 114), the most fruitful ground for musical detectives is libraries and archives, where even the most diligent librarian and cataloguer can ultimately be frustrated by a dearth of information about authorship and provenance. The Florentine Renaissance composer Alessandro Striggio (1536/37-92) was a court musician for the infamous Medici family, and combined his talents for composing madrigals and dramatic music with inventing the genre of madrigal comedy, an antecedent of opera. And yet it was only in 2005 when his most extraordinary work was discovered by the Berkeley musicologist and harpsichordist Davitt Moroney, who found it in the Bibliothèque nationale de France in Paris miscatalogued as a four-part Mass. *Missa sopra Ecco sì beato giorno* ('Mass on "Behold such a blessed day"') is of staggering polychoral scale, written for forty independent voices divided between five choirs of eight voices, with the final Agnus Dei section written for five choirs of twelve voices, totalling sixty simultaneous independent parts. In 1565-66, when *Missa sopra* was composed, this scale was unheard of, and it's thought that Striggio's is the largest polyphonic composition of the whole era. Lost for over 400 years, it received its first modern performance at the

Lost Music Found

A leaf from the manuscript of Beethoven's transcription of his composition for string quartet 'Grosse Fuge', with corrections in his own hand.

Royal Albert Hall on 17 July 2007 by the BBC Singers and The Tallis Scholars. Moroney conducted the piece himself, having spent months reconstructing it with a computer that frequently crashed under the strain of working with sixty staves.

On this theme of scale, over 5,000 manuscripts by the Bach family disappeared from the archives of the Berliner Singakademie during the Second World War, after being transferred to Silesia to avoid being damaged in the Allied bombardment. They were looted by the Red Army and stached by the KGB somewhere in Moscow. For over fifty years, there was no word of their location until Christoph Wolff, a music professor at Harvard University, came across a letter from 1950 that mentioned the manuscript trove was somewhere in Ukraine. He spent the next two decades following leads, until after three days of searching through the state museum's files, he discovered the Bach family archive. It has since been repatriated.

Finding Bach in Ukraine is unexpected; finding Beethoven in the American suburb of Wynnewood, Pennsylvania, is arguably even more of a surprise. A lost autograph manuscript of the composer's transcription of his 'Grosse Fuge' for string quartet suddenly appeared after 115 years, having languished on a bookshelf at the Eastern Baptist Theological Seminary, now the Palmer Theological Seminary. Beethoven wrote the piece in his later years when he was almost entirely deaf. The fugue was notorious at the time, as it was universally hated by every critic who attended a performance. A writer for the *Allgemeine musikalische Zeitung* in 1826 describes it as 'incomprehensible, like Chinese' and 'a confusion of Babel'. The late American critic Joseph Kerman has labelled it 'the most problematic single work in Beethoven's output and… doubtless in the entire literature of music'; while the violinist David Matthews lamented it as 'fiendishly difficult to play'. In fact, music critics past and present have variously described the 'Grosse Fuge' as 'inaccessible', 'eccentric', 'filled with paradoxes' and, most punchily, 'Armageddon'. Others consider it Beethoven's greatest composition. The value of the rediscovered manuscript is in the annotations and notes in Beethoven's own hand, providing glimpses into his thought processes during the final months before his death in 1827. It was sold at auction by Sotheby's on 1 December 2005 for £1.12 million.

In 1842, Felix Mendelssohn (1809-47) produced a composition titled 'The Heart of Man is Like a Mine' as a private commission for a friend who managed the Royal Theatre in Berlin, on one condition: that it would never be published. It never was. The manuscript was later sold in

Mendelssohn's lost manuscript of the private commission 'The Heart of Man is Like a Mine', 1842.

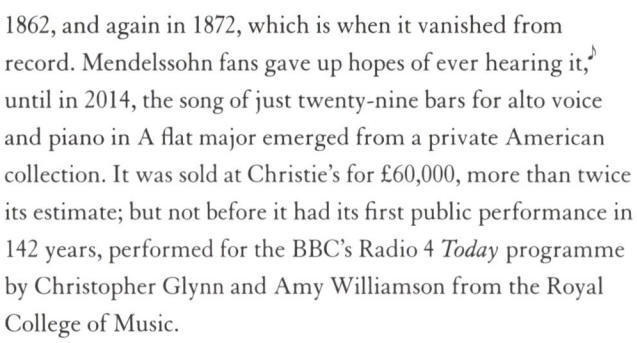

1862, and again in 1872, which is when it vanished from record. Mendelssohn fans gave up hopes of ever hearing it,♪ until in 2014, the song of just twenty-nine bars for alto voice and piano in A flat major emerged from a private American collection. It was sold at Christie's for £60,000, more than twice its estimate; but not before it had its first public performance in 142 years, performed for the BBC's Radio 4 *Today* programme by Christopher Glynn and Amy Williamson from the Royal College of Music.

It's especially exciting if a lost work emerges from hiding to fundamentally change the common understanding of the history in which it features. The popular conception of Antonio Salieri (1750-1825) is that he was the fierce bitter rival of Mozart (1756-91), who he drove to an early grave, perhaps even hastening his demise with a touch of arsenic, and that his

ABOVE-LEFT: *Antonio Salieri, painted by Joseph Willibrord Mähler, 1815.*

ABOVE-RIGHT: *Wolfgang Amadeus Mozart, painted by Johann Nepomuk della Croce, 1790.*

♪ Which brings to mind the American hip-hop group Wu-Tang Clan and their seventh studio album, *Once Upon a Time in Shaolin*. The rap group made a similar stipulation for their album in a nod to musical patronage of the Renaissance: only one copy should be created, which could be purchased directly from them for US$2 million on the condition it wouldn't be duplicated nor shared with the public. The album was purchased by Martin Shkreli, CEO of Turing Pharmaceuticals, who was notorious for acquiring the manufacturing licence for the lifesaving antiparasitic drug Daraprim and raising its price from US$13.50 to US$750.00 per pill. Two years later, Shkreli was convicted on two counts of securities fraud and one count of conspiracy, sentenced to seven years in prison and fined over US$70 million. The album was sold to help pay his debts, but is yet to be available to the public.

Korina Kilian of the Leipzig Municipal Libraries holds up another previously unknown music manuscript by Wolfgang Amadeus Mozart from 1760, which was discovered in the library's collection in 2024. The piece was later performed at the Leipzig Opera on 21 September the same year.

compositional skills were vastly inferior to his nemesis. This is largely thanks to the 1984 movie *Amadeus* and the Aleksandr Pushkin play *Mozart and Salieri* of 1830 that the film is partly inspired by, in which Salieri invites Mozart to dinner to poison him. The fact is there's no evidence of any acrimony, nor is there anything to say that the two were anything other than competitive contemporaries.

In 2015, the fictional nature of this legendary bitterness was confirmed by a remarkable discovery by the composer and musicologist Timo Jouko Herrmann in the Czech Museum of Music in Prague, who was astounded to find a musical collaboration by the two. The cantata titled 'Per la ricuperata salute di Offelia' ('For the recovering health of Ophelia') is a collaborative work by the two composers, along with the lesser-known composer Cornetti. The music was hailed as making clear what historians had already known, that the two were amicable colleagues, and that Salieri was the victim of centuries of calumny. By all reports, the latter was a perfectly benevolent man who was a driving force in the musical culture of Vienna. Having benefited himself from the generosity of a mentor who rescued him from the orphanage, Salieri taught composition to dozens of young musicians, including Beethoven and Schubert, for free. Today the appreciation of his music is being restored: of his forty or so operas, more than a dozen have been revived, and his grave in Vienna is regularly festooned with bouquets from admirers.

FOLLOWING SPREAD:
LEFT: Madonna and Child with Angels*, 1408-1427.*
RIGHT: Coronation of the Virgin*, 1420, both by Gentile da Fabriano.*

121 | Lost Music Found

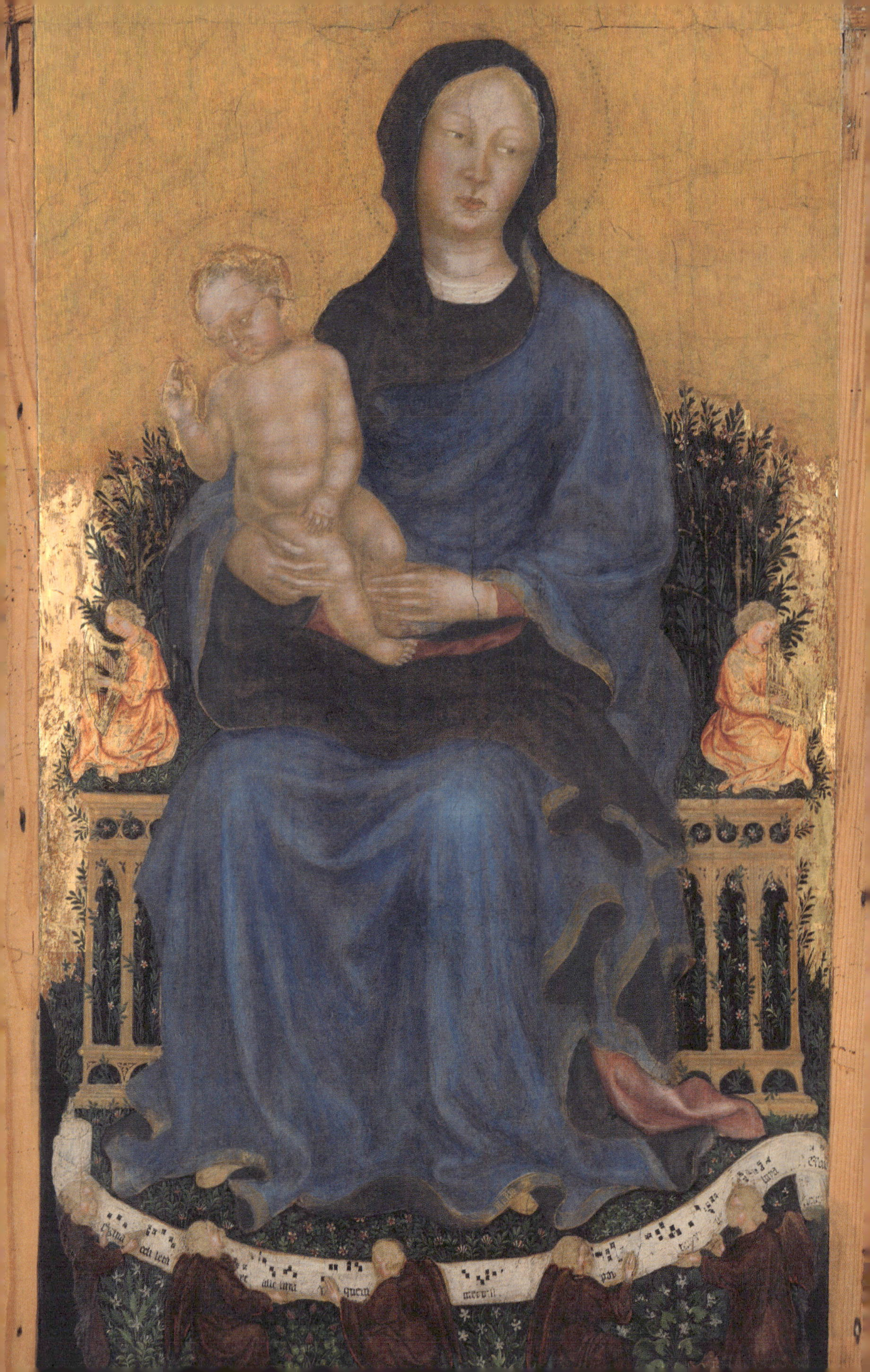

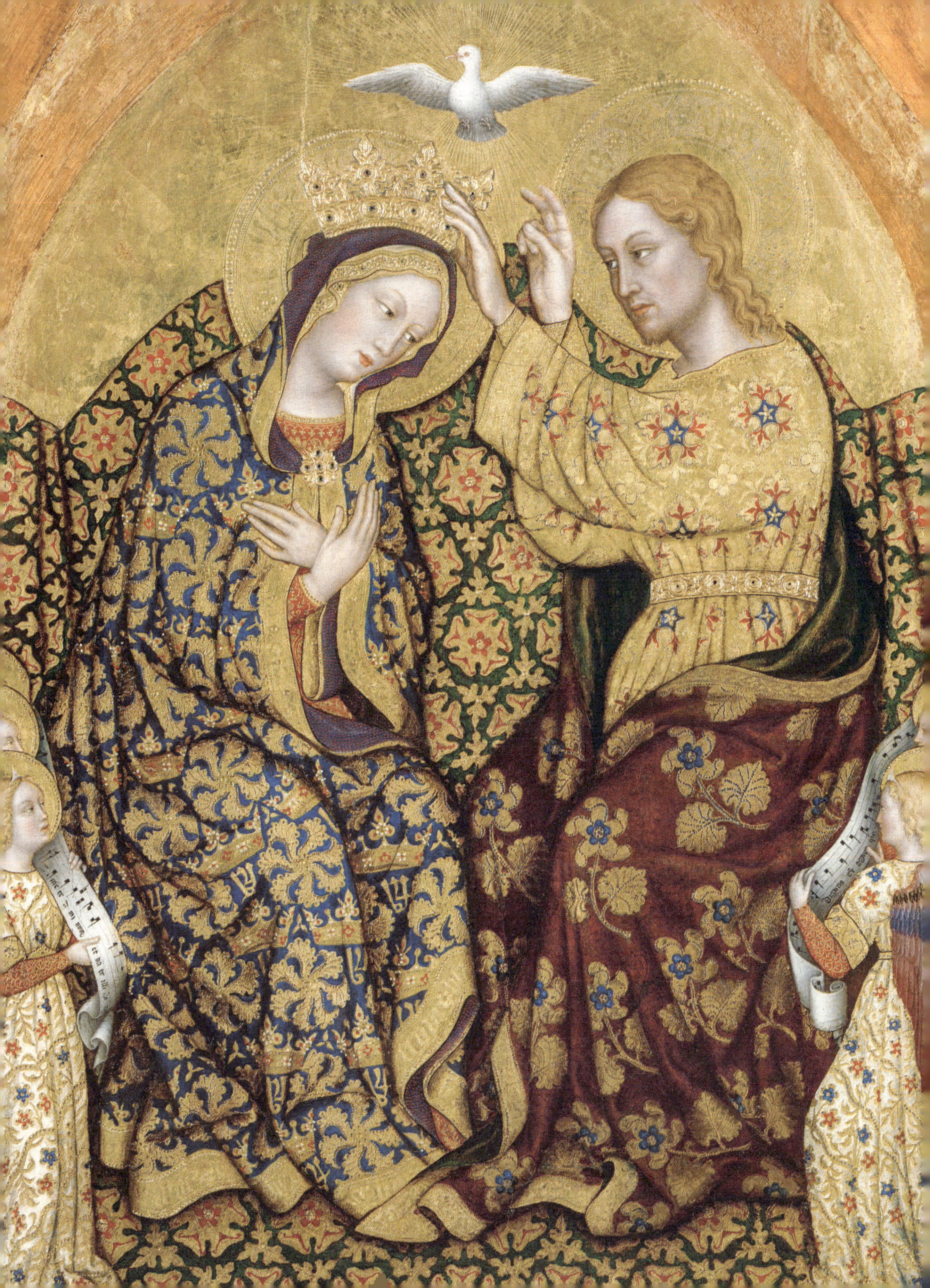

Sometimes music has been hidden in plain sight. The tradition of artists stashing real music notation inside their work began in the early fifteenth century as the Renaissance bloomed. One of the first painters to do this was the Italian artist Gentile da Fabriano (1370-1427), who includes the notation for the Marian antiphon (a short chant sung as a refrain) identified as the 'Regina caeli laetare' ('Queen of Heaven, rejoice'), found on the scroll at the base of the painting of the blue-clothed Virgin in his *Madonna and Child with Angels*, 1408-27 (see page 122), where she sits in the company of a harpist and organ player either side of her. Da Fabriano was so accurate with his musical painting that the notation featured on the first scroll in another of his works, the exquisite *Coronation of the Virgin*, 1420 (see page 123), was identified by the historian Jason Stoessel in 2013 as the first and last parts of the Latin 'Exhortatio ad Laudem Dei' ('Exhortation to the Praise of God'), a group of sung quotations from Revelation, Psalms, Daniel and other books of the Bible, attributed to St Francis of Assisi (1181/82-1226). Da Fabriano's accurate depiction of music allows it to be sung directly from his paintings. It has been concluded that the music on the second scroll is, therefore, also accurate, but, given the fact that no one has been able to identify it, it must be a piece of music that is now lost, with the painting the only evidence of its existence.

Almost nothing is known about the man with one of the most famous names in the history of Western art – and even that name was a later adoption. Hiëronymus Bosch (1450-1516) was born Jeroen van Aken in 's-Hertogenbosch, Netherlands, and later changed his forename to the Latinised form, and his surname to represent his city. His famous triptych *The Garden of Earthly Delights*, 1490-1500, is so dense with bizarre and devilish details that the cumulative effect is overwhelming, and so it's understandable how tiny features have been overlooked and understudied. In 2014, for example, particular attention was paid to musical notation that Bosch painted on the bare backside of a figure in the section of Hell reserved for musicians (to the left of the figure with the inserted woodwind instrument). This was spotted by Oklahoma Christian University student Amelia Hamrick, who transcribed it into modern notation for piano, a recording of which can be found on YouTube, under the title 'Hieronymus Bosch's Butt Song'. Her claim to be the first to transcribe it was met with anger from Laurinda S. Dixon, Professor in the Department of Art and Music Histories, Syracuse University, who pointed out that she had done the same in 1961, and had also observed Bosch's neat inclusion of a devil's tritone (see page 227 for more) in the notation.

While it's unlikely that the plodding 49-note piece will set fire to the charts, it is extraordinary to hear 500-year-old music emanate from a painting already rich in marvels, and one can't help but think that Bosch would be nothing but delighted with the amount of serious attention given by modern scholars to his bum notes.♪

♪ Speaking of bum notes, Joseph Haydn lets slip his own in his *Symphony No. 93*, completed in 1791. In the second movement, the music slows and quietens until the bassoonist is instructed to release a movement of their own and unexpectedly parp out a fart note as a joke. A bum-note footnote should also include a mention of *Three Hairs of the Wise Old Man*, which is a five-act opera originally composed entirely on toilet paper. The Czech composer Rudolf Karel (1880-1945) wrote the work while a prisoner-of-war at Theresienstadt in the Second World War, having to hand only toilet paper and the medicinal charcoal prescribed for his dysentery. He would eventually die from the illness, but his notes for the opera were kept by a sympathetic warden, and the orchestrations completed by Karel's pupil Zbynek Vostrák.

TOP: *The section of* The Garden of Earthly Delights *showing musicians in Hell.*

ABOVE: *The musical notation painted on the bare backside of an infernal inhabitant.*

125 Lost Music Found

126 *Madman's Orchestra*

Portrait of a Musician is an unfinished painting of *c.*1483-87, widely attributed to Leonardo da Vinci, that has captured particular interest over the years for the small detail of the folded piece of paper the man clasps in his hands. This curiosity came about after its restoration in 1904-05, when overpainting was removed to reveal the hand and piece of paper, which carries faint marks of musical notation. The identity of the sitter is unknown, but the music suggests the man might have been a musician. The mystery is sustained by the fact the notation has suffered too much erasure to be identified, if it is a real piece of music at all. However, given that Leonardo was himself a passionate musician and accomplished player of the *lira da braccio*, a bowed string instrument, it's exciting to consider the possibility that it could be an original composition by the artist himself.

Most poignantly of all, though, is a piece of music drawn not from a painting hanging on a wall, but from a wall itself. *Symphony No. 3*, or *Symphony of Sorrowful Songs*, 1976, is the work that brought fame to the Polish composer Henryk Górecki (1933-2010). Mournful cello leads the orchestra into a low build of strings until halfway through, when a solo soprano begins singing the first of three Polish texts, one for each movement. The second movement is especially devastating. Górecki had come across an inscription almost lost among the tangle of

OPPOSITE: *Leonardo da Vinci's* Portrait of a Musician, *c.1483-87.*

ABOVE: *The music held by the sitter of the portrait.*

127 *Lost Music Found*

hundreds of other laments written on the same cell wall in a German Gestapo prison in the town of Zakopane, which sits at the base of the Tatra mountains in southern Poland. The words were left by an 18-year-old woman of the highlands named Helena Wanda Błażusiakówna, who was incarcerated on 25 September 1944: *'O Mamo, nie płacz, nie. Niebios Przeczysta Królowo, Ty zawsze wspieraj mnie'* ('Oh Mamma do not cry, no. Immaculate Queen of Heaven, always support me'). Górecki was struck by the almost 'apologetic' tone of the message.

> In prison [he would later recall] the whole wall was covered with inscriptions screaming out loud: 'I'm innocent', 'Murderers', 'Executioners', 'Free me', 'You have to save me' – it was all so loud, so banal. Adults were writing this, while here is an eighteen-year-old girl, almost a child. And she is so different. She does not despair, does not cry, does not scream for revenge. She does not think about herself; whether she deserves her fate or not. Instead, she only thinks about her mother: because it is her mother who will experience true despair.

In 2024, a curator named Dr Robinson McClellan uncovered a previously unknown waltz written in the hand of composer Frédéric Chopin (1810-49) in the collection of the Morgan Library & Museum, New York City. The twenty-four notated bars are to be repeated once in their entirety, and the waltz is unusual for Chopin in that it begins with several moody dissonant bars culminating in a loud outburst.

128   *Madman's Orchestra*

▶ PLAYLIST: LOST MUSIC FOUND

Act 1: 'Norma viene' (Coro), *Norma*, 1831,
VINCENZO BELLINI, PERFORMED BY MARIA CALLAS

Act 2: 'Tu m'apristi in cor ferita', *Il Pirata*, 1827,
VINCENZO BELLINI, PERFORMED BY MARIA CALLAS

Bagatelle No. 25 in A minor, 'Für Elise', 1810,
LUDWIG VAN BEETHOVEN

'Butt Song' or 'Da Butt', 1987,
DEBESH SUVAT,
PERFORMED BY HIERONYMUS BOSCH ENSEMBLE

Canon in D major, 1680-90,
JOHANN PACHELBEL

Cello Concerto No. 1 in C major, 1756,
JOSEPH HAYDN

'Exhortatio ad Laudem Dei', 13th century,
TRADITIONAL LATIN MASS CHANT

'Funeral Song', 1908,
IGOR STRAVINSKY

'Ganz kleine Nachtmusik', mid-1760s,
WOLFGANG AMADEUS MOZART

Gloria in D major, RV 589, 1715,
ANTONIO VIVALDI

Kyrie: 'Orbis factor', *Gradual of Eleanor of Brittany*, mid-13th century,
ANONYMOUS (ORGANUM POLYPHONY)

'Grosse Fugue', op. 133, 1825,
LUDWIG VAN BEETHOVEN

'Hurrian Hymn to Nikkal', 1400-1200 BC,
PERFORMED BY TIM RAYBORN

'Let's Fall in Love Tonight', 1983,
LEWIS BALOUE

'Misere mei, Deus', 1638,
GREGORIO ALLEGRI (POLYPHONY)

Missa sopra Ecco sì beato giorno, 1565-66,
ALESSANDRO STRIGGIO

'Nottamun Town', 1969,
FAIRPORT CONVENTION

'Per la ricuperata salute di Offelia' ('For the recovering health of Ophelia'), 1785,
PAULO CORNETTI,
WOLFGANG AMADEUS MOZART,
ANTONIO SALIERI

'Regina caeli laetare', 12th-13th century,
TRADITIONAL LATIN MASS CHANT

'Song of Seikilos', 2019,
JAMIE LENMAN

'Sugar Man', 1969,
SIXTO RODRIGUEZ

Symphony in C, 1855,
GEORGES BIZET

Symphony No. 3, op. 36, 1976,
HENRYK GÓRECKI

Symphony No. 8, 'Unfinished', 1822,
FRANZ SCHUBERT

Symphony No. 93, 1791,
JOSEPH HAYDN

'Tantum Ergo Sacramentum', 1264,
THOMAS AQUINAS (PLAINCHANT)

'The Entertainer', 1902,
SCOTT JOPLIN

The Four Seasons, 1723,
ANTONIO VIVALDI

'Des Menschen Herz ist ein Schacht', 1842,
FELIX MENDELSSOHN

Waltz in A minor, 1843-48,
'Found in New York', 1860,
FRÉDÉRIC CHOPIN, PERFORMED BY LANG LANG

'Wo Gott der Herr nicht bei uns hält', BWV 1128, 1724,
JOHANN SEBASTIAN BACH

SOME MUSICAL UNAPPRECIATION

'Debussy's music is the dreariest kind of rubbish. Does anybody for a moment doubt that Debussy would write such chaotic, meaningless, cacophonous, ungrammatical stuff if he could invent a melody?'
New York Post, 1907

'It is probable that much, if not most, of Stravinsky's music will enjoy brief existence.' New York Sun, 16 January 1937

'Tchaikovsky's First Piano Concerto, like the first pancake, is a flop.'
Nicolai Soloviev, Novoye Vremya, 13 November 1875

'A horde of demons struggling in a torrent of brandy.'
Boston Evening Transcript, 24 October 1892, on Tchaikovsky's Fifth Symphony

'Tchaikovsky's Violin Concerto gives us for the first time the hideous notion that there can be music that stinks to the ear.' Critic Edvard Hanslick, 1881 (Tchaikovsky memorised Hanslick's review and would on occasion recite it word-for-word for the rest of his life.)

'Rigoletto is the weakest work of Verdi. It lacks melody. This opera has hardly any chance of being kept in the repertoire.'
Gazette Musicale de Paris, 22 May 1853

'Sure-fire rubbish.'
New York Herald Tribune on Porgy and Bess, 11 October 1935

'It will leave no great trace upon the history of our lyric theatre.'
Carlo Bersezio in La Stampa, on Puccini's La Bohème, 1896

'A blood-curdling nightmare.' Boston Herald, 23 February 1896, of Richard Strauss' 'Till Eulenspiegel lustige streiche'

'Something that I literally can't bear listening to because it absolutely reeks of cow shit, exaggerated Norwegian nationalism and trollish self-satisfaction!' Edvard Grieg in a letter in 1874 to a friend, on his own composition 'In the Hall of the Mountain King'

'[It] sounded as if a bomb had fallen into a large music factory and had thrown all the notes into confusion.'
The Berlin Tribune's critic on Wagner's *Tristan und Isolde*, 1871

'I've been told that Wagner's music is better than it sounds.'
Mark Twain

'I love Wagner, but the music I prefer is that of a cat hung up by its tail outside a window and trying to stick to the panes of glass with its claws.'
Charles Baudelaire

'A farrago of circus tunes.' E. Chapman, Tempo, September 1946, of Shostakovitch's Ninth Symphony

'But how did you get to understand Beethoven?' writes John Ruskin to John Brown in 1881. *'He always sounds to me like the upsetting of bags of nails, with here and there an also dropped hammer.'*

'A cat with catarrh.' Boston Evening Transcript, 17 April 1913, of Webern's 'Six Orchestral Pieces'

'The audience expected the ocean, something big, something colossal, but they were served instead with some agitated water in a saucer.'
Louis Schneider on Debussy's *La Mer*, 1903-05

'Strauss lets loose an orchestral riot that suggests a murder scene in a Chinese theatre.' H. T. Finck, 1910

'The music of Wagner imposes mental tortures that only algebra has a right to inflict.' Paul de Saint-Victor, La Presse, March 1861

'Sounded a good deal like a combination of early morning in the Mott Haven freight yards, feeding time at the zoo and a Sixth Avenue trolley rounding a curve, with an intoxicated woodpecker throw in for good measure.' Ernest Newman on Edgard Varèse's 'Intérales', New York Evening Post, 2 March 1925

'I am sitting in the smallest room of my house. I have your review before me. In a moment, it will be behind me.'
Max Reger, composer, in a written response to a critic

Some Musical Unappreciation

CRYPTOGRAPHIC MUSIC

Having examined *Portrait of a Musician* (see page 127), we can also find Leonardo da Vinci's love of music and composition evident – with a trademark Leonardo twist, of course – in a separate curious form. The Royal Collection at Windsor holds many sheets of sketches and doodles by the artist, including a number of rebuses, or picture-writing puzzles, in which words and letters are replaced with symbols and pictures. In other words, rebuses are a form of code-writing. Some of Leonardo's rebuses are of a musical nature, such as the one shown below. Most are too short to be performed, but several have been adapted in recent years. In 2019, Italy's Sensus Ensemble arranged two in a plain monody (solo vocal style) for performance at the Royal Opera House Mumbai to celebrate 500 years of Leonardo's genius; but, if you wish to hear them yourself, the Italian soprano Renata Fusco and the flautist Massimo Lonardi performed three of the musical puzzles in 2012, which you can find today under the title 'Vinci, Leonardo da: Tre Rebus musicali'.

Leonardo's musical puzzles bring us to the most secretive part of music history, as we move from a chapter about music hidden in time to one of music that hides secrets of its own in the form of 'musical cryptography'. The first European work on the subject of cryptography was written by the Franciscan friar Roger Bacon (1219/20–1292), in his *Letter Concerning the Marvelous Power of Art and of Nature and Concerning the Nullity of Magic*, written to a 'William of Paris', in which he outlines seven methods for disguising messages, while also dismissing necromancy and providing alchemical formulae. Thereafter, cipher systems and code-writing became an obsession of the

A scrap of puzzle-writing by Leonardo da Vinci, with a musical rebus at the top, followed by an attempt at pictographic translation, 1487-90.

132   Madman's Orchestra

scribes translating ancient texts, and then of Renaissance writers, along with musical puzzles like those of Da Vinci. But before all of this, we have the curious case of Hildegard of Bingen (1098-1179), the polymathic German Benedictine abbess, mystic and composer (see also The Horned Section, page 220). Hildegard is renowned for her hymns and antiphons for the liturgy, and, in fact, there are more existing chants by her than by any other composer from the Middle Ages. She is one of the few known to have written both the music and the text; but the most curious text she ever created was an entire language of her

A non-musical example of a pictographic rebus sheet of puzzle-writing by Leonardo da Vinci, 1490.

A possible 'hidden melody' in the pattern of the positions of the hands and bread, in Da Vinci's The Last Supper, *1495-98, to be played from right to left, as suggested by an Italian computer technician and musician named Giovanni Maria Pala in 2007. There is no consensus as to whether this is intentional or not, but the idea was deemed 'plausible' by Alessandro Vezzosi, a Leonardo expert and director of the artist's museum.*

own invention called the *lingua ignota* ('unknown tongue'). It is, in essence, an elaborate cryptographic system, for which – like all helpful cryptographers – she provides a key while describing the language in her work *Ignota lingua per simplicem hominem Hildegardem prolata*, which survives in two manuscripts, both dating to 1200.

The image shown opposite is taken from one of those manuscripts, the Wiesbaden Codex, a gigantic collection of Hildegard's works that weighs 15kg (33lb).♪ It shows her

---

♪ The breadth of Hildegard's writing is enormous. See, for example, her *Physica*, which is full of health advice such as: 'If someone has jaundice, strike a bat gently, so it does not die. Tie it over his loins, with the back of the bat turned towards the person's back. After a little while, take it off and tie it over his stomach. Leave it there until it dies.' Eating a heron's heart will cure sadness; applying the right ear of a lion to a deaf person's ear will restore hearing; eels are fine for healthy people to eat, but if you're ill they'll render you 'bitter in mind, crafty and evil.'

134 | *Madman's Orchestra*

invented alphabet for the lingua ignota and provides a glossary of 1,011 words to speak the lingua ignota, including:

Aigonz: deus (God)
Aieganz: angelus (angel)
Bischiniz: adolescens (adolescent)
Diueliz: diabolus (devil)
Falschin: vates (prophet)
Hilzmaiz: noverca (stepmother)
Hilzpeueriz: nutricus (stepfather)
Hilzscifriz: privignus (stepson)
Inimois: homo (human being)
Ispariz: spiritus (spirit)
Jugiza: vidua (widow)
Jur: vir (man)
Korzinthio: propheta (prophet)
Kulzphazur: attavus (great-great-great-grandfather)
Limzkil: infans (infant)
Linschiol: martir (martyr)
Liuionz: salvator (saviour)
Maiz: maler (sic, for mater, mother)
Pangizo: penitens (penitent)
Peuearrez: patriarcha (patriarch)
Peueriz: pater (father)
Phazur: avus (grandfather)
Scirizin: filius (son)
Sonziz: apostolus (apostle)
Vanix: femina (woman)
Vrizoil: virgo (virgin)
Zains: puer (boy)
Zanziuer: confessor (confessor)
Zunzial: iuvenis (youth)
Zuuenz: sanctus (saint)

Hildegard never revealed why she invented the lingua ignota. In the nineteenth century, it was thought to be a design for a universal language, but more recently it's been discussed as a secret language for text, and hymns, of divine inspiration. Sarah Higley at the University of Rochester describes it in a monograph as Hildegard's attempt at 'making the things of this world divine

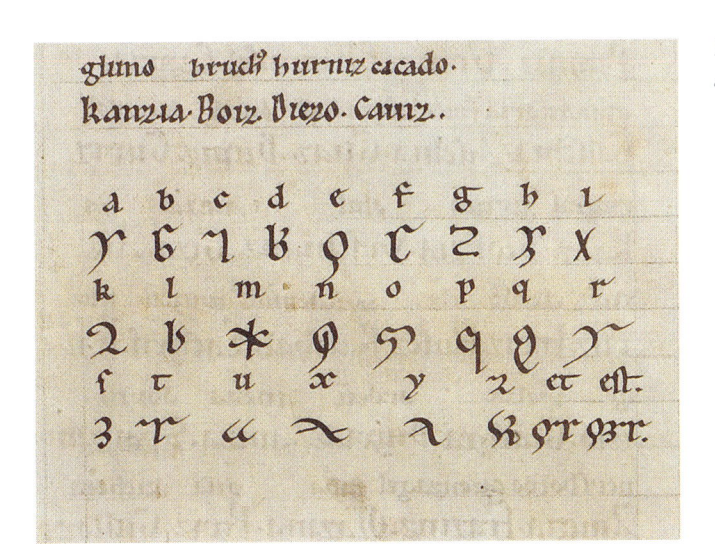

Hildegard of Bingen's invented alphabet for her lingua ignota.

again through the alterity of new signs'. It appears her contemporaries knew of the language, but there was no one to perpetuate it when she was gone: Hildegard's friend and provost, Volmar, wrote a letter to her in her final days, fearing her death approaching and asking worriedly '*ubi tunc vox inauditae melodiae? et vox inauditae linguae?*' ('Where, then, the voice of the unheard melody? And the voice of the unheard language?').

This idea of a constructed universal language – that is, one language that could be spoken the world over to transcend national boundaries – has a fascinating narrative in the history of music specifically. What if such a global language could be constructed with music, with all the depth and complexity of a complicated lingual system embedded and transmitted purely with notes?♪ The English polymath John Wilkins (1614-72) suggested in *Mercury, or the Secret and Swift Messenger*, 1641, the first English-language book on cryptography, that a musical instrument could be used for 'a general language as should be equally speakable by all nations and peoples.' Gottfried Leibnitz (1646-1716) proposed the same in 1678 for a musical language consisting simply of tones and intervals. Johann Ludwig Klüber (1762-1837) reported in 1809 of pupils at a Parisian school for the blind 'reading' messages played on the violin.

The fifteenth-century Lucca *(or* Mancini*) Codex is the only source for fifty-two early compositions, including this minimalist riddle canon of Johannes Ciconia,* Le ray au solely, *of the 1390s. Ciconia gives a Latin inscription at the end of the melody, hinting that three voices should be derived from this single line by rhythmically manipulating and superimposing it with itself.*

♪ In one sense, for a twentieth-century example of a musical universal language we can look to the Italian singer Adriano Celentano (b.1938) and his song 'Prisencolinensinainciusol', which charted in countries around Europe. At first it sounds like Celentano is singing in poorly annunciated English; in fact, he's singing nonsense, written to mimic the way English sounds to non-English speakers.

Madman's Orchestra

The most intriguing event in this experimental chronology is the innovation of Jean-François Sudre (1787-1862), who taught his students to communicate entirely through the use of their violins. By 1817, Sudre had achieved the remarkable: he had devised an entire artificial language he called Solrésol, with an alphabet and extensive vocabulary built entirely from the seven *solfège* syllables *do, re, mi, fa, sol, la* and *si*. These seven symbols could be used as many as five times per word, to the point that conversations could be held fluently. For example, some sample questions in Solrésol are:

Am I? – Fa-re-mi do-re?
Does he understand? – Fa-la-fa do-fa?
Are you learning? – Si-do-si do-mi?
Is your health good? – Re-do-fa-fa?
Will you go to the countryside this year? – Fa-do-re-mi?
Will you go to the theatre tonight? – Sol-do-re-mi?

Sudre formed a trio with Édouard Deldevez and Charles Larsonneur and trained them in the musical language. Together they gave performances around France, answering audience questions with their instruments. Ambitious plans were made for Solrésol. Perhaps, suggested Sudre, army buglers could broadcast orders to regiments on the field with encrypted melodies. He even devised a system of musical cannons. Ultimately, the plans never came to fruition. Solrésol was simply too flawed and complex. (For example, if you mistook just the first note of the word *fa-la-la-sol* for *sol-la-la-sol*, then instead of the word 'asthma' you would translate it as 'excrement'.) The other problem was the limited distance with which one could 'speak' the language. To solve this, Sudre came up with the idea of a huge musical instrument that could transmit Solrésol messages great distances, a device he labelled a *téléphone* (combining the Greek words for 'far' and 'voice') – three decades before Alexander Graham Bell was even born. Sudre spent three years compiling a dictionary of his invention, *Langue Musicale Universelle*, which was published in 1865, after his death and popularised the system into the twentieth century. Interest largely died out – although, even today, there are small groups of dedicated Sudre enthusiasts around the world that continue to converse musically in Solrésol.

In fact, music had already been used to hide and convey meaning for centuries before the universal languages of Sudre and co., with the field of musical cryptography. There was even

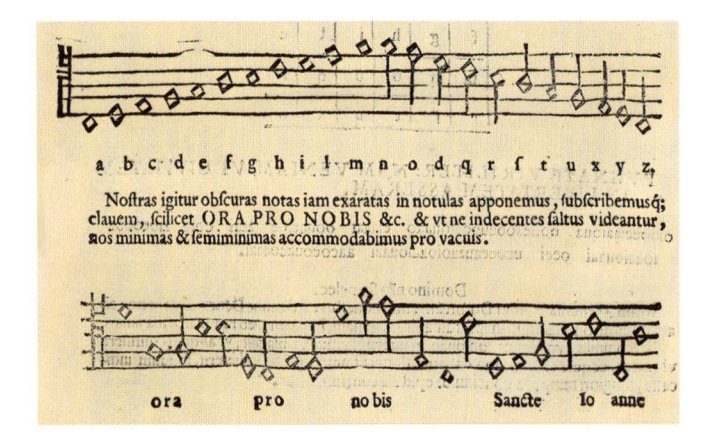

One of the earliest known musical ciphers for encrypting text as a musical melody, from Giambattista della Porta's De Furtivis Literarum Notis, *1563.*

a precursor to Sudre's idea of musical cannons in the suggestion by Giambattista della Porta (1535-1615), who authored the early cryptographic work *De Furtivis Literarum Notis* ('On the Secret Symbols of Letters') in 1563, and who revelled in the nickname of 'professor of secrets'. As well as devising techniques for passing secret messages, like writing on the inside of unbroken eggshells, he also describes a technique of communication with which a city under siege could send messages using the music of bell-ringing: ring one bell once = A, twice = B, thrice = C; a second bell once = D; and so on. Later in the seventeenth century, Athanasius Kircher transfers this idea of musical messaging to an orchestra by distributing up to four successive notes among six instruments, so one note from the first instrument would mean the letter A, two notes B, etc.

The systematic processes of cryptography, which is broken down into codes (a word or phrase that is swapped out with another word, number or symbol) and ciphers (substituting each letter, not just each word, with a new letter or symbol; in this case, a musical note) is markedly similar to the processes of writing music, itself a form of communication comprehensible only to those trained. Thus, numerous musicians from history have also dabbled in cryptography, from Giuseppe Tartini (1692-1770) writing in a cipher that remained unbroken for two hundred years, to Michael Haydn (1737-1806), Robert

Schumann (1810-56) and Edward Elgar (1857-1934) acting similarly. The British Secret Intelligence Service recognised the link when recruiting code-breakers in the Second World War: one of the interview questions was whether the candidate could read an orchestral score.

The earliest form of musical cryptography was the easiest to devise and still the most common: assigning letters to individual musical notes. This technique is recorded as early as the late fifteenth century, with the British Library manuscript Sloane 351 (f.15b) titled *Rules for Carrying on a Secret Correspondence by Cipher*. The trick to generating a sufficient variety of musical notes to substitute all the letters of the alphabet is to use five different pitches, or more, on a three-line stave and change the stem directions and note values. In 1596, the papal cryptographic service employed a music cipher of nine different pitches, each variable in eight ways, to produce a possible seventy-two symbols with which to write messages. When working with the chromatic scale, a greater number of note substitutes can be created by applying sharps and flats to the seven diatonic pitches, giving you twenty-one unique cipher symbols, and then generating the remaining required for a full alphabet by adding other features like octave register or duration. The latter code-writing technique is the one we find used by twentieth-century composers, as fully chromatic music itself was more usual.

Given its secretive nature, it's perhaps no surprise that musical cryptography was often referenced in occult works. The details shown on page 140 are a cipher from Gustav

Musical tones and their angelic rulers, from Gustav Selenus's Cryptomenytices et Cryptographiae Libri IX, *1624.*

Cipher notation from Cryptomenytices et Cryptographiae Libri IX, *1624.*

Selenus' *Cryptomenytices et Cryptographiae Libri IX*, 1624, a system of mixing demonology with music that is attributed to a certain Count who dressed music 'in the cloak of magic'. The solfège (the do-re-mi scale) table shows how each musical tone is governed by two angels: re, for example, is under the rule of the angel Lofaresiel, and at other times the angel Druziel. Selenus then details a magic ritual in which one should read the five-line invocation below the angelic table four times, each time facing in a different cardinal direction. In doing so, 'there is no doubt that you will find the angels obedient to your wishes, so that, with their help, though not a musician, you will suddenly become such, and there will come unbidden to your pen a melody, wherewith you can afterwards compose whatever song you will, whether sacred or profane, and even, by the union of four or five voices, render the same more sonorous still'. One must take care to do it correctly, though, 'for if you do not, you expose yourself to the ridicule of the angels'.

The instructions as to how to use the cipher are hidden in the spell itself. If you remove the first and last letter of each word of the five lines, and then read the remaining words backwards, you're left with a message informing you that the third letter in each angelic name is of significance, and pairs of notes linked with each angelic name form a key to ciphering and deciphering messages. As an example, he gives the cipher notation shown above a seemingly innocuous piece of music that can be translated using the key to read: '*Hiet dich for deinem Diener Hansen: Dan er sol dich bey nacht erwirgeni*' ('Beware your servant Hansen: for he plots to strangle you tonight.')

FOLLOWING SPREAD-LEFT:
A code-spinning musical cipher wheel, from Abraham Rees Cyclopædia, *1778.*

FOLLOWING SPREAD-RIGHT:
A demonstration of how to encrypt messages with music, from J. Bücking, Anweisung zur Geheimen Correspondenz… *('Instructions for Secret Correspondence'), 1804.*

140 Madman's Orchestra

In 1772, musical cryptography was promoted by the eighteenth-century writer and British Army officer Philip Thicknesse (1719-92), who published *A Treatise on the Art of Decyphering, and of Writing in Cyphers, With an Harmonic Alphabet* to enthuse on the benefits of using music to hide coded communiqués, 'for who that examined a suspected messenger would think an old song, without words, in which perhaps the messenger's tobacco or snuff might be put, contained a secret he was to convey?' Thicknesse presented his own cipher system of crotchets (or quarter notes if you're American) and semibreves (half notes) with treble clef and key signature, to create an 'harmonic alphabet' of reliable security, perfectly suited for espionage, as the melody would be convincingly functional.♪

In 1804, a German writer and cryptography enthusiast named Johann Bücking (1749-1838) concocted a compound cipher to generate musical compositions in the deceptive form of a minuet

ABOVE-TOP: *After retreating at the Battle of Worcester in 1651, Charles Stuart (later Charles II) fled from Oliver Cromwell's New Model Army and stopped at Boscobel House. This manuscript claims to be a coded message disguised as music notation that was passed to Charles at Boscobel by an unnamed woman to warn him of imminent danger. When folded correctly, the notation reads 'Conceal yourself, your foes look for you'.*

ABOVE-BOTTOM: *A nineteenth-century copy of this message, showing its solution and naming the author of the message as Jane Lane, who helped Charles escape England by disguising him as her servant.*

♪ Interesting fellow, Thicknesse. He lived out his later years in the gardens of St Catherine's Hermitage, Bath, as an 'ornamental hermit', a popular novelty of the time in which a wealthy landowner allowed an elderly man to live alone in a grotto in their garden as a living landscape feature. After Thicknesse died in 1792, he was buried near Boulogne, Pas-de-Calais, France, but in accordance with a remarkably pissy stipulation in his will his right hand was cut off and sent to his inattentive son, George, 'to remind him of his duty to God after having so long abandoned the duty he owed to a father, who once so affectionately loved him'.

141 Cryptographic Music

Fig. 5.

Let me know you are safe and easy, und ease my tortured mind

Tab 2.

§ 15. Fig. I. a.

a b c d e f g h i k l m n o p q r s t u v w x z

Fig. I b.

Fig. II a.

a b c d e f g h i k l m n o p q r s t u v w x z

Fig. II b.

FREUND.

§ 16. Fig. 1.

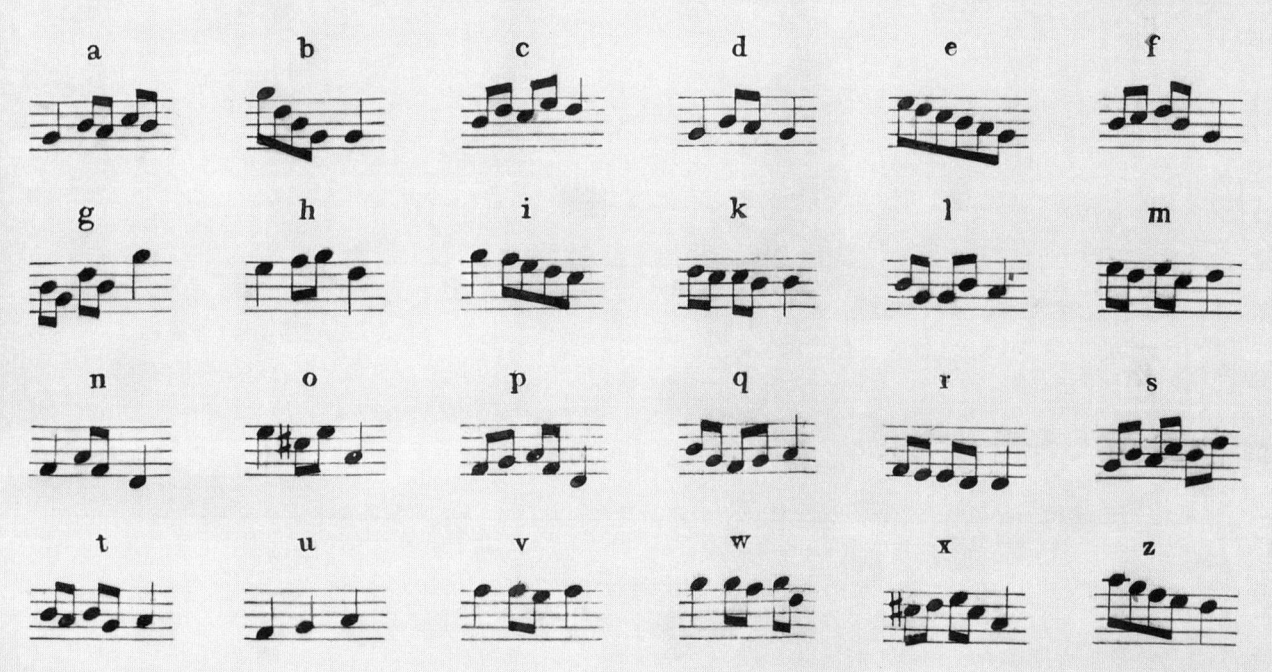

a b c d e f
g h i k l m
n o p q r s
t u v w x z

Nro. 1 der Anfang der Melodie   Nro 2 Finale   Fig. 1. § 16.

§ 16. Fig. 2.

in the key of G major. As shown on page 143, each letter of the alphabet is replaced not by a note but by a bar of music of between three and six notes, and then bookended with purely musical measures either end to disguise it. One can write a cipher, and simultaneously compose a full piece of music! Mozart had actually used a similar technique years earlier, in much more sophisticated form, but apparently as a parlour game rather than as a cipher with any real meaning.

Perhaps unsurprisingly, there are very few documented usages and surviving examples of these secretive musical ciphers. One is a message of the French diplomatic service (British Library manuscript Add 32259, f.180v), a correspondence between the Duke of Havré (1609-50) and the Duke of Lorges (1630–1702), which was written using a musical cipher system to produce a result that frankly isn't terribly convincing musically, nor secure cryptically. Nevertheless, this messaging system was used as late as 1800, and curiously is even found in the twentieth century in an unexpected situation: the first solved intercept by the New York City Police Department (as reported in a police science technical abstract titled *Codes are Fragile*, in April 1952) was a series of melodic lines in the treble clef that was found to be a note-for-figure encipherment of a bookie's records of illegal wagers – the criminal code-writer had even added flourishes of musical accents and pauses in an attempt to make it look more convincing.

Perhaps this musically minded (and swiftly imprisoned) bookmaker had been inspired by the great composers themselves, many of whom wove ciphers into the fabric of their compositions to leave traces of themselves in their work. We can look back as far as the early eighteenth century for this type of secretive code insertion. Johann Christoph Faber (1669-1744) enciphered the name Ludovicus in his *Neu-erfundene obligate Composition* with the number of notes allotted to the solo trumpet in each of the nine movements: the solo trumpet plays twenty notes in the first movement, under the written instruction 'L=20', then 200 notes in the second ('U=200') and so on.

In German, extra letters outside of A-G (and H, the German Bb) were found, like 'S' as an equivalent of Eb, as the German name of the note is 'Es' (this allowed, for example, Friedrich Fesca to 'sign' a piece for string quartet with F–E–Eb-CA). Johann Sebastian Bach inserted his own name into numerous compositions, including his final work 'The Art of the Fugue', with the usage shown opposite, known as the 'Bach

B A C H

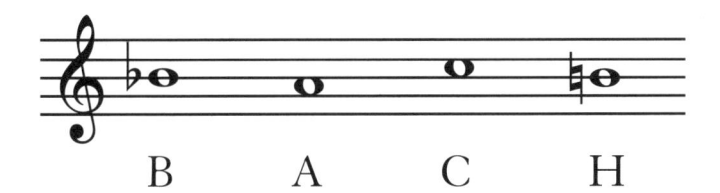

LEFT: *How to write 'Bach' in music notation, as hidden in composition by the composer himself.*

motif', which one also finds incorporated by Ludwig van Beethoven, Robert Schumann, Franz Liszt, Nikolay Rimsky-Korsakov, Ferruccio Busoni and others. Bach appears to have paid a subtle tribute to Faber with his seven-part canon using F–A–B–E, with the heading note 'FABERepetatur'. John Field (1782-1837), meanwhile, whose nocturnes had a clear influence on Liszt, Frédéric Chopin and Gabrial Fauré, paid grateful tribute to the culinary skills of his hostess Mme Cramer in the cipher form of two melodies using B–E–E–F and C-A-B-B-A-G–E.

Robert Schumann (1810-56) was prolific with cipher usage: take his famous work 'Carnaval', op. 9, 1834-35, as an example. The main theme is embedded with the musical letters S–C–H–A, while elsewhere in the piece you can find A–S–C–H (a reference to the hometown of his friend Ernestine von Fricken). A–S was enciphered by using A and Fb as equivalents, or simply by using As (Ab in German). In Schumann's various other pieces of music we can also 'read' ciphers containing A–B–E–G–G and G–A–D–E (for the names of friends); FA–E (which stands for *frei aber einsam*, 'free but lonely', a message hidden in music by Joachim, too); A–C–H, AD–E, B–E–D–A (a pet name for his wife Clara); B–E–SE–D–H (the closest he could do to representing the name of his friend Bezeth); and probably the longest musical cipher example on record: (L)–A–S–S D–A–S F–A–D–E, F–A–SS D–A–S A–E–C–H–D(T)–E – 'Leave what is trite, hold fast to the right.'

Schumann's friend Johannes Brahms (1833-97) also drew on music ciphers, with one in particular making for a poignant secret. Having fallen in love in 1858 at the age of twenty-five with a 23-year-old music director named Agathe von Siebold,

BELOW: *Louis Spohr's (1784-1859) musical signature, using the abbreviation for* portamento, *and an antique-style crotchet to resemble an 'r'.*

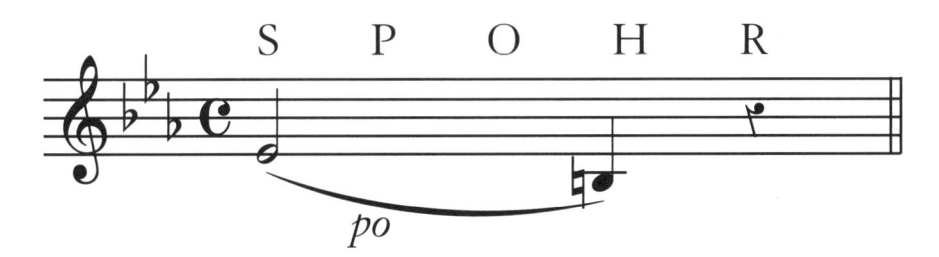

S P O H R

po

145   Cryptographic Music

the German composer broke off their engagement in 1859 to dedicate himself to music instead. As a formalised farewell, he stitched the wistful musical notes of her name A-G-A-H-E, A-D-E into the first movement of his String Sextet No. 2 in G major, in bars 162-168, at an emotional high spot in the piece; 'by this work, I have freed myself of my last love', Brahms writes in a letter to his friend Josef Gänsbacher about the sextet. Von Siebold later married, but Brahms would remain a bachelor.

Arnold Schoenberg (1874-1951) formed his signature hexachord (a six-note series), 6-Z44 (012569), known as the Schoenberg hexachord, as one transposition containing the pitches [A], Es, C, H, B, E, G (that is, A. Schoenberg). The Austrian-American composer uses the hexachord in his song 'Seraphita', op. 22, no. 1, 1913, and in the monodrama *Die glückliche Hand*, op. 18, 1913. Dmitri Shostakovich (1906-75), meanwhile, uses the eponymous DSCH motif as a cryptogram to bury in his music, employing the German equivalents of D, E flat, C, B natural to form 'D. Sch'.

In terms of mystery, the English composer Edward Elgar (1857-1934) is perhaps best known for his 'Enigma Variations' from 1899, which are made up of fourteen variations that each reimagine an original theme – an original theme that isn't actually given, and that Elgar never revealed. It was a well-known existing melody, writes Elgar; in fact it was 'so well known that it is extraordinary that no one has spotted

A comprehensive chromatic substitution cipher by Michael Haydn, brother of Joseph, from 1808. Not only did Haydn devise a way of substituting music for every letter of the alphabet, but he even added punctuation using rest signs, parentheses with clefs and word segmentation using bar lines.

it', adding: 'The Enigma I will not explain – its "dark saying" must be left unguessed.' At the same time, Elgar was also a fan of codes and ciphers. The most tantalising of these is one that has never been broken, known as the Dorabella cipher, which he writes in 1897 to Dora Penny, a family friend seventeen years his junior. It's possible that it's not even a text at all but a melody, the eight different positions of the semicircles, rotating clockwise, matching the notes of the scale. Some have confidently claimed to have cracked the code but often provide a solution even more nonsensical than the code: see that of Tim S. Roberts of Central Queensland University, for example: 'P.S. Now droop beige weeds set in it – pure idiocy – one entire bed! Luigi Ccibunud lovingly tuned liuto studio two.'

The list of great composers moonlighting as cryptographers goes on into the twentieth century: Joseph Maurice Ravel (1875-1937) created a complex cipher system that he used to hide the name 'Haydn' in a commemorative Menuet for piano in 1909, and again in 1922 for a tribute to Fauré. Claude Debussy (1862-1918), Paul Dukas (1865-1935), Reynaldo Hahn (1874-1945) and Vincent d'Indy (1851-1931) also did so. The most notable is the cipher work of the French composer Olivier Messiaen (1908-92) in the 1960s, when he created a cipher workable with all twenty-six letters in the alphabet that he used to make what he called a 'communicable language' to imitate the wordless language of the angels, as described by St Thomas Aquinas (1224/25-74). Messiaen, a deeply religious man, drew on the cipher to write his organ work, 'Méditations sur le mystère de la Sainte Trinité', 1967-69, in which he enciphered lengthy quotations of the French translation of Aquinas's *Summa theologica*, 1265-74. By mapping each letter of each message to

The unsolved Dorabella cipher, written by the composer Edward Elgar in 1897 to a young friend of his family, Dora Penny. The cipher has never been broken; it's possible that it's not even a text but a melody, the eight different positions of the semicircles, rotating clockwise, matching the notes of the scale.

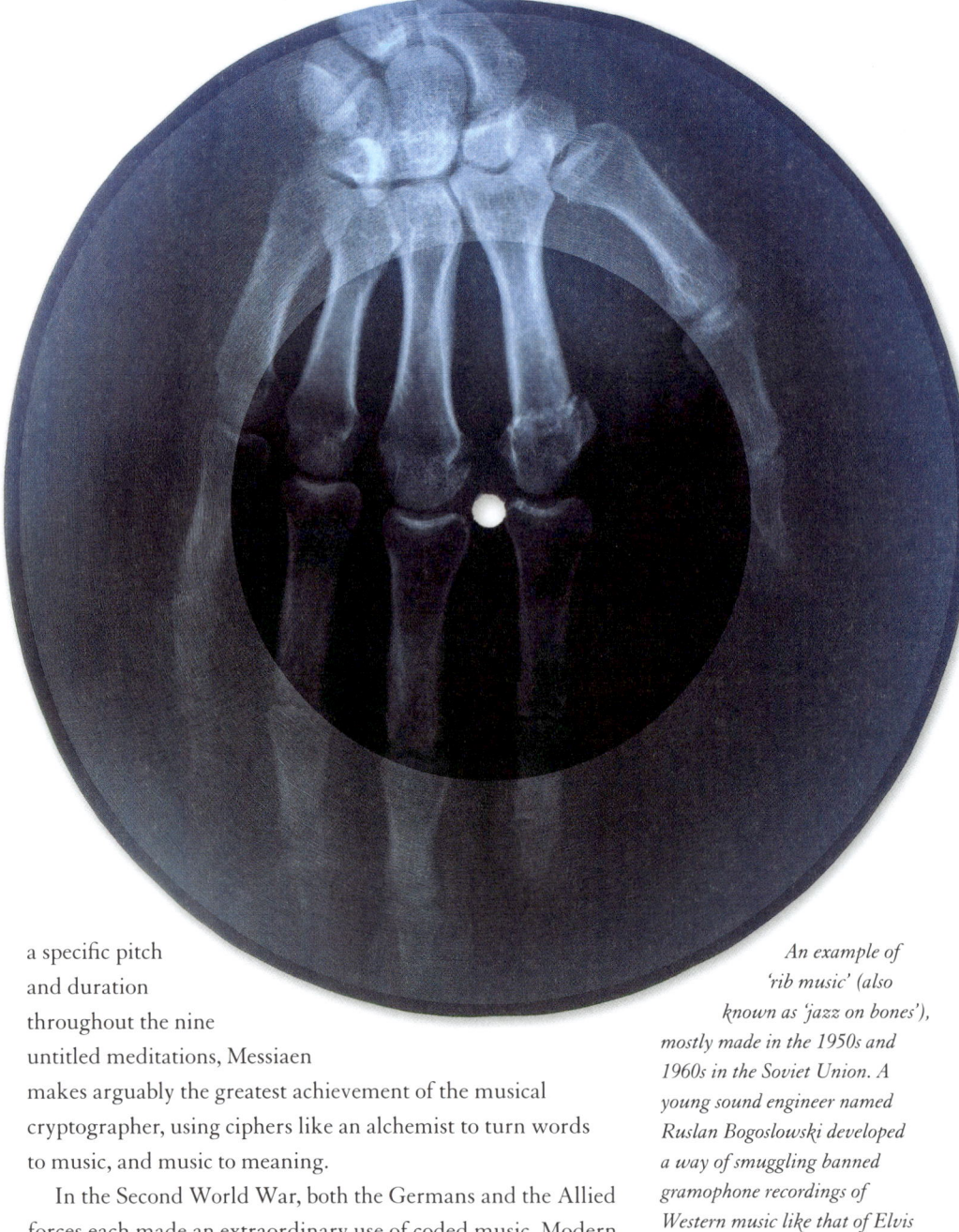

a specific pitch and duration throughout the nine untitled meditations, Messiaen makes arguably the greatest achievement of the musical cryptographer, using ciphers like an alchemist to turn words to music, and music to meaning.

In the Second World War, both the Germans and the Allied forces each made an extraordinary use of coded music. Modern listeners might not be familiar with the swing band Charlie and His Orchestra, who also went by the name of Bruno and His Swinging Tigers, but in 1940, the British radio audience could tune in to hear the band play every Wednesday and Saturday evenings from around 9 p.m. They performed popular British and American swing songs true to the original until about the second or third stanza. At this point, a keen-eared listener

An example of 'rib music' (also known as 'jazz on bones'), mostly made in the 1950s and 1960s in the Soviet Union. A young sound engineer named Ruslan Bogoslowski developed a way of smuggling banned gramophone recordings of Western music like that of Elvis Presley and the Beatles past censors by etching the recordings into discarded X-ray films.

might notice the singer Charlie (real name Karl Schwedler) straying from the original version and changing the lyrics to pro-German sentiment, crowing about Allied losses, mocking Winston Churchill and Franklin D. Roosevelt, insulting black and Jewish people and parroting Nazi propaganda. When singing Walter Donaldson's hit 'You're Driving Me Crazy', for example, Charlie begins crooning about new love; but in the third stanza sings: 'Here is Winston Churchill's latest tear-jerker: Yes, the Germans are driving me crazy / I thought I had brains / But they shot down my planes…' Charlie's cover of Louis Armstrong's 1930s hit 'I Double Dare You' featured the lines: 'I double dare you to venture a raid. I double dare you to try and invade. And if your loud propaganda means half of what it says, I double dare you to come over here.' Their rendition of the popular song 'Thanks for the Memory' featured the lines: 'Thanks for the memories / It gives us strength to fight / For freedom and for right / It might give you a headache, England / That the Germans know how to fight / And hurt you so much.'

At other times, Charlie would ditch the singing entirely and simply launch into a spoken propaganda speech. The band was dreamed up by propaganda minister Joseph Goebbels (1897-1945), who arranged for the broadcast of the music to reach the United Kingdom, and later, after the German declaration of war on 11 December 1941, to Canada and the United States as well. According to his staff, Winston Churchill enjoyed tuning in to listen to the shows.

The Allies, meanwhile, deployed their own musical plan – and, with magnificent irony, co-opted the work of one of the greatest German musicians to ever live. It was the exiled Belgian politician Victor de Laveleye (1894-1945) who, in 1941, came up with the idea of encouraging the people of Occupied Belgium to use the letter 'V' as a sign for not peace but 'Victory', a symbol of resistance. The idea was spread by the BBC's Radio Belgique, a special wartime service, until it was adopted throughout Europe. The letter V was painted on buildings, the hands of clocks were stopped in a V-shape, people even sat with their legs spread in a V to express solidarity with the resistance, and the raised two-fingered V-sign was immortalised by Winston Churchill in his palm-outward salute.

But how to spread the message audibly? Coincidentally, the Morse Code for the letter V is *dot-dot-dot-dash*, the same pattern as perhaps the most famous musical phrase in history: Beethoven's opening 'fate motif' in his Fifth Symphony – the

dun-dun-dun-dunnn
pattern of three short notes followed by one long one.

These opening notes of the Fifth Symphony became a rallying cry and a coded signal of defiance for the peoples of Nazi-occupied Europe. The notes were knocked on doors, windows and anywhere a secret show of solidarity was needed. The BBC used it as a time signal between news broadcasts to occupied territories, a perfect aid for tuning home-made radios in poor receiving conditions, as its sharp beats could be clearly heard. After the collapse of Nazi forces across Europe on 8 May 1945, this call-sign of the Overseas Service of the BBC was dramatically transformed in triumph, with James Blades – who had recorded the original wartime rhythm on an African slit-drum – re-recording the motif with a modern orchestral timpani, thundering out the call of victory across Europe.

A recording of Noel Gay and Harry Graham's 'The King's Horses', by the secret Nazi propaganda swing band Charlie and His Orchestra. The German Propaganda Ministry distributed their music on 78rpm records to prisoner-of-war (POW) camps and occupied countries.

▶ PLAYLIST: CRYPTOGRAPHIC MUSIC

Préambule, 'Carnaval', op. 9, 1837,
ROBERT SCHUMANN

Chopin, 'Carnaval', op. 9, 1837,
ROBERT SCHUMANN

'Berceuse sur le nom de Fauré', M. 74, 1922,
MAURICE RAVEL

'Collage sur B–A–C–H for chamber orchestra', 1964, ARVO PÄRT

La musica a Milano al tempo di Leonardo da Vinci: La figurazione delle cose invisibili, 1452-1519,
MASSIMO LONARDI AND RENATA FUSCO

'Die glückliche Hand', op. 18, 1913,
ARNOLD SCHOENBERG

Fugue No. 15 in D flat major, op. 87, 1952,
DMITRI SHOSTAKOVICH

'I Double Dare You', 1941-45,
'I Got Rhythm', 1941-45,
'Stardust', 1941-45,
'The Sheik of Araby',1941-45,
'Thanks For the Memory', 1941-45,
'You're Driving Me Crazy', 1941-45,
CHARLIE AND HIS ORCHESTRA

Leonardo da Vinci's Rebuses, 1489,
PERFORMED BY THE SENSUS ENSEMBLE

'Méditations sur le mystère de la Sainte Trinité',
OLIVIER MESSIAEN

'Menuet sur le nom de Haydn', M. 58, 1909,
MAURICE RAVEL

Nocturne No. 1 in E flat major, H. 24, 1812,
JOHN FIELD

'O Euchari in Leta Via', *Vision / The Music of Hildegard Von Bingen*, 1994, RICHARD SOUTHER

'Only the Devil Laughed (Sed Diabolus)', *Vision / The Music of Hildegard Von Bingen*, 1994, RICHARD SOUTHER

'Praise For the Mother (O Virga AC Diadema)', *Vision / The Music of Hildegard Von Bingen*, 1994, RICHARD SOUTHER

'Seraphita', op. 22, No. 1, 1913,
ARNOLD SCHOENBERG

String Quartet No. 5 in B flat major, op. 92, 1952, DMITRI SHOSTAKOVICH

String Quartet No. 6 in G major, op. 101, 1956,
DMITRI SHOSTAKOVICH

String Quartet No. 8 in C minor, op. 110, 1960,
DMITRI SHOSTAKOVICH

String Sextet No. 2 in G major, 1865,
JOHANNES BRAHMS

Symphony No. 10 in E minor, op. 93, 1953,
DMITRI SHOSTAKOVICH

Symphony No. 15 in A major, op. 141, 1972,
DMITRI SHOSTAKOVICH

Symphony No. 5 in C minor, op. 67, 1808,
LUDWIG VAN BEETHOVEN

'The Art of Fugue', BEV 1080, 1751,
JOHANN SEBASTIAN BACH

'Tre Rebus musicali', *La musica a Milano al tempo di Leonardo da Vinci: La figurazione*,
LEONARDO DA VINCI

Variations on an Original Theme, op. 36 ('Enigma Variations'), 1899, EDWARD ELGAR

Variations on the name 'Abegg', op. 1, 1829-30,
ROBERT SCHUMANN

Violin Concerto in B minor, D. 125, 'Lascia ch'io dica addio': III Allegro, 1740s, GIUSEPPE TARTINI

Violin Concerto in E major, D. 50: I. Allegro, 1724-35, GIUSEPPE TARTINI

Violin Concerto No. 1 in A minor, op. 77, 1947-48, DMITRI SHOSTAKOVICH

MUSICAL DISASTERS

Opening night nerves, hostile audiences, lack of rehearsal time, a conductor forgetting to fasten his trousers… While watching professional musicians at work, it can be easy to forget the sheer number of fragile moving parts to a live musical performance – be they human, technological or just the shaky cosmic mechanics of pure luck. Not every performance can meet with the same audience reaction as the 'Sinngedicht' ('Poems of the Senses or Epigrams'), op. 1, by Johann Strauss II (1825-99), the most encored work at one concert. At the Casino Dommayer in Vienna on Tuesday, 15 October 1844, this piece closed the programme, and was encored nineteen times. Similarly, when Domenico Cimarosa's (1749-1801) opera *Il matrimonio segreto* ('The Secret Marriage') opened at the Imperial Hofburg Theatre in Vienna in February 1792, Emperor Leopold II was so delighted by it that he demanded to hear it again. Immediately. And so the exhausted performers staged the entire opera from start to finish for a second time.

An advertisement for Johann Strauss II's record-breaking premiere of 'Sinngedicht' ('Poems of the Senses or Epigrams'), op. 1, in 1844.

The fact that disaster can strike any show at any moment is masked by polish and confidence, and yet the fearful knowledge of how quickly a masterpiece can turn into a disasterpiece lurks in the amygdala of every musician's brain. And when premiering a novel work, these risks are, of course, heightened massively – will the new music be rapturously digested by the public, or will there be some rather messy regurgitation?

Thanks to the endless Library of Babel that is the modern internet, you can watch the moment of disaster-panic strike in real time, with the most miraculous recovery of a public performer of recent times. In 1999, the Portuguese pianist Maria João Pires (b.1944) was invited at the last minute to perform a Mozart concerto at the Concertgebouw in Amsterdam by the Italian conductor Riccardo Chailly, in front of a full-house audience of 2,000 people. Over the phone, Pires heard the intended piece identified as 'K. 488', the 488 [Mozart's Piano Concerto No. 23 in A major] that she had played a couple of weeks before. It was only when the orchestra started playing on the night that she instantly realised it was the 466 (Mozart's Piano Concerto No. 20 in D minor), which she hadn't played for at least 11 months. The video recording of the live performance shows her horrified reaction, frantically whispering to Chailly while he conducts that she has prepared the wrong piece. 'You can do it, you played it, you can do it no problem, just do it,' he replies cheerfully, not pausing for a moment. Which is just what Pires proceeds to do, entirely from memory, with not a single note out of place. On that occasion, disaster was averted; the following are stories of some musicians rather less fortunate.

OPPOSITE: Destruction of Covent Garden Theatre by Fire, March 5th 1856. *The fire broke out during a musical masked ball organised by the Scottish magician J. H. Anderson, self-styled 'Wizard of the North', despite the manager of the theatre, Frederick Gye, having expressly forbidden it. The theatre was completely destroyed.*

Musical Disasters

The King's Theatre, London, scene of Haydn's 'Miracle'.

On 2 February 1795, the King's Theatre, London, was packed to the rafters with an audience eager to hear the music of the most famous man in the city at the time, Joseph Haydn, who was touring at the age of sixty-two. Haydn appeared in the orchestra and sat at the pianoforte to conduct the symphony himself. This obscured him from a section of the audience, who left their seats in the parterre and rushed up to the orchestra to get a better view of the composer. While this sounds like the recipe for a floor collapse, instead it was a twist of good fortune, as the great chandelier that fell from the centre of the ceiling crashed down onto empty seats, causing chaotic but non-fatal carnage. 'As soon as the first moment of fright was over', writes the contemporary German biographer Albert Dies in *Biographical News*, 'and those who had pressed forward could think of the danger they had luckily escaped and find words to express it, several persons uttered the state of their feelings with loud cries of "Miracle! Miracle!"… And the Londoners thus named the symphony the "Miracle".' For some reason, Dies mistakenly dated the incident to 1791, which has led to Haydn's Symphony No. 96 being labelled the 'Miracle' symphony. In fact' the chandelier crash took place in 1795 at the premiere of the tenth (and lesser known, but best) of Haydn's London symphonies, Symphony No. 102 in B flat major.

A famously disastrous premiere in the history of opera was that of Gioachino Rossini's (1792-1868) *The Barber of Seville* at the Teatro Argentina in Rome on 20 February 1816. In part, this was through the engineering of a rival. Much of the audience was said to have been composed of supporters of Giovanni Paisiello (1740-1816), who took Rossini's adaptation to be an insult to his own, offended by aspects like the use of a *basso buffo* (a bass singer of humorous roles), more common in lighter comic opera. Rossini was aware of the hatred and debuted the work disguised under the title 'Almaviva, or the Useless Precaution', to no avail. On a mission to sabotage, the audience hissed and jeered throughout the performance. Added to the hostile mob mentality was a string of accidents that had the audience roaring with unintended laughter. Basilio was forced to sing his aria with blood streaming from his nose after tripping over a trapdoor in the stage floor. In the Finale to Act 1, a cat wandered on stage and refused to leave, and so was hastily booted into the wings. The show ended with the audience chanting 'Paisiello! Paisiello! Paisello!' The second performance, however, was a massive success – but Rossini wasn't there to enjoy it. He couldn't face enduring the ridicule again. After the show, a crowd carrying torches gathered at his residence to congratulate him, but he hid in the stables, assuming they had come to burn the building down. Rossini later claimed that the disaster was one of only three times that he had cried in his life. The other two were when he heard a young Niccolò Paganini (1782-1840) play; and when he accidentally dropped his truffled turkey lunch into Lake Como while boating.

After three years of work, Ludwig van Beethoven debuted his String Quartet No. 12 in E flat major, op. 127, on 6 March 1825. One of three commissioned by the Russian Prince Demetrius Gallitzin, there was great anticipation. However, while tickets for the show had been sold for the end of February, the concert had been pushed back into March, as the quartet was given the music only two weeks before the new date, offering little in the way of rehearsal time. The performance was tentatively tested in a small hall,

ABOVE: *A falling chandelier adorns the cover of the Royal Philharmonic Orchestra's recording of Haydn's 'Miracle' Symphony, 1974.*

BELOW: *A rare survival from the time of Rossini, a painted fan celebrating his success with* The Barber of Seville, *inscribed with the title, character names and even part of the score of the opera.*

and the dazzlingly lyrical op. 127 was, at that time, described by both performers and listeners as baffling. A critic in Germany's *Allgemeine musicalische Zeitung* writes that the piece was an 'incomprehensible, incoherent, vague, over-extended series of fantasias and chaos, from which flashes of genius emerged from time to time like lightning bolts from a black thunder cloud'. Karl van Beethoven, nephew of the composer, blamed the failure on the playing of the Austrian violinist Ignaz Schuppanzigh (1776-1830): 'The first violin part went so badly', he writes. 'There were many disruptions. First nothing came together properly and then Schuppanzigh broke a string, which contributed to it a lot, because he didn't have a second violin at hand.'

In 1848, composer and piano virtuoso Frédéric Chopin was performing his Piano Sonata No. 2 in B flat minor, op. 35 at a private salon in Paris when he started having hallucinations so terrifying that he leapt to his feet and fled the room. In a letter he writes to French author George Sand later, he recounts how 'I was about to play the [Funeral] March when, suddenly, I saw emerging from the half-open case of my piano those cursed creatures that had appeared to me on a lugubrious night at the Carthusian monastery.' (George recalled how the monastery had been 'full of terrors and ghosts for him'.) Chopin's family and friends had always assumed the hallucinations were a side-effect of possessing such a brilliant mind, but in 2011, Spanish researcher Manuel Vázquez Caruncho published a paper offering the hypothesis that Chopin might have suffered temporal lobe epilepsy.

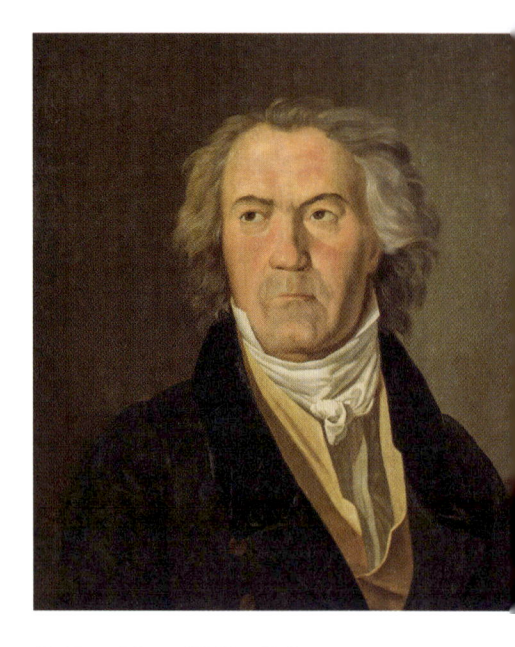

Ferdinand Georg Waldmüller's portrait of Ludwig van Beethoven in 1823, who looked this morose before the disastrous performance of his String Quartet No. 12 in E flat major, op. 127.

A watercolour of Chopin composing his last music, in his usual habit of leaning back and staying stock-still, with a dislike of pianists who swayed.

When Sergey Rachmaninoff's Symphony No. 1 in D minor, op. 13 premiered on 28 March 1897, the performance was so terrible that the symphony was never again performed in the composer's lifetime. The critic and composer César Cui compared it to the Seven Plagues of Egypt, and writes in the *St Petersburg News* that it would have delighted the members of the musical conservatory of Hell. Which seems a bit much. Rachmaninoff's wife, Natalie Satina (1877-1951), and other witnesses, blamed the catastrophe on the conductor, Aleksandr Glazunov, suggesting he had been drunk. Rachmaninoff fell into a three-year well of depression and writer's block, giving piano lessons to pay the bills while feeling 'like the man who had suffered a stroke and for a long time had lost the use of his head and hands'.

Giacomo Puccini (1858-1924) had written his opera *Madama Butterfly* over a two-year period, which included an

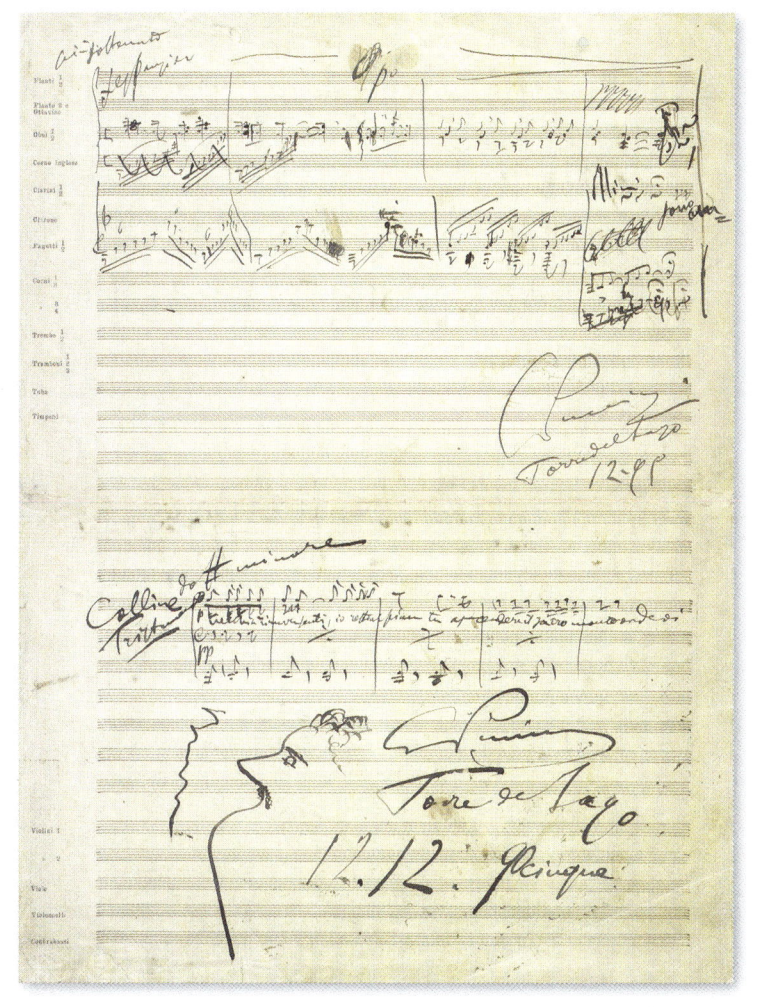

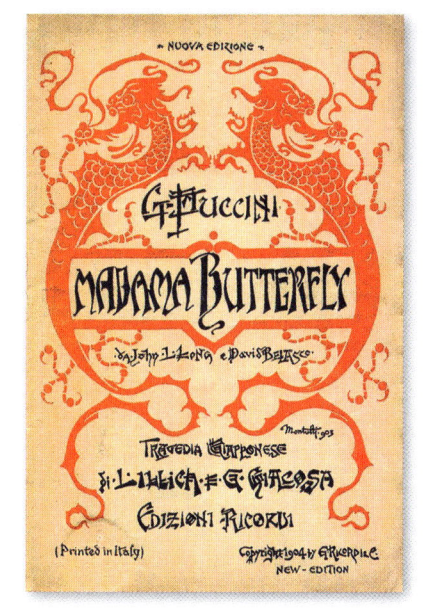

ABOVE: *The stunning artwork of the 1932 printing of* Madama Butterfly.

LEFT: *A sketch by Puccini of his music from* La Bohème, *Act 4, written on 12 December 1895 and signed, with a self-caricature.*

157 *Musical Disasters*

eight-month break to recover from a car crash that left him with a permanent limp. So it must have been particularly heartbreaking to endure the boos and hisses at the premiere on 17 February 1904 at La Scala in Milan. The audience were already irritated by the secrecy around the plot. The song 'Quanto cielo! Quanto mar!' marking Butterfly's entrance sounded so similar to his previous work that the audience took up the mocking chant of 'Bohème, bohème!' When the kimono of soprano Rosina Storchio billowed from a gust of wind, a heckler got a raucous laugh by shouting 'Butterfly is pregnant!' (The popular gossip at the time was that Storchio was having an affair). The final straw came when it was time to signal dawn, for which the actors had been handed bird whistles. The audience as one burst out laughing, and joined in with farm animal noises. Puccini branded the opening night 'a lynching'.

Edward Elgar had written the first melody for what would be his Cello Concerto in E minor the night after he returned from hospital after a tonsillectomy. The premiere of the concerto, at the opening concert of the London Symphony Orchestra's

Henry Cowell demonstrating his technique of playing tone clusters by slamming his forearm down on the keys, 1924-1926.

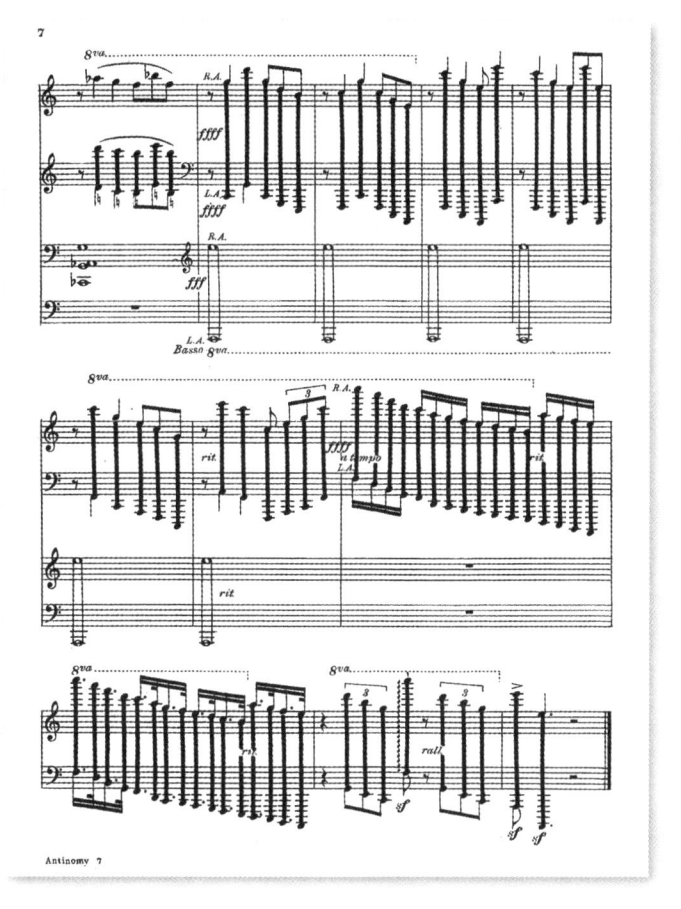

The climax of Cowell's piece 'Antinomy' from Five Encores to Dynamic Motion, *1917, showing five-and-a-half octave chromatic clusters that require both forearms to be played.*

1919–20 season on 27 October 1919, was even more painful. The bulk of the orchestra's rehearsal time was taken up by English composer Albert Coates (1882-1953), who was conducting the rest of the programme, leaving Elgar little time with his musicians. 'That brutal selfish ill-mannered bounder… that brute Coates went on rehearsing', writes Lady Elgar. The performance was a shambles. Ernest Newman of *The Observer* writes: 'There have been rumours about during the week of inadequate rehearsal. Whatever the explanation, the sad fact remains that never, in all probability, has so great an orchestra made so lamentable an exhibition of itself… The work itself is lovely stuff, very simple – that pregnant simplicity that has come upon Elgar's music in the last couple of years – but with a profound wisdom and beauty underlying its simplicity.' Elgar said that, if it had not been for the all the preparation done by his soloist Felix Salmond, he would have cancelled the performance.

The American experimental composer Henry Cowell (1897-1965) made his first tour of Europe in 1923, playing an infamous concert of his *Five Encores to Dynamic Motion* in

Leipzig, Germany, on 15 October. There he introduced his audience to his 'tone clusters', chords that spread across so many octaves that they required both forearms, and sometimes the involvement of other limbs, to play. Cowell recalled hearing gasps, screams, catcalls and pleas for him to stop playing. A man in the front row threatened to physically remove him from the stage if he didn't cease playing. 'The audience was yelling and stamping and clapping and hissing until I could hardly hear myself', he told a journalist later. 'They stood up during most of the performance and got as near to me and the piano as they could. Some of those who disapproved of my methods were so excited that they almost threatened me with physical violence. Those who liked the music restrained them.' One man shouted 'Do you take us for idiots in Germany?', while others threw programme notes at Cowell's head. Finally, the audience rushed the stage. Cowell remembered that 'the police came onto the stage and arrested twenty young fellows, the audience being in an absolute state of hysteria – and I was still playing!'

French composer Edgard Varèse (1883-1965), 'Father of Electronic Music' and 'stratospheric Colossus of Sound' as

Edgard Varèse in 1910.

Kaikhosru Shapurji Sorabji in 1917.

Henry Miller called him, debuted 'Hyperprism', a piece for wind, brass and percussion, at an International Composers' Guild concert at the Klaw Theatre on 4 March 1923. The audience broke out in laughter at his 'organised sound' aesthetic throughout the show, hissed during the ovation and did exactly the same again when they were urged to take it seriously and the performance was repeated. William James Henderson writes in the *New York Herald*: 'It remained for Edgard Varèse (to whom all honor) to shatter the calm of a Sabbath night, to cause peaceful lovers of music to scream out their agony, to arouse angry emotions and tempt men to retire to the back of the theatre and perform tympani concertos on each other's faces.'

When the pianist John Tobin played part 1 of Kaikhosru Shapurji Sorabji's (1892-1988) immensely demanding 'Opus Clavicembalisticum' in 1936, word reached the English composer that, despite Tobin's best efforts, the performance had been less than perfect. Sorabji therefore imposed a performance ban on his own music, prohibiting any musician from publicly playing his work without his permission. 'No performance at all is vastly preferable to an obscene travesty', he stated. It wasn't until the late 1970s, when Sorabji allowed pianists Yonty Solomon and Michael Habermann to perform his work, that his compositions became better known. The 'Opus Clavicembalisticum' remains the most intimidating to pianists. 'The work is only intended for pianist-musicians of the highest order', writes Sorabji. 'Indeed, its intellectual and technical difficulties place it beyond the reach of any others – it is a weighty and serious contribution to the literature of the piano, for serious musicians and serious listeners only.' Composing the opus had left him physically exhausted. He told his friend Erik Chisholm in a letter dated 26 June 1930 that 'the closing four pages are so cataclysmic and catastrophic as anything I've ever done – the harmony bites like nitric acid – the counterpoint grinds like the mills of God'.

Fifteen years later: 'Those who experienced this Donaueschingen première will remember the scandal as long as they live,' writes the musicologist Antoine Goléa after attending the premiere concert of Pierre Boulez's (1925-2016) 'Polyphonie X' on 6 October 1951 at the Donaueschingen Festival. 'Shouts, caterwauling and other animal noises were unleashed from one half of the hall in response to applause, foot-stamping and enthusiastic bravos from the other.' Boulez had not been able to attend, but word quickly reached him, and after he listened to a tape of the concert, he withdrew the work, conceding that it suffered from 'theoretical exaggeration'. ' "Polyphonie X" was the greatest scandal I went through after the war', grumbles Boulez. 'Unfortunately, the press, in writing about the work today, still uses some of the pejorative phrases it used at the premiere. But those who knew anything at all knew that this was a very special work, one that in both structure and colour opened completely new paths.'

When the Italian opera singer Cesare Siepi (1923-2010) played the part of Don Giovanni, for which he would be renowned, in the Vienna State Opera in 1958, he set the gold standard for how to keep an audience on his side while experiencing an unexpected technical error. In rehearsals, Don Giovanni had successfully descended into Hell using a stage-lift with no problem. Only with a live audience did plans go awry. Cesare bid his goodbyes to the land of the living, stepped back and began his descent to the underworld. Unfortunately, halfway down the lift got stuck, leaving him visible to the audience from the waist up. Below, stage technicians frantically

Pierre Boulez conducting in Amsterdam in 1963.

worked to dislodge the lift, raising and lowering him again, but again it lodged halfway down and finally he was returned to stage level. Unfazed, Cesare sang in Italian, 'Oh, how wonderful – Hell is full!'

Steve Reich's (b.1936) 'Four Organs' lasts for around sixteen minutes. With just four organs and a maraca for rhythm, the instruments harmonically play with a dominant eleventh chord (E–D–E–F♯–G♯–A–B), taking it apart by playing its components in sequence while the chord slowly increases in length from a 1/8 note at the beginning to 200 beats at the end. This is the technical description of what's going – to an audience member not briefed on what to expect, the physical sensation left by the stabbing and droning 'Four Organs' is akin to being hit over the head with four organs. At a performance on 18 January 1973 at New York's Carnegie Hall, the audience

A presumably trousered Muhai Tang conducting in Prague in 2011.

heckled and sarcastically applauded to hasten the end of the performance. Michael Tilson, one of the organists, recalls that as the piece ended: 'One woman walked down the aisle and repeatedly banged her head on the front of the stage, wailing "Stop, stop, I confess."'

And finally, it should be noted that, while a successful performance can bring the house down, on rare occasions it can apparently also bring the conductor's trousers down. On 20 October 2019, the Chinese conductor Muhai Tang (b.1949) was leading La Scala's Orchestra at the Teatro Dal Verme in Milan through a powerful brass fanfare to celebrate the seventieth anniversary of the founding of the People's Republic of China, when the unusual incident took place in front of an audience of 3,000 people. As the orchestra played, Tang's trousers dropped to the floor, leaving the 70-year-old standing in his boxer shorts. Without missing a beat, Tang hoisted up his trousers with one hand while waving in a drum roll with the other. Unfortunately for Tang, the incident was caught on video, in which we can hear an audience member exclaim 'Oh my God', and one of the violinists corpse with laughter and try and hide her face behind her music stand, as the conductor continues to wrestle with his waistband.

▶ PLAYLIST: SOME DISASTROUS PERFORMANCES

'Antinomy', *Five Encores to Dynamic Motion*, 1916, HENRY COWELL

Artaxerxes, 1762, THOMAS ARNE AND PIETRO METASTASIO

Benvenuto Cellini, 1838, HECTOR BERLIOZ

Carmen, 1875, GEORGES BIZET, HENRI MEILHAC AND LUDOVIC HALÉVY

Cello Concerto in E minor, 1919, EDWARD ELGAR

Choral Fantasy, op. 80, 1808, LUDWIG VAN BEETHOVEN

Don Giovanni, 1787, k.527, Act II: No. 24, Finale: c. 'Don Giovanni, a cenar teco' WOLFGANG AMADEUS MOZART, PERFORMED BY VIENNA STATE OPERA, FEATURING CESARE SIEPE

'Four Organs', 1970, STEVE REICH

Gran Concerto Futuristico, 1917, LUIGI RUSSOLO

'Hyperprism', 1923, EDGARD VARÈSE

K. 466 Piano Concerto No. 20 in D minor, 1785, WOLFGANG AMADEUS MOZART

K. 488 Piano Concerto No. 23 in A major, 1786, WOLFGANG AMADEUS MOZART

La Traviata, 1853, GIUSEPPE VERDI

'Maggie's Farm', 1965, BOB DYLAN

Mercure, 1924, ERIK SATIE

'Opus Clavicembalisticum', KSS 50, 1930, KAIKHOSRU SHAPURJI SORABJI

Piano Sonata No. 2 in B flat minor, op. 35, 'Funeral March': III. Marche funèbre, 1840, FRÉDÉRIC CHOPIN

'Polyphonie X' for eighteen instruments, 1951, PIERRE BOULEZ

'Quanto cielo! Quanto mar!' *Madama Butterfly*, 1898, GIACOMO PUCCINI

Rise and Fall of the City of Mahagonny, 1930, KURT WEILL AND BERTOLT BRECHT

'Sahst du nach dem Gewitterregen den Wald?', *Fünf Orchesterlieder nach Ansichtskarten von Peter Altenberg*, 1913, ALBAN BERG

Second Sonata, 'The Airplane', 1921, GEORGE ANTHEIL

String Quartet No. 12 in E flat major, op. 127, 1825, LUDWIG VAN BEETHOVEN

Symphony No. 1 in D minor, op. 13, 1895, SERGEI RACHMANINOFF

Symphony No. 96 in D major, 'Miracle', 1791, JOSEPH HAYDN

Symphony No. 102 in B flat major, 1794, JOSEPH HAYDN

Tannhäuser und der Sängerkrieg auf Wartburg, WWV 70, 1845, RICHARD WAGNER

The Baber of Seville, Act I: 'Cavatina: Super bramate' (Count Almaviva, Rosina), 1782, GIOVANNI PAISIELLO

The Barber of Seville, Act I, Scene 2: 'La calunnia è venticello' (Basilio), 1816, GIOACHINO ROSSINI

The Rite of Spring, 1913, IGOR STRAVINSKY

'Über die Grenzen des All', *Fünf Orchesterlieder nach Ansichtskarten von Peter Altenberg*, 1912, ALBAN BERG

SOME CURIOUS COMPOSER INSTRUCTIONS

Larghissimo, 'extremely slow', is the slowest tempo instruction for playing at a speed of 24 beats per minute (bpm) and under. (For context, Beethoven's Fifth Symphony of 1808 hovers at around 132bpm). At the opposite end of the speedometer is *prestissimo assai possibile* – a frightening indication that literally translates to: 'as extremely very fast as possible'.

One of the longest indications, and perhaps the most ambivalent, is found in Kyrie (the first of six mass movements) of Beethoven's Mass in C, op. 86, 1808: *Andante con moto assai vivace, quasi Allegretto, ma non Troppo* ('Andante (walking pace) with very lively motion, almost Allegretto (moderately fast), but not too much').

Mahler's Symphony No. 5 of 1904 contains the record-holding instruction on the most instruments that one performer can play in a single piece, excluding percussion – it calls for one nimble clarinetist to play six different instruments.

Percy Grainger commands that the French horn be played 'as violently and roughly as possible' in his 'Children's March: Over the Hills and Far Away', 1918. Other Grainger instructions include 'Louden lots', 'Lower notes of woggle well to the fore', 'Glassily', 'Sipplingly', 'Rollikingly' and 'Easygoingly but very clingingly'.

Another classical extreme is the quietest indication, *pppppp* – an abbreviation of *più più più più più più piano* ('more more more more more more quiet') – that's found in the first movement of Tchaikovsky's Symphony No. 6, 1893, and in bar 37 of the duet for Otello and Desdemona in Act 1 of Verdi's *Otello*, 1887.

Play *imbibet* (drunkenly) and *corpulentus* (fatly), advises Erik Satie for 'Limp Preludes (for a Dog)', 1912; while another of his piano pieces is 'to be played with both hands in the pocket'.

John Cage's 'A Flower', 1950, has no text, but instructs the singer to sing basic phonemes like 'uh' and 'wah' without vibrato; while other passages should be played 'like a pigeon' and 'like a wild duck', among others. The pianist never opens the piano, instead playing it by hitting the lid in different ways with fingers and knuckles.

Madman's Orchestra

Frank Zappa's piano composition 'Penis Dimension', 1971, includes the instruction: '(Both buttocks) Sit on keyboard and jump back to normal position without losing the tempo.'

David Maslanka's 'Symphony No. 4', 1994, includes the unusual instruction: '*Suddenly faster* reassemble clarinet', after a section in which the clarinetist is instructed to disassemble their instrument at the barrel and slide their finger in and out of the barrel to change the pitch, producing a sound not dissimilar to an air-raid siren.

'Groovy mysterioso' – Henry Mancini's direction for *The Pink Panther* theme, 1963.

To perform 'Skeleton Appreciation Day', 2015, by Will Wood and the Tapeworms, you must 'play like you are about to start crying', and at bar 82, 'Scream maniacally, and with pain'.

Symphony No. 1, 1993, by Daniel Bukvich instructs: 'Solo – Flute 1 ("Muffled sobs", 3 or 4 times)'.

'4. Bagpipe slam – (bagpipe solo but everyone plays and kids scream)' notes Dave Soldier in his 'The Most Unwanted Song', 1997.

La Monte Young's instructions for 'Piano Piece for Terry Riley', 1960, are: 'Push the piano up to a wall and put the flat side up against it. Then continue pushing into the wall. Push as hard as you can. If the piano goes through the wall, keep pushing in the same direction regardless of new obstacles and continue to push as hard as you can whether the piano is stopped against an obstacle or moving. The piece is over when you are too exhausted to push any longer.'

Also by La Monte Young is 'Piano Piece for David Tudor No. 1', 1960, for which one must 'bring a bale of hay and a bucket of water onto the stage for the piano to eat and drink. The performer may then feed the piano or leave it to eat by itself. If the former, the piece is over after the piano has been fed. If the latter, it is over after the piano eats or decides not to.'

'Live completely alone for four days, without food, in complete silence, without much movement, sleep as little as necessary, think as little as possible. After four days, late at night, without conversation beforehand, play single sounds WITHOUT THINKING which you are playing, close your eyes, just listen.' – Karlheinz Stockhausen's instructions for 'Goldstaub' ('Gold Dust'), from *Aus den Sieben Tagen* ('From the Seven Days'), 1968.

And finally, when playing Kevin Wooding's 'The Egyptian Level', 2018, the composer indicates that you must play 'Egyptically'.

Some Curious Composer Instructions

EXPERIMENTAL ODDITIES

For the vast majority of music aficionados, the term 'experimental music' is most strongly associated with the genre of the modernists and avant-garde movements of the twentieth century – in fact, the most famous experimental musical work is probably the one that contains no actual music. As seen on page 194, John Cage, one of the first to use the term 'experimental music', caused shockwaves with his infamous four and a half minutes of silence that he titled '4'33"' in 1952.

However, an interesting challenge is to take this banner philosophy of rejecting the status quo and look farther back through time for what else might qualify as 'experimental' before the term officially existed. Some famous pieces arguably qualify: Beethoven's 'Grosse Fuge', for example (see Lost Music Found, page 112), is often pointed to as a work at least a century ahead of its time, and moved Igor Stravinsky (1882-1971) to describe it as: 'an absolutely contemporary piece of music that will be contemporary forever'. Some of the first movements of Franz Schubert's later piano sonatas, like Piano Sonata in G major, D 894, 1826, and Piano Sonata in A major, D 959, 1828, are also admired for startling qualities one would expect to hear in compositions of later decades. But I think we can go back even earlier, and stranger, on a search for historical music of especial imagination.

In fact, an apt starting point might be 'Rondeau 14, "Ma fin est mon commencement" ("My End is My Beginning")' by the fourteenth-century French poet and composer Guillaume de Machaut (1300-77), a pillar of the *ars nova* musical style of the Kingdom of France during the late Middle Ages. Machaut was such a significant figure that the ars nova period officially ends with his death and transitions to the *ars subtilior* ('subtler art') period. With 'Ma fin est mon commencement', Machaut creates a musical *ouroboros*, the circular symbol of a serpent or dragon eating its own tail to represent eternity. The vocal piece is a crab canon (named for the crab's ability to walk in multiple directions) over a palindrome, which refers to the ingenious device of arranging two musical lines that complement each other, with one played or sung forward, while the other is played or sung in reverse simultaneously (e.g. C–A–B–A–F–A–C–E and E–C–A–F–A–B–A–C

OPPOSITE-TOP: *Guillaume de Machaut's 'Rondeau 14, "Ma fin est mon commencement" ("My End is My Beginning")', from a manuscript copied in the 1370s, specifically the last system of the first page and on through the top four systems of the second page.*

BELOW: *An accompanying illuminated miniature from the same manuscript, depicting Machaut on the right being introduced by Nature to her children Sens, Retorique and Musique (Meaning, Rhetoric and Music).*

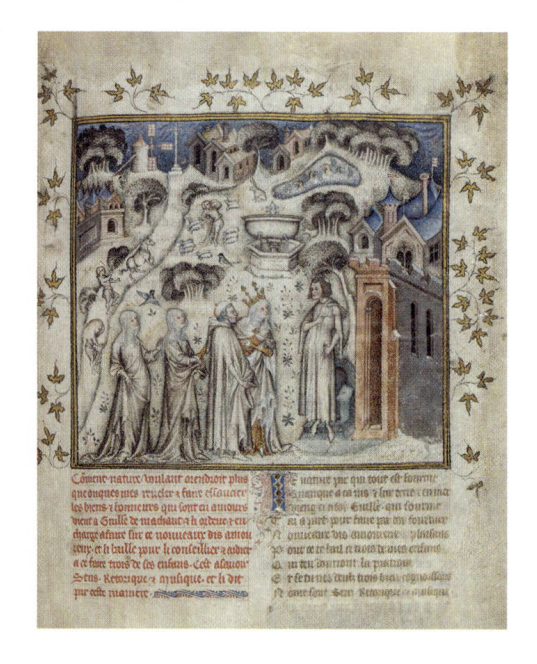

168 | Madman's Orchestra

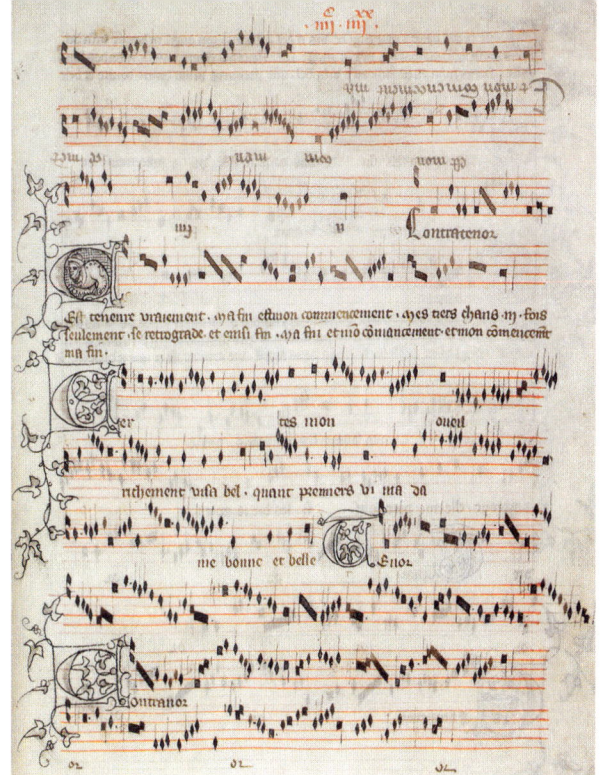

together).♪ With Machaut's three-part composition, when the singers reach the end of the line, the tenor (the lowest part) reverses direction and sings his music backwards from right to left, followed by the triplum (top line) and the cantus (middle line), who swap parts. They arrive back where they started, like the tail in the mouth of the serpent, with the beginning becoming the end, and the end the beginning. Machaut weaves the nature of the masterful piece into the lyrics as well, which translate to:

> A. My end is my beginning
> B. And my beginning my end
> a. And this holds truly
> A. My end is my beginning
> a. My third melody three times only
> b. Reverses itself and thus ends
> A. My end is my beginning
> B. And my beginning my end

♪ Musical palindromes are far from rare, of course, but there are a couple of neat examples in opera that are worth mentioning. Paul Hindemith's (1895-1963) *Hin und Zurück* ('Back and Forth'), 1927, is a tragedy of jealousy, murder and suicide that is then repeated with the music and the story performed in reverse, so that it concludes with a happy ending (the beginning). And the second act of Alban Berg's 1937 opera *Lulu* includes a three-minute sequence that's a musical and dramatic palindrome: three people arrest and imprison Lulu, and then as the music pauses and is played in reverse, three release her. The palindromic déjà vu is amplified by the fact that her husbands in Act I are played by the same singers who play her clients in Act III.

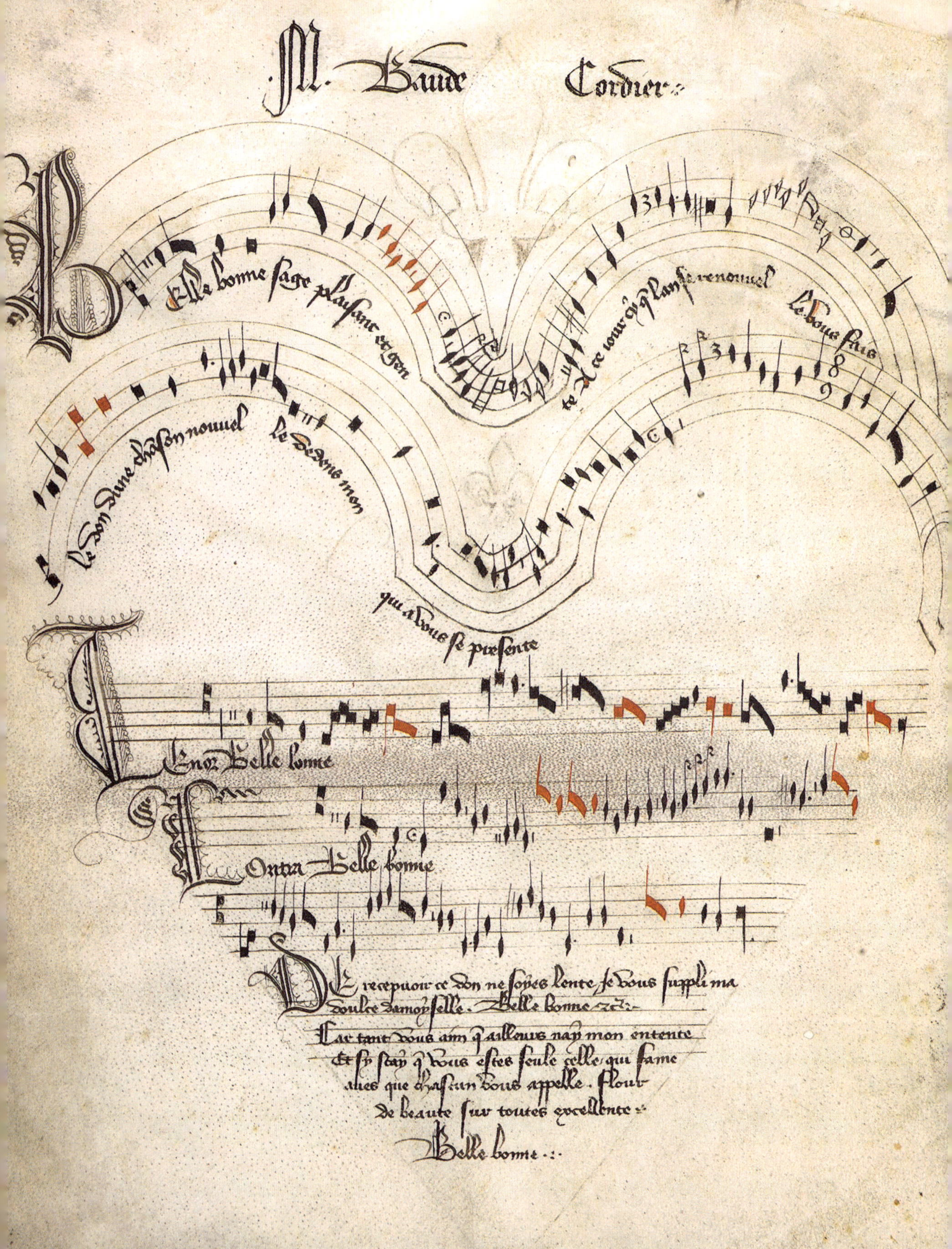

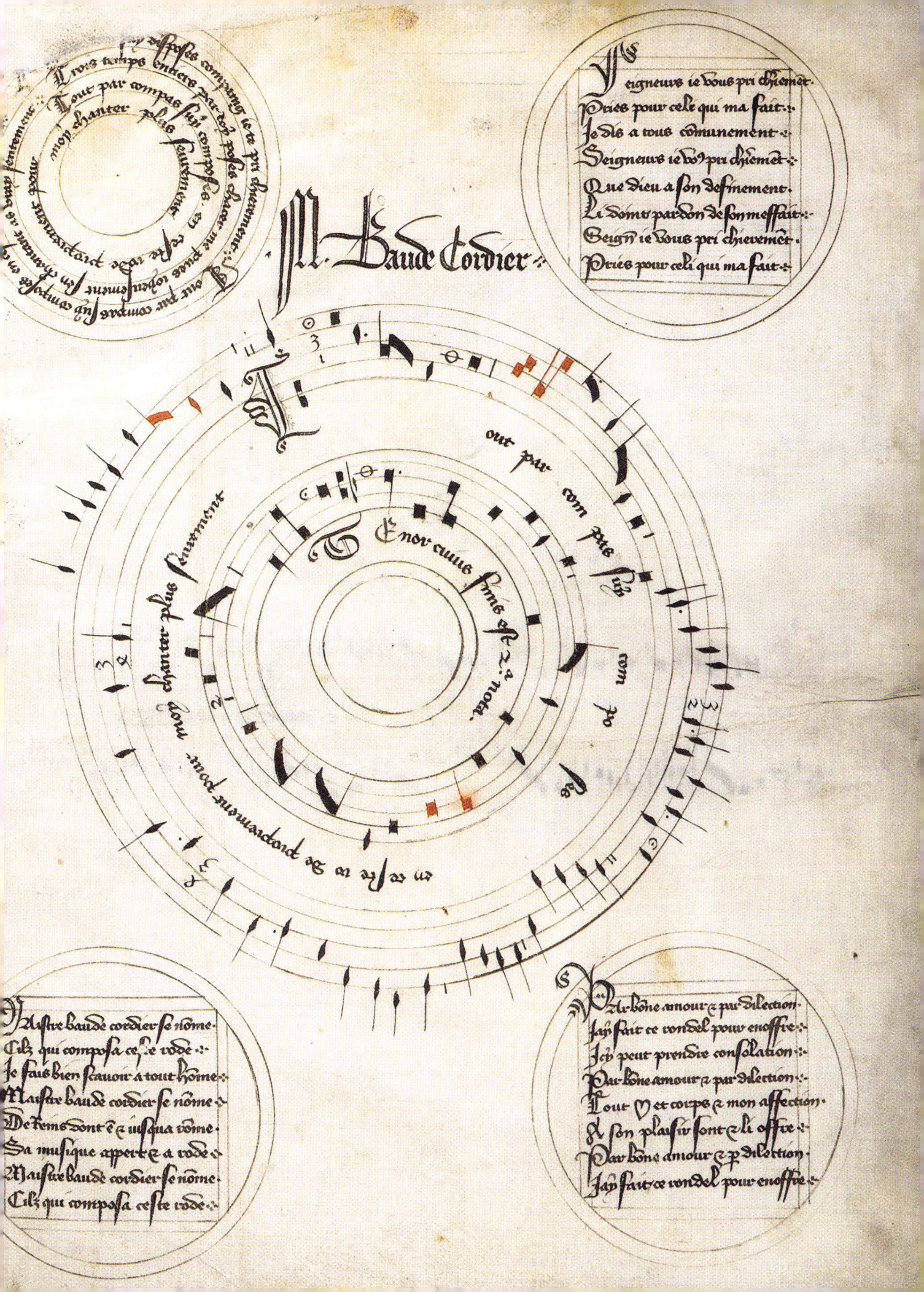
M. Baude Cordier
Seigneurs ie vous pri chierement
Pries pour cele qui ma fait
Je dis a tous comunement
Seigneurs ie vo9 pri chierement
Que dieu a son definement
Li doint pardon de son meffait
Seign9 ie vous pri chierement
Pries pour celi qui ma fait
Tout par compas suy composee
Tenor cuius finis est ad 2a notam
Maistre baude cordier se nome
Cilz qui composa ce rondel
Je fais bien scavoir a tout homme
Maistre baude cordier se nome
De Reims dont est jusqua Romme
Sa musique appert et a rondel
Maistre baude cordier se nome
Cilz qui composa ceste rondel
Par bone amour et par dilection
Jay fait ce rondel pour enoffre
Icy peut prendre consolation
Par bone amour et par dilection
Tout cuer et corps et mon affection
A son plaisir sont et li offre
Par bone amour et par dilection
Jay fait ce rondel pour enoffre

As the ars subtilior period then begins, a trend of experimental notation rather contrary to the name of the style springs up, credited to the French composer Baude Cordier (*fl.* early fifteenth century). Virtually nothing is known about Cordier other than an inscription revealing his place of birth as Rheims and that he had a Master of Arts. In musical notation terms, Cordier was a crackpot scientist centuries ahead of his time, producing graphic scores in a style that would be considered avant-garde in the twentieth century. Cordier saw the basic page layout of horizontal staves as merely a starting point to leave far behind, twisting his music into shapes that matched the theme of the composition. His notation for 'Belle, Bonne, Sage' found in the late fourteenth-century manuscript known as the *Chantilly Codex* is a love rondeau (a medieval poetic structure of repeated verse and refrain) cleverly arranged in the shape of a heart. This heart music also demonstrates his use of red music notation, a technique that uses the shift in colour to indicate a change in rhythm. Alongside this piece in the *Chantilly Codex* is collected Cordier's 'Tout par compas suy composes' ('With a Compass Was I Composed'), a circular canon (a composition in which the melody is accompanied by mimicking lines begun at staggered times) in which the music notation is beautifully written in a large central circle. Smaller circles orbit the music like celestial bodies. In the upper-left corner, the lyrics are also presented in circular fashion; in the upper-right, Cordier implores the reader to pray for him; while a circle in the lower-right corner contains Cordier's explanations of his motive for creating the work ('I have made this rondel for an offering… Here, one can take consolation by good love and dilection'); and in the lower-left circle he proudly identifies himself as the author.

Cordier's are the most influential examples of what would become known as 'eye music', innovative graphic notations that are a secret hidden from the audience, and exist only for the benefit for the reader/performer. The visible experimentation of eye music fitted perfectly with the Renaissance obsession with puzzles, codes and measurements, and the form swiftly evolved to blend with 'puzzle canons'. Also known as riddle canons or enigma canons, these are compositions in which only one voice line is notated, leaving the performers to deduce or guess the time intervals, accompanying vocal lines and other important components of the composition. Sometimes, instructions and clues are provided (like the lines from Machaut's 'Ma fin est

ABOVE: *A leaf from the remarkable Berkeley Theory Manuscript, created in 1375. In this illustration, the well-known French ballade 'En La Maison Dedalus' ('In the House of Dedalus') is presented highly unusually, with both music and lyrics written in circular form. It represents the labyrinth of the story, with the captive Ariadne the red dot at the centre.*

PREVIOUS SPREAD – LEFT: *The heart-shaped romance composition 'Belle, bonne, sage' from the* Chantilly Codex *by the French composer Baude Cordier, with a string of red notes forming a second heart.* RIGHT: *His circular canon 'With a Compass Was I Composed'*

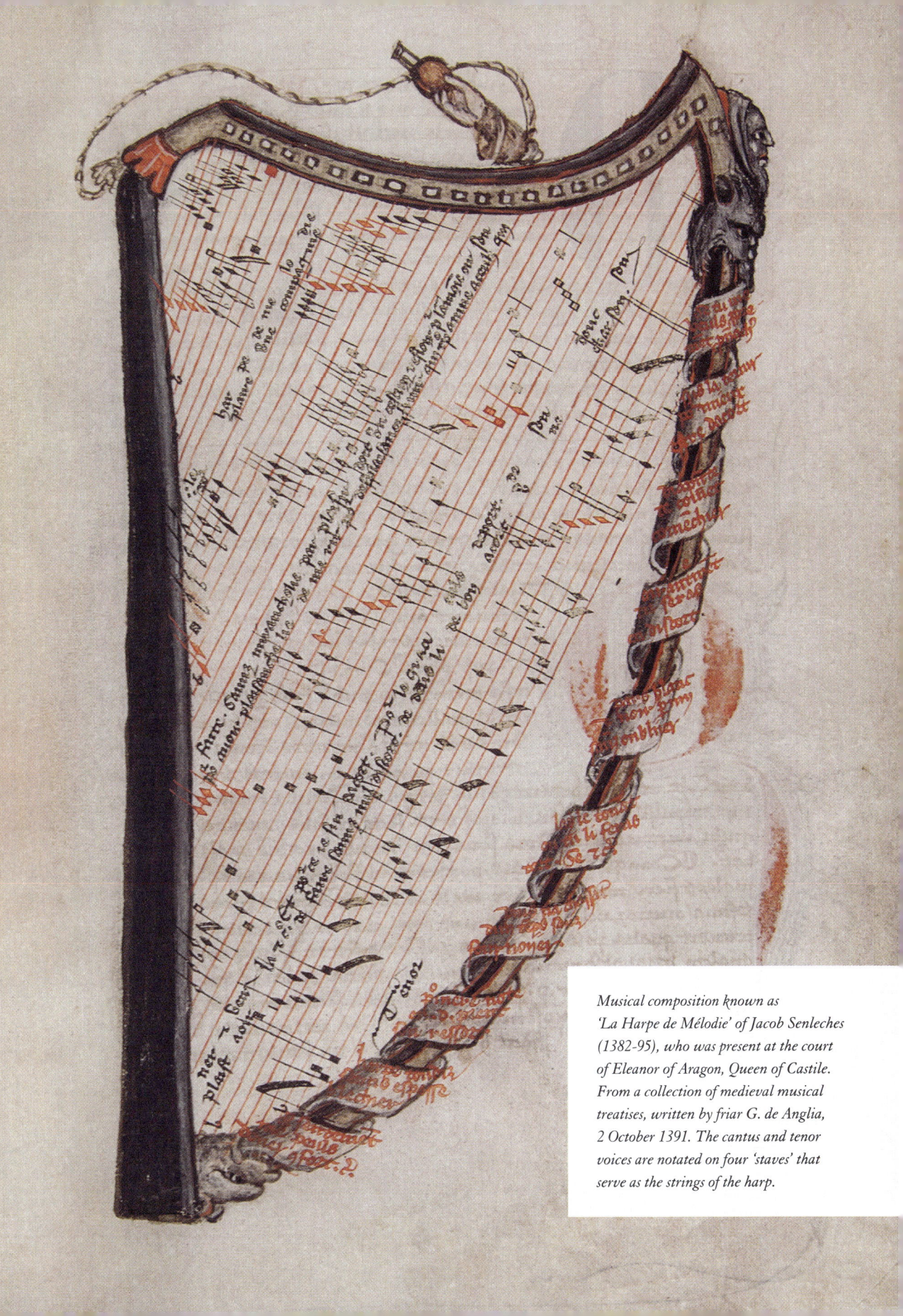

Musical composition known as 'La Harpe de Mélodie' of Jacob Senleches (1382-95), who was present at the court of Eleanor of Aragon, Queen of Castile. From a collection of medieval musical treatises, written by friar G. de Anglia, 2 October 1391. The cantus and tenor voices are notated on four 'staves' that serve as the strings of the harp.

mon commencement': 'My third melody three times only / Reverses itself and thus ends.') Sometimes no clues are given and the musician is left scratching their head.

We can find one eye-music puzzle canon in a curious place, the painting *Allegory of Music*, 1530, by Dosso Dossi (1486-1542), which hangs on the wall of the Horne Museum, Florence. In the lower-right corner is a circular canon painted on a board, and on the other, to the right, a faint depiction of something even more unusual, a 495-year-old triangular puzzle canon that one has to squint to make out. This triangular notation, so easy to miss when first viewing the painting, is part of a simplified version of a puzzle canon by the great Renaissance composer Josquin des Prez (1450-1521), in his Agnus Dei II from his *Missa l'Homme Armé Super Voces Musicales* canonic mass. The triangle offers the superscript 'trinitas in un[um]' ('three in one', i.e. the Holy Trinity) as a clue to how one can solve it. It's a mensuration canon (a type of canon in which the voices proceed simultaneously with the same subject, but at different speeds) of 3:1, with one voice taking part at the interval of a fifth, or 3:2. Hence the triangular representation. As far as we are aware, this representation is unique.

Not everyone was a fan. The English composer Thomas Morley (1557-1602), famed for his madrigals, moaned that, after working hard to solve puzzle canons, sometimes the answer 'which being founde (it might bee) was scant worth the hearing'. With respect to Master Morley, however, anything that's good enough for J. S. Bach should be good enough for us all. We can find crab canons and other puzzles hidden in one of Bach's most famous collections of keyboard canons, fugues and other compositions, *The Musical Offering*, BWV 1079. This came about from a meeting between King Frederick of Prussia (1727-1786) and Bach in 1747, when the monarch wanted to show off a new experimental instrument – the fortepiano. During Bach's visit to the palace in Potsdam, Frederick decided to conduct an experiment of his own, and surprised him with a long and complicated musical theme, tasking the composer with improvising a three-voice fugue from it on the spot. Bach complied, and an enraptured Frederick challenged him to expand it to a six-voice fugue. Bach said he would need a bit of time to work on it, and sure enough sent a six-voice fugue to the king soon after.

Four months later, Bach published a set of pieces around the theme that came to be known as *The Musical Offering*.

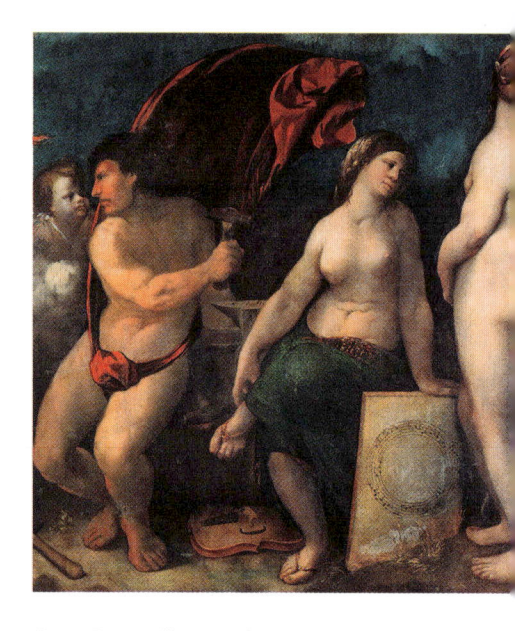

Dosso Dossi, Allegory of Music, *1530. In the lower-right corner is an unidentified canon written in circular notation, and just to its right a canon by Des Prez faintly notated in a triangle form.*

FOLLOWING SPREAD: *Two of six* empresas enigmatáticas *('enigmatic devices') from a c.1667 book of lectern masses by Spanish composer Juan del Vado (1625-91) of the Royal Chapel. Each has a short legend, usually in Latin, at the beginning of the composition to indicate the rule to be followed for its resolution.*

Madman's Orchestra

Among these pieces are ten different puzzle canons, all variations on the '*Thema Regium*' ('theme of the king'). While the solutions are far too complicated to lay out here, the clues that Bach provides are generally hidden in the Latin titles; in the use of G, F and C clefs to subtly indicate the placement and directionality of the accompanying voices; and even delicately presenting clefs and notes in mirror image to indicate when the lines should be sung in reverse. The knowledge of just how much of the music *The Musical Offering* is fabricated with riddles and geometrical experimentation makes for a completely different listening experience.

Mozart enjoyed solving the musical puzzles of the Italian friar Giovanni Battista Martini (1706-84) so much that he composed his own, writing '4 Puzzle Canons', K. 73r, with Latin epigrams such as *Sit trium series una* and *Ter ternis canite vocibus* ('Let there be one series of three parts' and 'sing three times with three voices'). Things get even more complex in the trio section of Mozart's Serenade for Wind Octet in C, K. 388, 1782, which is actually a double mirror canon. The second oboe introduces a line and, after two bars, the first oboe joins in, playing the same line inverted or 'upside down'; then the first bassoon begins a line and the second bassoon follows, playing that upside down. All four parts end up simultaneously playing with the same theme, though they are offset by two bars each

ABOVE: The Flute Concert of Sanssouci *by Adolf von Menzel (1815-1905), 1852, showing King Frederick II of Prussia playing flute, accompanied by Bach's son Carl Philipp Emanuel playing a harpsichord-shaped piano.*

BELOW: *Johann Sebastian Bach, painted in 1746 by Elias Haussmann.*

175 | *Experimental Oddities*

ARMONIA ❁ DE DIOS

Omnia per ipsum facta sunt.

Maria Santissima Concebida sin peccado original, alcanza Armonia.
Et qui creauit me requieuit in tabernaculo meo.
En que forma Vn Duo (Singular en lo comun) Con su sacratissimo hijo quanto es
permitido a la ynfinita distancia de Criador a Criatura por la acion de
la felicissima maternidad; nace Vna Voz de Otra quedando Y essa de
qua natus ̄est.
Iesus qui Vocatur Christus.

(circular musical notation surrounding central text:)

in Sole posuit tabernaculum.
El Sol Ylustra mis pasos.
Que el tabernaculo Soy.
donde fue al primer ynstante.
Mi primero Punto el Sol.

Ecce ancilla Domini.
Ecce Virgo concipiet, et pariet filium, &c.
quando por la dignacion
de Criador quedo Criatura
en el Virginal quedo el Sol.

Quam pulchri sunt passus tui
Me sublima Nota Altta.
En mi Compas quies Yo.
donde por las blancas Claues.
Sus pasos Alumbran Sol.

ab eterno Ordinata Sum.
Dios me Ordeno y me compuso.
musica de Su eleccion
A donde En el tres Eterno.
Echo el Compas el Amor.

(center:)
Benedicite Omnia Opera Dñi Dño.

Haze Otro Duo La Naturaleza humana Con su Comun Padre a quien sigue:
Juntanse Los Dos Duos y hazen Vn Quatro por Venir todos por Vn Camino, o Linea
Con tal diferencia que al primero Duo de los dos individuos Seles Conzede a Vno por
Gracia, y a Otro por Naturaleza Preuilegio Que no pasen por las notas negras Y solo
Su Camino Sea por las blancas Y de mas Valor: Viniendo a incluso todo en Primer Mouimi.o en
glosa es lo mismo en sentido alegorico Que Juntar Naturaleza Y gracia de preseruacion

Laus Deo, imaculatæ que Virgini Mariæ, eius dulcissimæ, Matri.

Competencia del abismo.
De Virtudes que vio el mundo.
Carlos soy, y aunque segundo.
Emulo soy, y él el mismo.

La naturaleza ayuda al arte

Vado soi y mis caudales, de todos voy recogiendo, pues dándoles aprendiendo, multiplico mis caudales...

PLVS VLTRA

El Carlos.

Operibus Credite.

~ 18. Duos. ~ 36. ~ tercios. ~ y 28 Quatros. ~

Este canon tan Sucinto.
Ochenta y dos Casos, son.
Miralos Con Atencion.
Busca el ylo al laberintho.
Diez y ocho Duos te pinto.
Treinta y Seis, tercios Veras.
Veinte y ocho Quatros, mas
En distintas posiciones.
Doctrina Sin Opiniones.
Que Maestro aprobaras.
Que doctrina da probaras.

Gesualdo Castle, in the Campania region of Italy.

and two of them are inverted. The pianist Erik Smith (1931-2004) marvellously likened this to 'the visual image of two swans reflected in the still water.'

For the avoidance of migraines, we should perhaps move on from riddle compositions; and in our search for other inventive mindsets, we now find the Italian nobleman and composer Carlo Gesualdo da Venosa (1566-1613), Prince of Venosa and Count of Conza. Gesualdo is known as much for producing the most experimental music of the Renaissance as he is for the tragic stories of murder and madness that suffuse his work. His madrigals and sacred music pieces are told with wildly chromatic language and progressions so advanced for their time that nothing similar would be heard again until the late nineteenth century. In his most famous works, six books of madrigals published 1594-1611, and his 'Tenebrae Responsoria', of 1611, which is based on texts from the Passion of Christ, his use of uniquely brutal dissonance and chromatic juxtapositions are shockingly jarring in comparison to the works of contemporaries.

This drama is amplified with Gesualdo's use of 'word painting', in which notes are used to reflect the literal meaning of the word they accompany – think Handel's *Messiah*, in which 'valley' is sung with a low note, 'mountain' with a peaking high note and 'straight' with one sustained note, etc. In Gesualdo's case, it's with the extremes of emotion, of love, pain, ecstasy and a recurrent theme of guilt, fuelled by the events of his biography. On the night of 16 October 1590, he caught his wife, Donna Maria, *in flagrante delicto* with Fabrizio Carafa, third Duke of Andria at the Palazzo San Severo in Naples. Gesualdo murdered them both in a fit of rage. The Gran Corte della Vicaria found that Gesualdo had not committed a crime, but he was tortured by guilt and depression for the rest of his life. He lived in self-isolation at his castle from 1595, paying musicians and singers to visit and perform his own music just for himself. According to Tommaso Campanella (1568-1639), Gesualdo ordered his servants to beat him daily, with one given the duty of beating him 'at stool'; while he also desperately sought to collect the bones of saints and other religious relics to atone for his crimes. His late setting of Psalm 51, the 'Miserere', with its monotonous chants and stabs of chromatic polyphony, paints his pained state of mind before his lonely death at his castle in 1613.

So far, we've looked at unusual compositions, but we should introduce the theme of inventive approaches to playing instruments, too. As we're currently hovering around the turn of the seventeenth century, this offers the perfect excuse to cut to one of my favourite musical curiosities in history – an Elizabethan lute duet that is unique in that it necessitates one player to sit on the other's lap. 'My Lord Chamberlain,

Perhaps the most spectacular ending to a piece of notation, from Johann Jakob Froberger's (1616-67) Suite II in C major, 'Lamento sopra la dolorosa perdita della Real Msta di Ferdinando IV, Re de Romani'. The soul of Ferdinand IV ascends a scale of three octaves to enter the clouds of heaven. Froberger also marks the fatal tumble taken by the lutenist Charles Fleury in 1652 down a flight of stairs with a descending scale of two octaves.

Experimental Oddities

His Galliard (an invention for two to play upon one lute)' is a piece by the English Renaissance composer John Dowland (1563-1626). It was printed in Dowland's *First Booke of Songes or Ayres*, 1597, and, fittingly enough for this chapter theme, its descriptive title is the first use in English of the term 'invention' in reference to music. It's also the only lute duet of the time not composed by Thomas Robinson (1560-1610), although duet might not quite be the right term for a piece uniquely designed for two players with one lute. The piece calls for the instrument to be shared between the two, apparently romantically, and thereby at one point (in the words of the historian Matthew Spring, author of *The Lute in Britain*, 2001): 'allows the possibility of an intimate embrace' as one player sits on the other's lap (and indeed online searches for performance footage turn up some frankly adorable results). It has been suggested that perhaps the piece was designed to be played by father and son, but somehow this seems – if you'll pardon the pun – like a bit of a reach.

'Battalia à 10' is a baroque piece of chamber music written in 1673 and scored for three violins, four violas, two violones and continuo, that is famous for its unconventionality. Written by the Bohemian-Austrian composer Heinrich Ignaz Franz Biber (1644-1704), it's thought the composer was motivated by the extraordinarily high casualty rates of the Thirty Years' War, in which an estimated 4.5–8 million soldiers and civilians died from battle, famine or disease, and regions of Germany saw population declines of over 50 percent. The 'Battalia' is an uncharacteristically radical tangent for Biber, as he dreams up ways of representing both fighting and life in an army camp through various musical effects. In the second movement, 'Die liederliche Gesellschaft von allerley Humor' ('The Profligate Society of Common Humor'), the orchestra plays various melodies of folk songs (including 'Cabbage and Turnips Have Driven Me Away') in eight different keys and time signatures simultaneously, to represent drunkenness. 'Here it is dissonant everywhere', read Biber's instructions, 'for thus are the drunks accustomed to bellow with different songs.' In 'Der Mars' ('The March'), the violin plays trills and ornaments while the bass viol is instructed to imitate a snare drum by placing sheets of thick paper under the strings to create a rattling rasping sound, conjuring the image of a military drum and the boots that march to it. Richard Strauss would aim for a similar result years later, with the double bass (the descendant of the bass viol), which should be bowed below the bridge in *Salome*, 1905, to represent the death-rattle of Jokanaan. (These double basses should breathe a sigh of relief that this was all that was asked of them, unlike those required by Charles Ives (1874-1954) to be played slap-bass style with vigour that he humorously called *con fistiswatto*; or those used by Lou Harrison (1917-2003) for 'Labyrinth 3', 1941, which the American experimental composer instructs must be hit with mallets.) Albert Siklós (1878-1942) loved the double bass so much that he composed the remarkable Symphony No 3 'Aetherique' in 1899. The piece is scored entirely for twelve double basses.

With the 'Battalia à 10', Biber was the first to direct string players to play *col legno* ('with wood'), with the bow played upside down so that it's the wood that makes contact with the strings. He also appears to be the first to specifically call for the technique of *scordatura*, which is the deliberate mistuning of one or more of the strings of instruments, for his fifteen short *Rosary Sonatas*, or *Mystery Sonatas*, 1676, for violin. These interestingly are identified not by titles, but by a copper-engraved religious illustration, each relating to a prayer of the Christian rosary practice, and survive today in just one manuscript. The sonatas are grouped into three sets: five joyful mysteries, five sorrowful mysteries and five glorious mysteries, matching with the spoken prayers of the rosary. (The final, sixteenth work is a melancholy *passacaglia* for solo violin, which is almost unbearably beautiful.) Aside from the first and last sonata, each one has a different scordatura tuning, which makes possible strange sonorities, colours, altered ranges and new harmonies. The actual notation is written as normal, which means that the performer sees familiar notes but, when playing, hears them in an unfamiliar way.

Vivaldi, Haydn, Paganini and Mahler are among others who have employed scordatura most effectively. Haydn incorporates the technique in his Symphony No. 67 in F, 1778, but the most famous work to draw on it is 'Mars' from Gustav Holst's *The Planets*, op. 32, 1914-16.

Georg Philipp Telemann's (1681-1767) 'Gulliver Suite', 1728-29, for two violins without bass. The chaconne *(a style that is normally slow) movement of the tiny Lilliputian people is written in a weird, time-brisk signature of 3/32 with very short notes for a scampering effect; while the gigue (normally fast) of the giant Brobdingnagians is written in the equally weird, lumbering time signature of 24/1.*

In 'Battalia à 10', to represent musket shots, Biber also invents the *pizzicato* technique, in which the player plucks the strings of their instrument so hard that it snaps against the body of the instrument. Gioachino Rossini has his violinists hit their lampshades or music stands with their bows as part of his Overture 'Il Signor Bruschino', 1813, while in 1968, George Crumb (1929-2022) would instruct his violinists to loosen the hairs of their bow while performing his 'Songs, Drones and Refrains of Death', 1968, in order to produce a morbidly weak, disembodied sound. With the horn section, meanwhile, Carl Maria von Weber (1786-1826) makes the first official use, in his Horn Concertino in E minor, 1815, of a strange technique in which a horn player can produce a four-note chord. This is done by blowing one note while simultaneously humming a lower note, which results in another tone emerging (known as the 'difference tone'), while a fourth (the 'resultant tone') is also formed from the two played notes. Perhaps von Weber would have enjoyed Robert Watts's (1923-88) 'Duet for Tuba' (date unknown), which requires coffee and cream be served from two of the instrument's spit-valves; or his 'F/H TRACE', 1963, in which a player enters the stage with a French horn under his arm and takes a bow, causing ping pong balls to cascade out of the instrument. (Watts also has another curious piece called 'Trace for Orchestra', 1964, in which the performers take their seats in front of their music stands. The lights are extinguished and the musicians promptly set fire to their sheet music.)

An equally surprising (to modern listeners, at least) appearance of an instrument is found in the Concerto for Jew's Harp, Mandora and Orchestra in E major, 1782, by the Austrian composer Johann Georg Albrechtsberger (1736-1809), which is one of the best recordings to play to baffle those unfamiliar with classical music. Things start off with unremarkable strings playing in the confident stride of the *galant* style, until the Jew's harp♪ enters, the sound of which can really only be described as

ABOVE: *Sonata No. 1 in D minor, C. 90, 'The Annunciation', from the only surviving manuscript of Heinrich Biber's* Rosary Sonatas, *or* Mystery Sonatas, *each with no official title but identified by a different illustration at their header.*

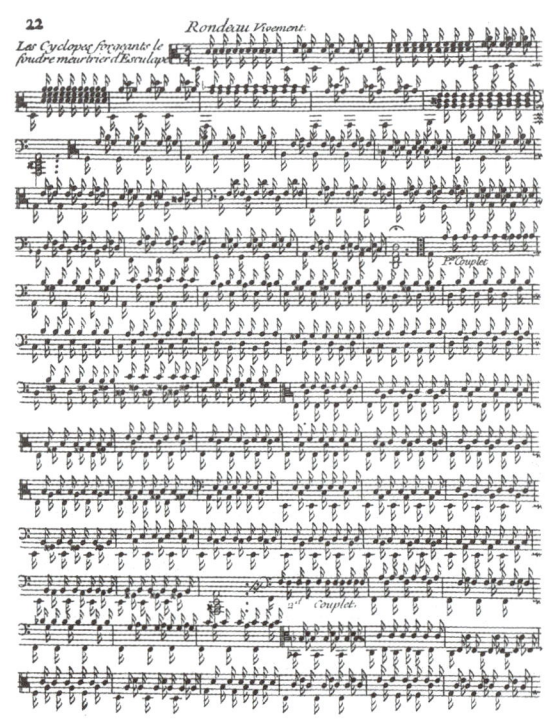

♪ Despite its name, the instrument has no relation to the Jewish people (nor does it resemble a harp for that matter), and is thought to have originated in Siberia, in the region of the Altai mountains.

182 | Madman's Orchestra

a metallic 'boing'. The wild juxtaposition of the instrument is so alien as to be comical, as if a clockwork automaton has infiltrated the orchestra's ranks and quietly begun to self-destruct, pinging springs around the room. Albrechtsberger, who taught Ludwig van Beethoven, actually composed at least six other concerti for Jew's harp and strings, and reader, I'll be honest: I have not out sought their recordings.

At the other end of the scale, so to speak, of the modest Jew's harp is the composer said to have created the noisiest symphonies in history, the Italian Abbé Giovanni Pietro Maria Crispi (1737-97). Sixteen of his symphonies are all in the cheerful military key of D major (with two others in the equally chipper G major). Charles Burney (1726-1814) said of Crispi's music that it was 'too furious and noisy for a room or, indeed, for any other place'.

The German composer Peter Cornelius (1824-74) took a different approach in 1854 with his own experiment: 'Ein Ton' ('The Monotone'), which features a vocal melody of just a single note, B, repeated eighty times across forty-two bars. The effect is surprisingly wistful and haunting. The rich harmonic

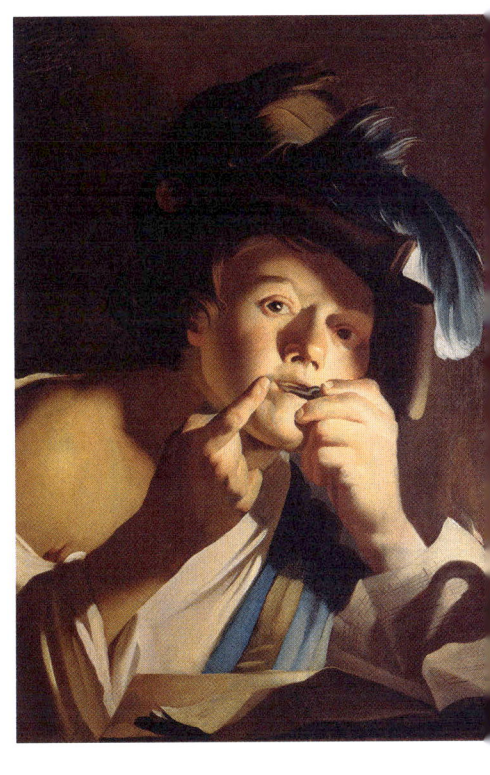

ABOVE: Young Man with a Jew's Harp, 1621, by Dirck van Baburen (1594-1624).

LEFT: Peter Cornelius's 'Ein Ton' ('The Monotone')

OPPOSITE-BOTTOM: *Christophe Moyreau's (1700-74) 'The Cyclops forging the murderous thunderbolt of Aesculapius', which replicates the mythical creatures' hammering with a headache-inducing repetitive and pounding score.*

183 | Experimental Oddities

line of the accompanying piano makes up for much of the monotony, and, as recordings like those of Alma Gluck in 1914 and Felicity Lott in 2001 show, the skilful performer can convey the requisite grief and hopelessness via a single note, while gently singing the beautiful lyrics:

> A sound sounds so wonderful to me,
> in my heart and mind, forever.
> Is it the breath that escapes you,
> when your mouth trembled once more?
> Is it the dull sound of the little bell,
> that followed you along the way?
> The sound sounds so full and pure to me,
> as if it enclosed your soul.
> As if you were descending lovingly
> and singing my pain in peace.

In 1948, the Italian composer Giacinto Scelsi (1905-88) took a similar approach while recuperating in a sanatorium in the Swiss Alps. Sat at the institution's piano, he spent hours striking the same piano key over and over again until he was completely lost in the note. 'Reiterating a note for a long time, it grows large', he says later, 'so large that you even hear harmony growing inside it… When you enter into a sound, the sound envelops you and you become part of the sound. Gradually, you are consumed by it and you need no other sound… All possible sounds are contained in it.' 'Four Pieces, Each on a Single Note', 1959, for chamber orchestra was the resulting composition, in which the movements are constrained by a single pitch, but roar, shudder and whisper with a full range of tricks. For context as to how skilful it is to make these one-note pieces so impactful, and how things can actually go terribly diabolically wrong, a helpful contrast can be found on YouTube. 'Never Gonna Give You Up But All the Notes Are C' is, frankly, the work of a madman, uploaded under the account name Content Creator Man. Rick Astley's pop hit from 1987 is compressed entirely to the note of C. 'If the feeling of pure nausea was converted into a song, this would be it', reads one user comment beneath the video. 'He sounds like he's being held at gunpoint and is on the verge of crying', states another.

We last encountered Aleksandr Scriabin while exploring 'colour music' (see page 81), but we can briefly revisit him here for his final and most experimental work that his death would

ABOVE: *Ignaz Moscheles's (1794-1870) piano piece 'The Way of the World', 1837, is invertible – the music reads (and plays) the same upside down.*

BELOW: *Scriabin's sketch of the* Mysterium *set, 1914.*

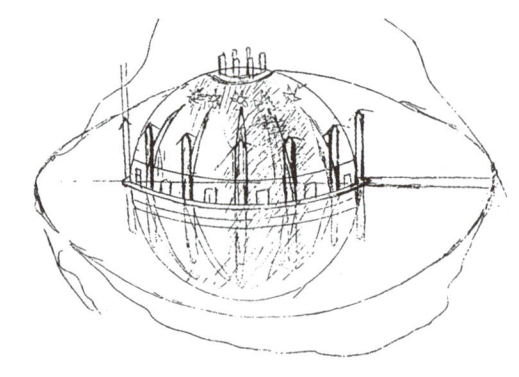

Madman's Orchestra

leave unfinished. Had he succeeded in realising *Mysterium*, he would no doubt be spoken of as one of the great multimedia artists in history. His original plan was for the piece to be a new art form, a *Gesamtkunstwerk* ('total work of art') featuring 'an orchestra, a large mixed choir, an instrument with visual effects, dancers, a procession, incense and rhythmic textural articulation', with theosophical poetry, coloured light shows and other choreographed sensorial delights to create the ultimate synaesthetic experience. The sunrise would be the prelude; the sunset the coda. Which honestly all sounds fairly reasonable until one learns that this was to be housed in a giant cathedral custom-built for the performance at the foothills of the Himalayas, which would 'continually change with the atmosphere and motion of the *Mysterium*'. Huge bells would hang from the clouds and ring for seven days straight, drawing attendees from around the world. The finale performance would bring about the Apocalypse, when humans would be replaced with 'nobler beings'. Having begun work in 1903, by the time of his death in 1915 of septicaemia, at the age of forty-three, he was far from finished.

In this period of the late nineteenth/early twentieth century, a compiler of a playlist of experimental music is spoilt for choice when it comes to startling piano compositions. Franz Liszt (1811-86), who coined the terms 'transcription' and 'paraphrase', enjoyed the 'Lisztomania' superstardom garnered by displaying his technical brilliance on tours of Europe in the 1830s and 40s. The stories of this fame often overshadow his contributions to music, like the concept of the symphonic poem that would so obsess Scriabin; innovations with thematic transformation and musical impressionism; and inventing the idea of the 'masterclass' as a way of teaching. In his later years, it was experiments with atonality (music that lacks a tonal centre, or key) with which Liszt was preoccupied, and which foreshadowed the atonal obsession that would grip the twentieth century. Any Liszt fan listening to his Bagatelle sans tonalité, S. 216a of 1885 for the first time would be hard pressed to identify it as having the same author as Liszt's 'Consolations' S. 171a/172 series of nocturnes of 1844-50, for example.

The influence of Liszt's innovations and showmanship flooded the musical landscape of his time and set the standard for new superstars: when the Italian pianist Ferrucio Busoni (1866-1924), composer of magnificent works like 'Java Suite', 'Triakontameron' and 'Passacaglia', boasted of his own

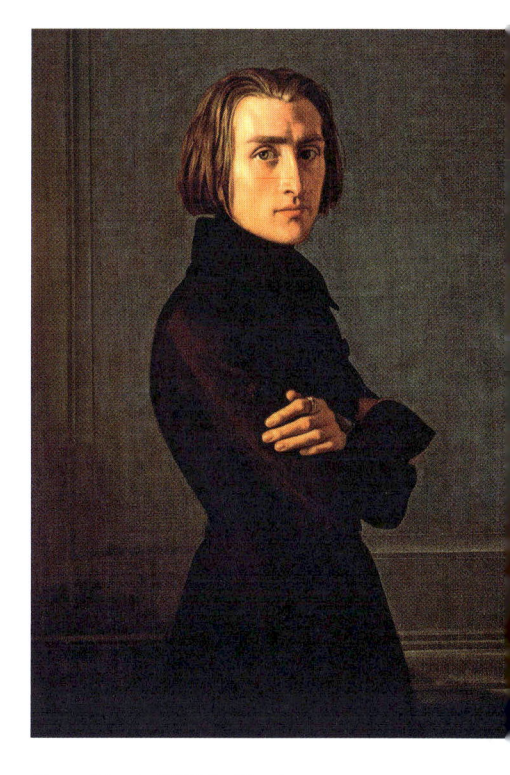

Franz Liszt in 1839, by Henri Lehrman (1814-82).

Experimental Oddities

importance, it was to say that it was himself and one other man who were 'the only composers to have added anything of significance to keyboard writing since Franz Liszt'. That other composer was the Lithuanian-American Leopold Godowsky Sr (1870-1938), whose proficiency was so highly regarded by his peers that he was known by the nickname 'Buddha of the Piano'. 'I would be very glad could I have stated with truth that I was a pupil of Liszt or any other great man', Godowsky writes in his autobiography, 'but I was not. I have not had three months lessons in my life. I have been told I was playing the piano before I was two. I think, however, an imaginative family perpetrated this story.'

Some of Godowsky's most remarkable work are his *Studies on Chopin's Études*, 53 arrangements of Chopin's études composed 1894-1914 that are breathtakingly complicated. The critic Harold C. Schonberg (1915-2003) describes them as 'the most impossibly difficult things ever written for the piano'. 'Ignis Fatuus', a study on Chopin's Étude in A minor, op. 10, No. 2, puts the original right-hand part into the left hand, for example. Two studies even combine two études – 'Badinage' combines the G flat (the 'Black Key') Étude of op. 10 and the 'Butterfly' Étude of op. 25 to form a hybrid requiring a virtuoso's skill to play. But perhaps most impressive to see performed are the several Godowsky studies like the 'Revolutionary' étude transposed to C sharp minor that demands the entire étude to be played with the left hand alone, unforgivingly, at tremendous pace. The pianist Arthur Rubenstein (1887-1982) once said that it would take him 'five hundred years to get a technique like Godowsky's'. The Italian musician Francesco Libetta (b.1968) is the only pianist to have ever performed the entire four-hour series of Godowsky's *Studies on Chopin's* Études in concert – and he did it entirely from memory.

In terms of originality, however, there are few composers' names to exalt above Erik Satie (1866-1925), whose work would influence Maurice Ravel (1875-1937), Claude Debussy (1862-1918) and Francis Poulenc (1899-1963), as well as John Cage and John Adams (b.1947). Young composers were magnetically drawn to Satie, who for most of his adult life lived in a small room in Montmartre, and then in Arcueil outside Paris, wearing identical grey velvet suits, and later adopting a signature bowler hat, wing collar and umbrella (he owned over 100). He carried a hammer under his coat for self-defence. 'My

Erik Satie in 1909.

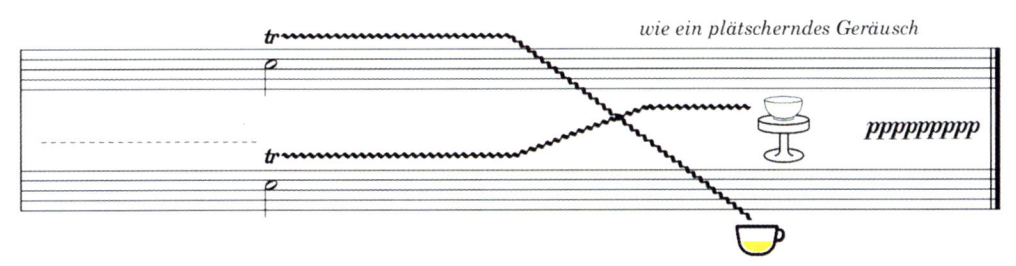

only nourishment consists of food that is white', he writes in *Memoirs of an Amnesiac*, 1912-24. 'Eggs, sugar, grated bones, the fat of dead animals, veal, salt, coconuts, chicken cooked in white water, fruit-mould, rice, turnips, camphorated sausages, pastry, cheese (white varieties), cotton salad and certain kinds of fish (without their skin). I boil my wine and drink it cold mixed with the juice of the Fuchsia. I am a hearty eater, but never speak while eating, for fear of strangling.'♪

His works have absurd titles like 'Desiccated Embryos', 1913, 'True Flabby Preludes (for a Dog)', 1912, and 'Sketches and Exasperations of a Fat Man Made of Wood', 1913. For our purposes, it's Satie's 1893 piece 'Vexations' that is particularly notable, comprising just a few bars of music of 20 seconds on a single sheet of music, that are to be repeated 840 times. 'In order to play the theme 840 times in succession', reads its inscription, 'it would be advisable to prepare oneself beforehand, and in the deepest silence, by serious immobilities.' Should this indeed be interpreted as requiring the repetition of the theme 840 times, a performance takes 12-24 hours in one sitting, depending on how one interprets the tempo 'Très lent'. Despite how tough it is on both performer and audience, complete performances have been staged a number of times. The first was organised by John Cage at the Pocket Theater, New York, in 1963, and lasted 18 hours 12 minutes, performed by a group of ten pianists in relay. The most recent was by Igor Levit (b.1987) in May 2020, who attributed his attempt to boredom from the coronavirus lockdown. He copied out the piece on 820 sheets of paper, and laid each one on the floor after each repetition.

One experimental musical avenue that was explored by theorists in the twentieth century was microtones, which are intervals smaller than a semitone. These could be described as sliver notes, found *between* the standard notes of a piano, with

'Sonata Erotica', 1919, by the Austro-Czech composer and Dadaist Erwin Schulhoff (1894-1942), features six-and-a-half minutes of the female vocalist making loud sex noises, before a finale in which the audience listens to the sound of her urinating into a chamber pot. The piece was feared lost after Schulhoff was caught fleeing by the Nazis and died of tuberculosis at Wülzburg prison in Bavaria, Germany, but it was rediscovered and given its premiere in 1993.

♪ Conventionality didn't find Satie at night, either. He also mentions in his memoirs his unusual way of sleeping: 'I sleep with only one eye closed, very deeply. My bed is round, with a hole to put my head through. Once every hour a servant takes my temperature and gives me another.'

which one can expand the customary Western tuning of twelve equal intervals per octave to include the microtones between these standard notes. One does, of course, require a specially tuned, or specially fabricated, keyboard to find the in-between music. For this we can go back at least as far as the Renaissance composer and experimental theorist Nicola Vicentino (1511-76), who was so obsessed by microtones that he built a harpsichord keyboard he called the archicembalo with thirty-six keys to the octave instead of the standard twelve. The double-rowed keyboard had black keys between B and C, and between E and F, and every black key was divided in two, so one could distinguish between a sharp or flat note. Vicentino used the archicembalo to test his theories of tuning, and discovered it to be useful in accompanying vocalists, as it could match the subtle variations in intonation in a way other keyboards couldn't.

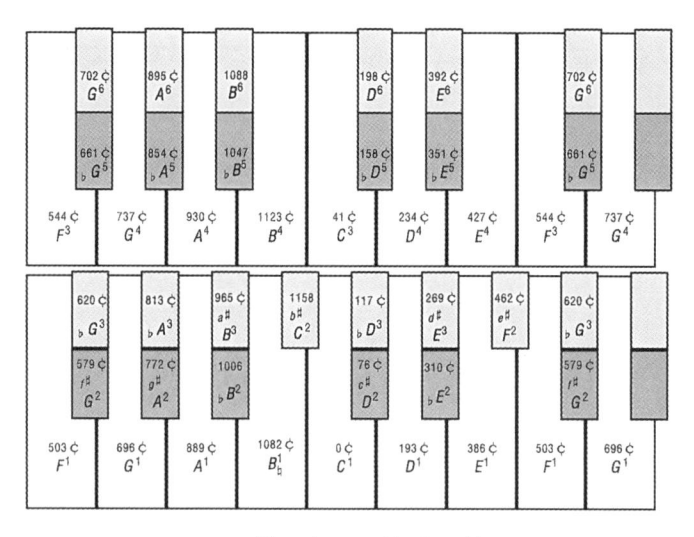

The microtonal keyboard layout of Vicentino's archicembalo.

Composers of the 1920s and 30s explored things farther: Alois Hába (1893-1973) had keyboards and woodwind instruments specially built to work with quarter tones, though he went as far as working with twelfth tones. The Mexican composer Julián Carrillo (1875-1965) built a series of expanded pianos that could play from twenty-four intervals per octave, through to ninety-six equal pitches; while the American composer Harry Partch (1901-74) went haywire and built his own unique musical instruments, including the chromelodeon, the quadrangularis reversum and the zymo-xyl, to be capable of playing microtonal scales divided into forty-three unequal tones. He created large-scale, theatrical pieces for his own microtonal chamber orchestra, in which the performers were expected to sing, dance, speak and play instruments. Partch was as eccentric as his instruments. From 1935, for example, as the Great Depression hit its nadir, he spent nine years living as a travelling vagrant, picking up bit-jobs and keeping a journal that was published after his death as *Bitter Music*. From reading this, we discover that Partch had a habit of writing notation of the speech inflections of people he met in his travels. A listen of 'Barstow', 1941, one of his earliest surviving and (believe it or not) most accessible pieces, perfectly introduces all the unique colours and tones of the Partch musical universe and is based around an inscription that he noticed on a highway railing in the Mojave Desert junction town of Barstow, which reads: 'It's January 26. I'm freezing. Ed Fitzgerald. Age 19. Five feet, 10 inches. Black hair, brown eyes. Going home to Boston, Massachusetts. It's 4:00, and I'm hungry and broke. I wish I was dead. But today I am a man.'

The American modernist Charles Ives (1874-1954) brought much publicity to composition with microtones; and also to bitonality, in which two or more instruments are tuned slightly apart to play in different keys simultaneously. His short composition 'Hallowe'en', 1907, is of a duration of only 2-3 minutes, but is intended to be played several times, each in a different tempo. The first violin plays in C major, the second violin in B major, a viola in D flat, a cello in D major and there is an atonal piano. A sixth member can be added in the form of a drummer, who joins in the last repetition, which should be played 'as fast as possible without disabling any player or instrument'. Ives's 'Unanswered Question', 1808, meanwhile, features three separate ensembles of strings, brass and flutes, all playing 'together' in completely different rhythms and keys. Ives even instructs that the string section be hidden from the audience, for added eeriness. 'Three Quarter-Tone Pieces', 1923-24, is particularly notorious for being a difficult listen, calling for two pianos to be tuned a quarter-tone apart. To Ives, this reduced pitch distance had a powerful meaning: it represented the proximity of God being much greater to us than we are aware.

Ernst Toch (1887-1964) established himself as one of the great avant-garde composers of the 1920s Weimar Germany, but of special mention is his Symphony No. 3, op. 75, which was premiered by the Pittsburgh Symphony Orchestra in 1955, and went on to win him the Pulitzer Prize for Music. The assembly of instruments required for its performance looks more like an inventor's workshop than an orchestra. At one point, the symphony calls for the sound of escaping steam, which is performed by operating a device powered by a carbon dioxide tank invented by Gerard Hoffnung (1925-59) called the Hisser, which its inventor claimed had 'all the venom and threat of a wild jungle creature spitting at its enemy'. Other instruments for the piece include an octagonal wooden drum filled with croquet balls, a vibraphone, a xylophone and a Hammond organ.

ABOVE: *Harry Partch directing Mills College students in March 1952.*

BELOW: *Miss Margaret Cotton operates the Hisser during a performance of Ernst Toch's Symphony No. 3 in 1958 at London's Royal Festival Hall.*

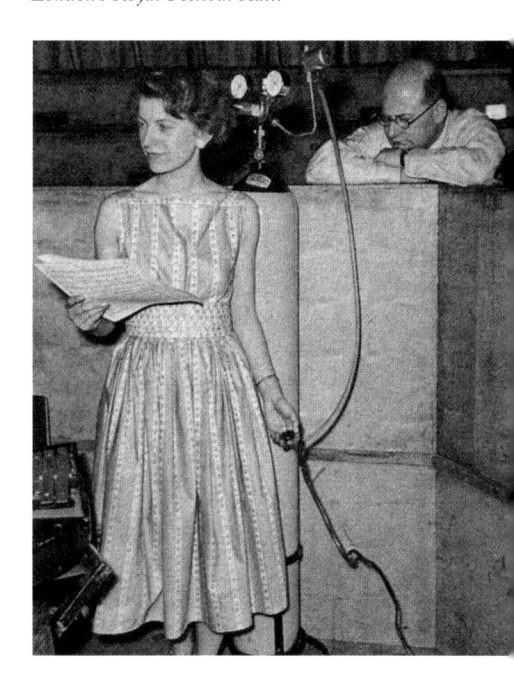

189 *Experimental Oddities*

Satie's *Parade*, 1917, involves the use of a roulette wheel and office machines. Children's toys are used in Lejaren Hiller's (1924-94) *Machine Music*, 1964 – of which 'Solo V' is often spoken about as being the hardest work to perform in all percussion literature. Police whistles feature in Mauricio Kagel's (1931-2008) 'Match', 1964, and a referee's whistle in Jacque Ibert's (1890-1962) 'Divertissement', 1930. The Italian composer Luciano Berio's (1925-2003) 'Rossignolet du bois' ('Little nightingale of the woods'), 1964, features clarinet, harp and crotales cymbals, as well as chords played on car suspension springs. A sound that is impossible for the listener to identify features in the score by Tristram Cary (1925-2008) for the animated feature film *I Vor Pittfalks*, 1974, which was achieved by stretching a condom over a microphone and scratching it with fingernails.

Salvator Martirano (1927-95) must surely qualify to compete for the title of composer working with most diverse array of instruments, scoring not only for standard orchestra but also for electronic music with instruments of his own invention, as well as for marimba, celesta, amplified night-club singer, tape, three film projectors, gas-masked politico and helium bomb. Which reminds me of Malcolm Arnold's (1921-2006) 'A Grand Grand Overture' written for the 1956 Hoffnung Music Festival, as a parody of pompous nineteenth-century concert overtures. Scored for full symphony orchestra and organ, it also features three vacuum cleaners, a floor polisher and four loaded rifles, which fire during the piece and again at the climax in an execution of their vacuum rivals. The work also has several horrendous juxtapositions of key, and a ridiculously prolonged coda.

Mauricio Kagel's 'Transition II', 1959, instructs that the two pianists play their instruments entirely by hitting the inside of their instrument with drumsticks and other devices, and for 'Und so weiter…', 1966. Luc Ferrari (1929-2005) requires that objects including billiard balls should be placed on the strings and soundboard. In David Bedford's (1937-2011) 'Music for Albion Moonlight', 1965, the soprano must scream the word 'Hell' as loud as they're able into the interior of the piano to make the strings resonate.

In his 'Ellora Symphony', written in 1958, the Japanese composer Yasushi Akutagawa (1925-89) allows for the twenty movements to be spontaneously played in any order. Symphony No. 4: 'A Wine Symphony', 1979, by Derek Bourgeois (1941-2017) is written in nine movements, with each one representing a different region of wine-growing. The music begins with all

One of three vacuum-cleaner-players rehearsing for a performance of Malcolm Arnold's 'A Grand Grand Overture' at the Birmingham Symphony Hall, UK, in May 2010.

FOLLOWING SPREAD: *'Faerie's Aire and Death Waltz', 1980, by composer John Stump (1944-2006), crammed onto a single page featuring the directions 'Add bicycle', 'Duck' and 'Cool timpani with small fan'.*

the players putting their fingers in their mouths, and pulling them out to imitate the 'pop' of corks being released. The Polynesian symphonist Dai-Keong Lee (1915-2005) composed the only symphony to include a part for a dancer, Polynesian Suite, 1959, in which a Tahitian dancer appears on stage. Zsolt Durko's (1934-97) 'Dartmouth Concerto', 1966, for mezzo and orchestra is a piece about the reported habit of lemmings marching off cliffs to their death. The Belgian composer Henri Pousseur (1929-2009) wrote his piano work 'Caractères I', 1961, with the idea that a piece of paper with holes randomly cut into it should be placed over the music score, and the pianist must play only the parts of visible through the holes. 'Goldstaub' from *Aus den Sieben Tagen*, 1968, by Karlheinz Stockhausen (1928-2007) is even more demanding on its players, requiring that the four performers must live in isolation without food for four days before the concert.

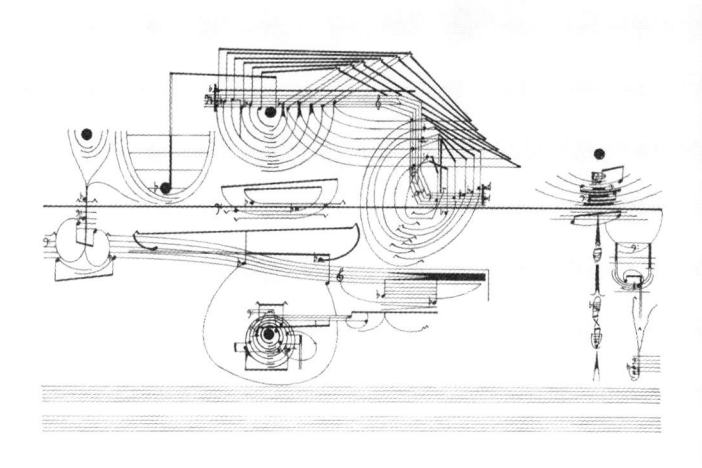

The score for 'Treatise', 1967, by British composer Cornelius Cardew (1936-81), who provides no instructions for how to play the 193 pages of abstract and geometric shapes, other than suggesting the players come up with a plan together before the performance.

Even if you had never heard the music of Kaikhosru Shapurji Sorabji (1892-1988) (see page 161), you would likely guess as to the experimental nature of his music from his eccentric biographical details. Born to an Indian father and English mother, the largely self-taught composer felt a complete outsider to English society and opted for seclusion, leaving London (which he called the 'International Human Rubbish Dump') in 1956 and moved to a house he built for himself in Dorset called The Eye, which he rarely left. A 'Tower of Granite', as he describes it, 'with plentiful supplies of boiling oil and molten lead handy to tip over the battlements onto the heads of unwanted and uninvited intruders.' Legend has it he posted a sign on his front door reading 'Certain nuns welcome; all others not.'

As mentioned (on page 161), after hearing of John Tobin doing an inadequate job of performing part one of his 'Opus Clavicembalisticum' (1930) in 1936, Sorabji would forbid musicians to perform in public his compositions in his lifetime, for fear they would ruin them. 'No performance at all is vastly preferable to an obscene travesty,' he explains. For many performers, this prohibition was mutually agreeable, as Sorabji had a talent for composing pieces so complex and inhumanly

FAERIE'S AIRE and DEATH WALTZ
(from "A Tribute to Zdenko G. Fibich")

Words and Music by John Stump
Arranged by Accident

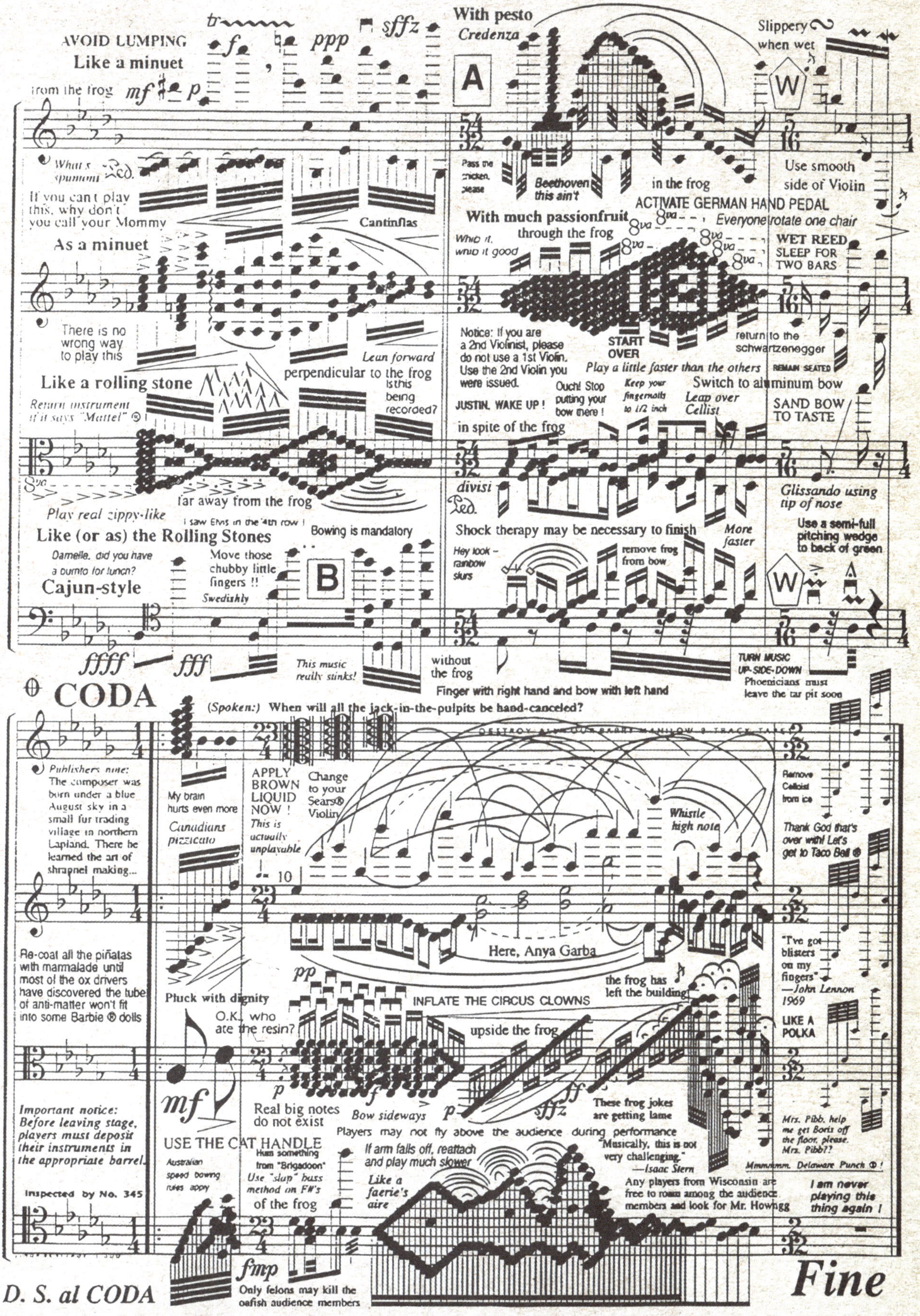

AVOID LUMPING
Like a minuet
from the frog
With pesto
Credenza
A
Slippery
when wet
W
What's spumoni
If you can't play this, why don't you call your Mommy
Pass the chicken, please
Beethoven this ain't
in the frog
Use smooth side of Violin
Cantinflas
ACTIVATE GERMAN HAND PEDAL
With much passionfruit
through the frog
Everyone rotate one chair
As a minuet
Whip it, whip it good
WET REED
SLEEP FOR TWO BARS
There is no wrong way to play this
Lean forward
Notice: If you are a 2nd Violinist, please do not use a 1st Violin. Use the 2nd Violin you were issued.
START OVER
return to the schwartzenegger
Play a little faster than the others
REMAIN SEATED
Like a rolling stone
perpendicular to the frog
Is this being recorded?
Return instrument if it says "Mattel" ®
JUSTIN, WAKE UP!
Ouch! Stop putting your bow there!
Keep your fingernails to 1/2 inch
Leap over Cellist
Switch to aluminum bow
SAND BOW TO TASTE
in spite of the frog
divisi
far away from the frog
Glissando using tip of nose
Play real zippy-like
I saw Elvis in the 4th row!
Bowing is mandatory
Shock therapy may be necessary to finish
More faster
Use a semi-full pitching wedge to back of green
Like (or as) the Rolling Stones
Darnelle, did you have a burrito for lunch?
Move those chubby little fingers!!
Swedishly
B
Hey look – rainbow slurs
remove frog from bow
W
Cajun-style
This music really stinks!
without the frog
TURN MUSIC UP-SIDE-DOWN
Phoenicians must leave the tar pit soon
Finger with right hand and bow with left hand
CODA
(Spoken:) When will all the jack-in-the-pulpits be hand-canceled?
DESTROY ALL YOUR BARRY MANILOW 8 TRACK TAPES
Publishers note: The composer was born under a blue August sky in a small fur trading village in northern Lapland. There he learned the art of shrapnel making...
My brain hurts even more
APPLY BROWN LIQUID NOW!
Change to your Sears® Violin
This is actually unplayable
Canadians pizzicato
Whistle high note
Remove Cellist from ice
Thank God that's over with! Let's get to Taco Bell ®
Here, Anya Garba
"I've got blisters on my fingers" —John Lennon 1969
Re-coat all the piñatas with marmalade until most of the ox drivers have discovered the tube of anti-matter won't fit into some Barbie ® dolls
the frog has left the building
Pluck with dignity
INFLATE THE CIRCUS CLOWNS
O.K., who ate the resin?
upside the frog
LIKE A POLKA
Important notice: Before leaving stage, players must deposit their instruments in the appropriate barrel.
Real big notes do not exist
Bow sideways
These frog jokes are getting lame
Mrs. Pibb, help me get Boris off the floor, please. Mrs. Pibb??
Players may not fly above the audience during performance
USE THE CAT HANDLE
Hum something from "Brigadoon"
If arm falls off, reattach and play much slower
"Musically, this is not very challenging." —Isaac Stern
Mmmmmm. Delaware Punch ®!
Australian speed bowing rules apply
Use "slap" bass method on F#'s
Like a faerie's aire
Any players from Wisconsin are free to roam among the audience members and look for Mr. Howigg
I am never playing this thing again!
Inspected by No. 345
of the frog
Only felons may kill the oafish audience members
D. S. al CODA
Fine

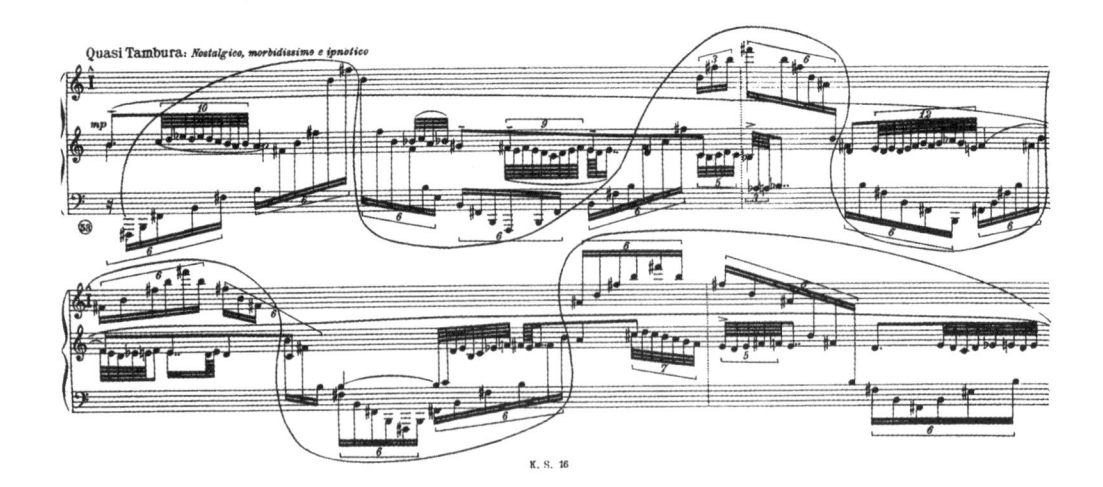

ABOVE: *An excerpt from Sorabji's gargantuan 'Opus Clavicembalisticum', 1930, IX [Interludium B]. Note the extraordinary slur (a curved line that connects two or more notes of different pitches), perhaps the most complicated of any composition with a total of ten inflection points, spanning three systems, and repeatedly crossing three staves (perhaps also the most staves in a single system, too); and even running backwards, from right to left, at several points.*

long that they were virtually impossible to play. His 'Messa Grande Sinfonica', 1961, is written across 1,001 pages. Organ Symphony No. 2, 1932, a work for solo organ, lasts nine hours. When Jonathan Powell was asked by the *Guardian* newspaper, ahead of his performance of the 'Opus Clavicembalisticum' in 2003, how he would describe the piece, he simply laughs and says 'That's like saying: "How would you describe the world?"'

Conlon Nancarrow (1912-97) deemed human ability insufficient to perform the music he heard in his head, so he composed for automatic player pianos, punching hundreds of thousands of holes in their reels by hand. This meant he could insist on far greater accuracy than other composers. Take the time signatures for his Study No. 41 (shown opposite), for example, which is in three parts for two pianos: the first canon has a time signature of (*see* FIG. 1) for the first piano; the second is in (*see* FIG. 2) for the second piano; and the third is in (*see* FIG. 3) for both pianos.

Twelve years before Simon and Garfunkel were singing the 'Sound of Silence' in 1964 (which Simon later explained came from his love of sitting in his bathroom in the dark), the most famous of the avant-garde composers, John Cage, was premiering his famous experimental piece '4'33"', for any instrument or combination of instruments, as the score instructs the players not to touch their instruments across the three movements. Cage wasn't the first to play with silence, however: a previous example is the 'In Futurum' movement for solo piano from *Fünf Pittoresken*, 1919, by the Czech composer Erwin Schulhoff, which is made entirely of rests. The score instructs that the performer play 'the whole piece with free expression and feeling, always, until the end'. (Which once prompted the pianist Philippe Binconi (b.1960) to ask 'Should

FIG. 1
$$\frac{1}{\sqrt{\pi}} / \sqrt{2/3}$$

FIG. 2
$$\frac{1}{3\sqrt{\pi}} / \sqrt[3]{13/16}$$

FIG. 3
$$\frac{\frac{1}{3\sqrt{\pi}} / \sqrt[3]{13/16}}{\frac{1}{\sqrt{\pi}} / \sqrt{2/3}}$$

I just sit here?') The French humourist Alphonse Allais (1854-1905) also wrote 'Funeral March for the Obsequies of a Deaf Man' in 1897, which consists of twenty-four empty bars.

An audience at a programme of all these silent pieces would be unlikely to confuse them with that of Cage's, however, as contrary to popular belief, silence was not his intention for the piece. Speaking of the 1952 premiere, he later says: 'What they thought was silence, because they didn't know how to listen, was full of accidental sounds. You could hear the wind stirring outside during the first movement. During the second, raindrops began pattering on the roof, and during the third the people themselves made all kinds of interesting sounds as they talked or walked out.' The title of the piece is also misleading, as Cage later said the work may be performed to last any length of time. As well known as the piece is, performances can still cause potential difficulties – in 2004, when BBC Radio 3 broadcast the first UK orchestral performance of '4'33"', at the last minute a quick-thinking station employee remembered to shut off the emergency backup system that interprets silence as dead air and automatically begins playing music of the audible variety.

Some pieces are even less suited to radio. We can't end this chapter without mentioning the American composer La Monte Young (b.1935), who was born in a log cabin in Bern, Idaho, where his experimental approach was formed by listening to the drones of his environment, from the wind blowing under the eaves to the six-cycle-per-second hum of the step-down transformers on telephone poles. An exploration of his strange work would fill several thick volumes, but of particular note are his *Compositions 1960*. No. 2, for example, is titled 'Build a Fire', which is what the performer is instructed to do in front of the audience, and watch it burn for the duration of the composition. For No. 5, the performer must, according to Young's instructions: 'Turn a butterfly (or any number of butterflies) loose in the performance area. When the composition is over, be sure to allow the butterfly to fly away outside. The composition may be any length but if an unlimited amount of time is available the doors and windows may be opened before the butterfly is turned loose and the composition may be considered finished when the butterfly flies away.' This is arguably a lot more enjoyable to sit through than No. 7, which involves playing only two notes, a B3 and F#4, with each 'to be held for a long time' using any amount of instruments. A forty-five-minute performance of the piece was performed by a string trio in New York in 1961.

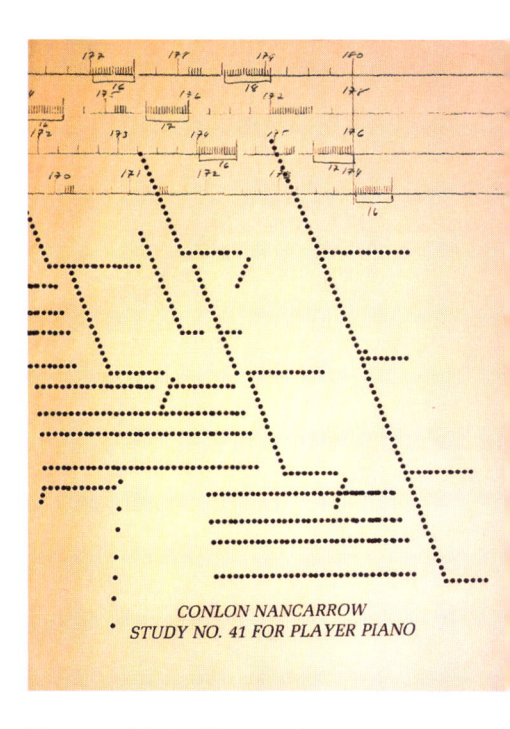

The cover of Conlon Nancarrow's Study No. 41 for Player Piano.

III. In futurum.

Zeitmaß-zeitlos.

tutto il canzone con espressione e sentimento ad libitum, sempre, sin al fine!

G.P.
(Marschall Pause.)

OPPOSITE: *Silent music before John Cage: the 'In Futurum' section of Erwin Schulhoff's 1919 composition* Fünf Pittoresken *features only rests.*

LEFT-TOP: *The Danish violinist Robert Karlsson of the aquatic music ensemble Between Music plays underwater in a tank during a concert at the Tramway in Glasgow, 25 October 2017. Each of the five musicians perform in their own giant aquarium on stage.*

LEFT-MIDDLE: *Alan Pierson, centre, and members of Alarm Will Sound perform Hungarian composer György Ligeti's (1923-2006) 'Poème Symphonique for 100 Metronomes', 1962, at Zankel Hall in March 2018. The mechanical metronomes are wound to their limit, set to different tempos and activated simultaneously, for the audience to watch wind down. Ligeti was inspired by a childhood story of a widow living in a house full of clocks.*

LEFT-BOTTOM: *Karlheinz Stockhausen's 'Helicopter Quartet' requires each of the four players to perform in a separate helicopter circling the audience. Here a video wall shows an airborne string quartet in four helicopters performing the concert on Friday 22 in August 2003, as part of the Salzburg Festival at the opening of Hangar 7 at Salzburg Airport. The performance ends when the helicopters land and the musicians return to the stage to the sound of rotor blades winding down.*

197 | *Experimental Oddities*

▶ PLAYLIST: EXPERIMENTAL ODDITIES

4 Puzzle Canons, K. 73r, 1770 or 1772,
WOLFGANG AMADEUS MOZART

'A Grand Grand Overture', 1956,
MALCOLM ARNOLD

'Agnus Dei II, *Missa l'Homme Armé Super Voces Musicales*', 1489,
JOSQUIN DES PREZ

'Bagatelle sans tonalite' S.216a, 1885,
FRANZ LISZT

'Barstow' (from *The Wayward*), 1941-1955,
HARRY PARTCH

'Battalia à 10', 1673,
HEINRICH IGNAZ FRANZ BIBER

'Belle Bonne Sage', early fifteenth century,
BAUDE CORDIER

'Caractères I', 1961,
HENRI POUSSEUR

Compositions 1960,
LA MONTE YOUNG

Concerto for Jew's Harp, Mandora and Orchestra F major, 1782,
JOHANN GEORG ALBRECHTSBERGER

'Dartmouth Concerto', 1966,
ZSOLT DURKO

'Desiccated Embryos', 1913,
ERIK SATIE

'Divertissement', 1930,
JACQUES IBERT

'Duet for Tuba', 1963,
ROBERT WATTS

'Ein Ton' ('The Monotone'), 1854,
PETER CORNELIUS

'En la maison Dedalus', 14th century,
FRENCH TRADITIONAL BALLAD

'Ellora Symphony', 1958,
YASUSHI AKUTAGAWA

'Faerie's Aire and Death Waltz', 1980,
JOHN STUMP

'F/H TRACE' 1963,
ROBERT WATTS

'Four Pieces, Each on a Single Note', 1959,
GIACINTO SCELSI

'Funeral March for the Obsequies of a Deaf Man', 1897,
ALPHONSE ALLAIS

Fünf Pittoresken, 1919,
ERWIN SCHULHOFF

'Goldstaub', *Aus den Sieben Tagen*, 1968,
KARLHEINZ STOCKHAUSEN

'Grosse Fuge', op. 133, 1825,
LUDWIG VAN BEETHOVEN

'Gulliver Suite', 1728-29,
GEORG PHILIPP TELEMANN

'Hallowe'en', 1907,
CHARLES IVES

'Helicopter Quartet', 1995,
KARLHEINZ STOCKHAUSEN

Horn Concertino in E minor, 1806,
CARL MARIA VON WEBER

I Vor Pittfalks soundtrack, 1974,
TRISTRAM CARY

'Labyrinth 3', 1941,
LOU HARRISON

Machine Music, 1964,
LEJAREN HILLER

'Match', 1964,
MAURICIO KAGEL

Messiah, HWV 56, 1741,
GEORGE FRIDERIC HANDEL

'My Lord Chamberlain, His Galliard', 1597,
JOHN DOWLAND

'Never Gonna Give You Up But All the Notes Are C', 2017,
CONTENT CREATOR MAN,
https://www.youtube.com/watch?v=cSAp9sBzPbc

'Opus Clavicembalisticum', 1930,
KAIKHOSRU SHAPURJI SORABJI

'Organ Symphony No. 2', 1932,
KAIKHOSRU SHAPURJI SORABJI

Overture 'Il Signor Bruschino', 1813,
GIOACHINO ROSSINI

Parade (1917),
ERIK SATIE

'Piano Piece for David Tudor', 1959,
SYLVANO BUSSOTTI

Piano Sonata in G major, D 894, 1826,
FRANZ SCHUBERT

'Preparation for the Final Mystery',
ALEXANDER SCRIABIN (completed in 1973 by ALEXANDER NEMTIN)

Rondeau 14, 'Ma fin est mon commencement' ('My End is My Beginning'), fourteenth century,
GUILLAUME DE MACHAUT

Rosary Sonatas, c.1676,
HEINRICH IGNAZ FRANZ BIBER

Salome, 1905,
RICHARD STRAUSS

'Sketches and Exasperations of a Fat Man Made of Wood' (1913),
ERIK SATIE

'Sonata Erotica', 1919,
ERWIN SCHULHOFF

'Songs, Drones and Refrains of Death', 1968,
GEORGE CRUMB

Studies on Chopin's Études, 1894-1914,
LEOPOLD GODOWSKY SR

'Study for Player Piano 3a', 1988,
CONLON NANCARROW

Study No. 41, 1982,
CONLON NANCARROW

Suite II in C major, 'Lamento sopra la dolorosa perdita della Real Msta di Ferdinando IV, Re de Romani', 1654,
JOHANN JAKOB FROBERGER

Symphony No. 3 'Aetherique', 1899,
ALBERT SIKLOS

Symphony No. 3, op. 75, 1955,
ERNST TOCH

Symphony No. 4: 'A Wine Symphony', 1979,
DEREK BOURGEOIS

Symphony No. 67 in F, *c*.1778,
JOSEPH HAYDN

'Tenebrae Responsoria', 1611,
CARLO GESUALDO DA VENOSA

'The Cyclops forging the murderous thunderbolt of Aesculapius', *c*.1753,
CHRISTOPHE MOYREAU

'The Musical Offering', BWV 1079, 1747,
JOHANN SEBASTIAN BACH

'The Way of the World', nineteenth century,
IGNAZ MOSCHELES

'Three Quarter-Tone Pieces' (1923-24),
CHARLES IVES

'Tout par compas suy composes' ('With a Compass Was I Composed'), early fifteenth century,
BAUDE CORDIER

'Trace for Orchestra',
ROBERT WATTS

'Treatise', 1967,
CORNELIUS CARDEW

'True Flabby Preludes (for a Dog)', (1912),
ERIK SATIE

'Unanswered Question', 1908,
CHARLES IVES

'Vexations', 1893,
ERIK SATIE

'Water Walk', 1959,
JOHN CAGE

MUSICAL HOAXES

On 17 May 1991, an estimated 11.3 million people in the Soviet Union tuned into the television programme *Pyatoe Koleso* ('The Fifth Wheel') to learn that Vladimir Lenin was in fact a mushroom. Over the course of an extensive, 30-minute interview with the journalist Sergey Sholokhov on Leningrad Television, a historian laid out his recent findings about the 'main secret of the October Revolution': that Lenin had consumed so many psychedelic mushrooms he had physically morphed into one. 'I have completely irrefutable proof that the October Revolution was made by people who had been eating certain mushrooms for many years. And in the process of being eaten by those people, the mushrooms supplanted their personalities, and the people became mushrooms. In other words, I am simply stating that Lenin was a mushroom. A mushroom. And furthermore, he wasn't just a mushroom, he was also a radio wave.'

The 'historian' was Sergey Anatolyevich Kuryokhin (1954-96), a Russian composer, pianist and keyboardist for the rock group Аквариум ('Aquarium') who came up with the idea for the hoax after watching a documentary on the poet Sergey Yesenin (1895-1925) that featured wild and unfounded claims. The best part of the reaction to the joke was that, as with all great hoaxes, people didn't know whether to take it seriously or not. According to Sholokhov, the Leningrad Regional Committee of the Communist Party of the Soviet Union was inundated with requests to verify the information. The official response was that the first and founding head of Soviet Russian government 'could not have been a mushroom' because 'a mammal cannot be a plant'.

Hoaxes are most commonly associated with news media, literature and the visual arts, but there is a surprisingly deep and glitteringly rich vein of deliberate deceptions in music history. Kuryokhin's masterpiece serves to illustrate just how suitably inventive the musical imagination is for this genre.

One of the earliest examples of musical hoodwinking came during a particular episode in France in 1753 known as the *Guerre des Bouffons* ('War of the Comic Actors'), when rival factions of French and Italian music quarrelled over whose was the superior form. To the Italians, the art had its pinnacle in the *opera buffa* ('comic opera') *La Serva Padrona*, 1733, by Giovanni Pergolesi (1710-36), the best of a tradition that French composers could never hope to approach. As if to reinforce their

LEFT: *A* trompe l'oeil *by the Dutch artist Jan van der Vaardt (1647-1721) in 1723 at Chatsworth House in Derbyshire, UK. In* Anecdotes of Painting, *1762, Horace Walpole writes: 'In old Devonshire-house in Piccadilly, he painted a violin against a door that deceived every body. When the house was burned, this piece was preserved, and is now at Chatsworth.'*

BELOW: *Leopoldo Franciolini (1844–1920) was an antiques dealer and prolific forger of historical musical instruments. This clavicytherium, sold by Franciolini, is unlike any authentic example, and was used as evidence by the prosecution at his criminal trial in 1910.*

point, a new comic opera in one act appeared in 1753 called *Les Troqueurs* ('The Barterers'). Written by a French-speaking Italian living in Vienna, it was an instant smash-hit. Both the French and the Italian partisans received it proudly. Only then did Jean Monnet, head of the Théâtre de la Foire Saint-Laurent, reveal that he had commissioned composer Antoine Dauvergne (1713-97) to write a new French opera in the style of Pergolesi: the result was *Les Troqueurs*. Monnet revealed in his memoirs that he had invented and spread the rumour of its Italian authorship himself.

From his Austrian seat at Schloss Stuppach near Gloggnitz, Count Franz von Walsegg (1763-1827) was particularly focused on commissioning musical compositions to perform at his ancestral home. Every Tuesday and Thursday at Schloss Stuppach, a quartet would play for three hours, sometimes joined by the Count himself, who played the violoncello as well

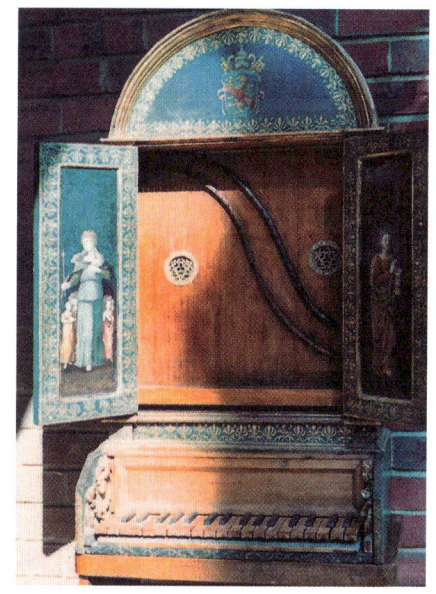

Musical Hoaxes

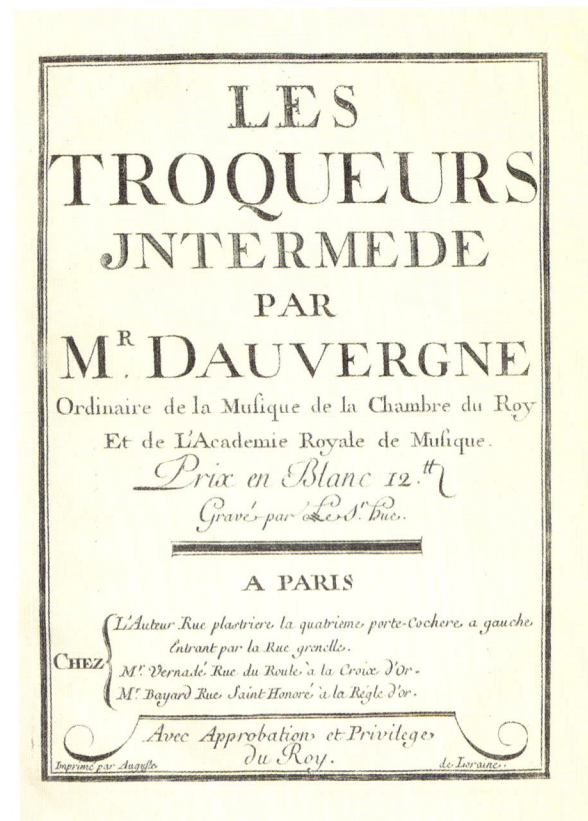

as the flute in wind ensembles. Unfortunately, Von Walsegg had a relentless habit of passing off these commissioned pieces as his own. Most famously, he attempted to do this with a requiem mass he had hired Wolfgang Amadeus Mozart to write in 1791 in honour of his twenty-year-old wife, Anna. Anton Herzog, a school teacher in Wiener Neustadt who claimed to have attended performances of this requiem, published an account with first-hand information on the Count's habits. (The document was censored in 1839 and would only appear in print in 1925.) 'So that we would not lack for new quartets', Herzog writes, 'in view of so frequent productions of them, Herr Count not only procured all those publicly announced but was in touch with many composers, yet without ever revealing [their] identit[ies]… they delivered to him works of which he retained the sole ownership, and for which he paid well.'

Mozart devised what we know today as his Requiem in D minor, K. 626 for Von Walsegg but died before he could finish it. A completed version was then delivered in 1792 by Franz Xaver Süssmayr to the Count, who would have passed it off as 'Von Walsegg's Requiem' if it wasn't for Mozart's widow

ABOVE: *The title page and first page of the score to* Les Troqueurs, *1753, an influential work of opera buffa.*

BELOW: *Portrait of composer Antoine Dauvergne.*

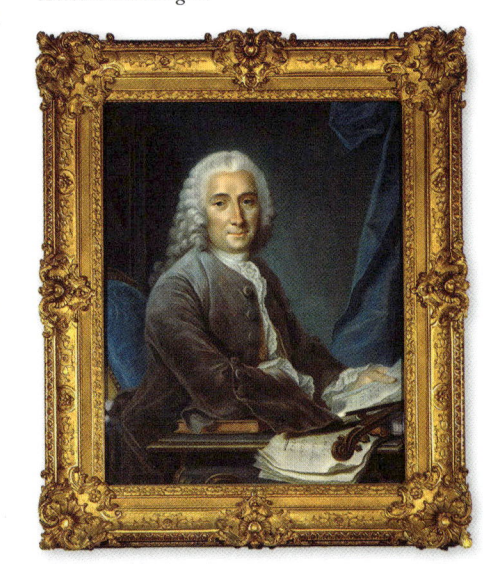

ABOVE: *A section of a page from the manuscript of Mozart's Requiem in D minor, K 626, 1791, showing Mozart's heading for the first movement. It was supposedly written for his own funeral.*

BELOW: *Silhouette portrait of Count Franz von Walsegg.*

Constanze organising a public benefit performance of the piece. She claimed that the commission came to Mozart from a mysterious messenger who did not reveal the identity of his employer, and Mozart came to believe that he was writing it for his own funeral.

Mozart himself had previously dabbled with the satirical side of hoaxing in 1787 with his 'Ein musikalischer Spaß' (traditionally translated as 'A Musical Joke', but more accurately meaning 'Some Musical Fun'); although first it's worth mentioning how his humour shines through more obviously in a couple of lyrical pieces designed not to be taken seriously. One is titled, improbably, 'Leck Mich im Arsch' ('Lick Me in the Arsehole') K. 231 (K. 382c).♪ The canon in B flat major was written in 1782 to be sung by six voices as a three-part round, and likely as a drunken singalong party piece. Another to add to this humorous heap is his 'Bona Nox, Bist a Rechta Ochs' (which translates as 'Good Night, You Are Quite

---

♪ For a long time the related composition 'Leck mir den Arsch fein recht schön sauber' ('Lick My Arse Right Well and Clean') was logically assumed to also have been written by Mozart, but it's now believed to be the work of the Austrian-Czech composer Wenzel Trnka (1739-91) that was bundled up with the original Mozart pieces sent by his widow Constanze to his publishers after his death. And on a loosely related note, the name of the Irish band The Pogues is a shortening of *pogue mo chone*, which in Gaelic means 'kiss my arse'.

203 | *Musical Hoaxes*

an Ox'), a canon of similar kind and quality. This was also heavily bowdlerised – below are the sanitised lyrics, followed by Mozart's original version for comparison:

Gute Nacht!	Good night!
bis der Tag erwacht!	Until the morning breaks!
Alle Sorgen	All you sorrows
ruht bis morgen!	Rest till morrow!
Euch gute Nacht!	Good night to you!
Schlaf wohl!	Sleep well!
schliess(t) nur die Augen (jetzt) zu	Close the eyes now fast
schlaf mein Liebchen	Sleep, my darling
fein sanft, schlaf in guter Ruh	Very gently, sleep resting well
gute Nacht!	Good night!
Schlaft fein süss	Have sweet dreams
bis nun der Tag erwacht!	Until the morning breaks!
Bona nox!	Good night! [Latin]
bist a rechta Ochs	You are quite an ox
bona notte	Good night [Italian]
liebe Lotte	My dear Lotte
bonne nuit	Good night [French]
pfui, pfui	Phooey, phooey
good night, good night	Good night, good night [English]
heut müßma noch weit	We still have far to go today
gute Nacht, gute Nacht	Good night, good night
scheiß ins Bett daß' kracht	Shit in your bed and make it burst
gute Nacht, schlaf fei g'sund	Good night, sleep tight
und reck' den Arsch zum Mund	And stick your ass to your mouth

Mozart's rather blunt method of correcting his English pupil Thomas Attwood, writing 'You are an ass' by his work. From Add. MS 58437, a manuscript of exercises in theory and composition in the British Library.

204 | *Madman's Orchestra*

But back to Mozart's jape 'Ein musikalischer Spaß', which even to those unfamiliar with an eighteenth-century German's sense of humour has instantly discernible oddities woven skilfully into the fabric of the 20-minute piece. The discords in the horns, the shifts to wrong keys and deliberately ham-fisted orchestration are jarring to anyone's ear – the sarcastic clumsiness was hilarious to a contemporary audience. Finally, it wraps up with one of the earliest instances of polytonality (the wince-inducing use of more than one musical key simultaneously), to give the impression that all the players collectively collapse in a heap when finished. Although Mozart didn't record his intentions behind the piece, it is today believed to be a satire of inept composers and musicians.

The Danish composer Rued Langgaard (1893-1952) was rather more pointed with his mockery, composing several pieces purely out of sarcasm, the most biting (and, frankly, brilliant) of which is 'Carl Nielsen – vor store komponist' ('Carl Nielsen – Our Great Composer'), 1948, for orchestra and choir, which has to be the most sarcastic piece in the history of music. Outraged by the adulation (undeserved, as he saw it) that Denmark continued to heap on Nielsen (1865-1931) sixteen years after his death, and the lack of admiration of his own work, Langgaard responded with the musical equivalent of a schoolyard taunting. The choir simply repeats the phrase 'Carl Nielsen our great composer' in dripping sarcasm over and over again, which they are instructed to do 'for all eternity' by Langgaard in the notes, although most performances seem to wind down at around nine minutes for general preservation of sanity.

Sometimes a musical hoax has been concocted not as criticism but as protection against criticism. In 1850, Hector Berlioz invented a composer named Pierre Ducré as an alter ego. To be fair to Berlioz, this unusual move is perfectly understandable given the critical flak he had been taking. In 1843, a journalist of the London *Dramatic and Musical Review* writes: 'Berlioz, musically speaking, is a lunatic; a classical composer only in Paris, the great city of quacks. His music is simply and undisguisedly nonsense.' The Paris critic Pierre Scudo says of him: 'Not only does Berlioz not have any melodic ideas, but when one occurs to him he does not know how to handle it, for he does not know how to write… There is nothing in these strange compositions but noise, disorder, a sickly and sterile exaltation. He gasps, he prances, he fidgets, he behaves like a demon disinherited of divine grace.'

Rued Langgaard in 1918.

Carl Nielsen c.1908.

The title page of Berlioz's autograph manuscript of La Fuite en Égypte, *attributed to Pierre Ducré, imaginary choirmaster.*

In 1850, Berlioz was set to release a new four-part choral work entitled 'L'adieu des bergers' ('The Shepherds' Farewell'), which by his account had originated from improvising a fireside piece on organ during an evening spent with his friend Pierre Duc. Wanting to sneak it past those critics loaded for bear, and also to amuse himself, he invented the wittily named Pierre Ducré (*cré* in French meaning 'created'), an ingenious but forgotten music master of the Parisian church Sainte-Chapelle in 1679. The aged music manuscript of 'L'adieu des bergers', Berlioz announced, had been found in a secret compartment behind a wall during a renovation of the church. Due to it being written in an outdated form of notation, it had been a challenge to decipher, but here it was for the listening pleasure of a concert audience for the first time in nearly 200 years.

That first performance of 'L'adieu des bergers' took place on 12 November 1850, where Berlioz maintained the fiction, and it met with instant success. The critics were fooled: Edmond Viel in the *Ménestrel* remarks that the work 'breathed a fragrance of archaic style and naïvety which was not devoid of charm', while Léon Kreutzer in the *Revue et Gazette musicale de Paris* comments (rather more cautiously) that 'the piece seemed to me quite pretty and modulated rather felicitously for a period when composers did not modulate'. Paris clamoured to know more of the lost brilliance of Ducré, but Berlioz would confess soon after. When 'L'adieu des bergers' was published two years later, as part of the larger *La Fuite en Égypte*, it was with the note: 'Fragments of a Mystery in antique style, attributed to Pierre Ducré, imaginary master of music at the Sainte-Chapelle, and composed by Hector Berlioz.'

The largest web of hoaxes in music history is weaved with this spider silk of misattribution – to invented figures like Ducré, and also deceitful attribution of new pieces to old masters by those seeking acclaim, not caring if that glory is technically heaped on another's name. Mozart's Twelfth Mass, K. Anh. 232, for example, is no longer credited to Mozart, but to either the prolific Austrian composer Wenzel Müller (1767-1835) or the German composer Carl Zulehner (1770-1841), who was an early champion of the Mozart attribution but has a tainted reputation of passing off several of his own compositions as Mozart's original work.

Berlioz's invented tale of 'rediscovering an old manuscript' is a well-worn tool of this subterfuge, particularly in the nineteenth century. There were famous true instances of this happening at the time – one of the best-known being Felix Mendelssohn's revival of J. S. Bach's *St Matthew Passion* in Berlin in 1829, after being sent a copy of the 100-year-old music by his grandmother. The credulity of audiences was charged up by these stories, and even today we are still re-evaluating and revising suspicious works that slipped through. The 'Dank sei Dir, Herr' ('Thanks Be to God') is still commonly attributed to George Frideric Handel (1685-1759), for example, even though most musicologists believe that it's actually the work of the German choral conductor and composer Siegfried Ochs (1858-1929). Giovanni Pergolesi, who we met earlier for his role in the *Guerre des Bouffons* (see page 200), was credited by the composer Alessandro Parisotti (1853-1913) with writing the aria 'Se tu m'ami' – but no early manuscripts of this music have ever been found, and it's believed that Parisotti wrote the song himself to beef up his 'historical' collection *Antique Arias*, Milan, 1885-88.

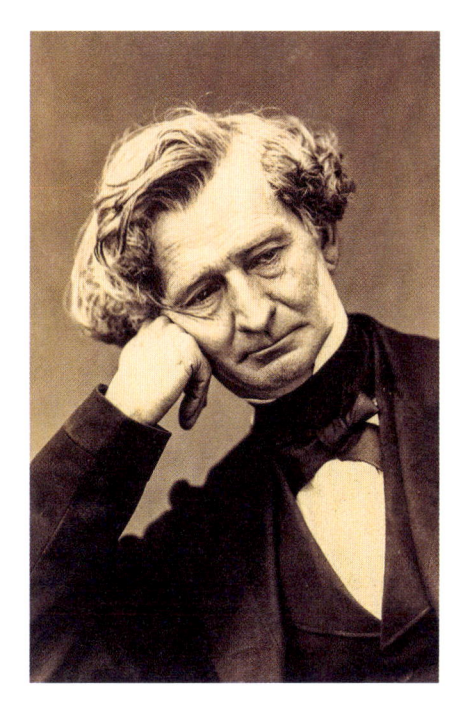

Hector Berlioz in 1863.

The most notorious of these rediscoveries was made in the twentieth century, when in 1933 the Hungarian violinist Jelly d'Arányi (1893-1966)♪ debuted in London a never-before-heard violin concerto by Mozart, known as the 'Adélaïde' concerto. The arrangement had been made by the French violinist Marius Casadesus (1892-1981), who said he had copied it from an autograph manuscript written by Mozart at the age of ten, dated 'Versailles May 26, 1766', and dedicated to 'Madame Adélaïde de France', eldest daughter of Louis XV. The concerto was published that same year under Mozart's name, with Casadesus credited as 'editor.' Its authenticity was widely accepted; it was allocated a place in the Köchel-Verzeichnis (the catalogue of Mozart's works) as 'K. Anh. 294a' ('Anh.' denotes *Anhang* or 'appendix'); and the great violinist Yehudi Menuhin (1916-99) released a recording of the concerto in 1976. It was only during a legal dispute that Casadesus admitted that there was no 'Adélaïde' manuscript – he had composed the entire concerto himself.

The skill to convincingly imitate the abilities of Mozart would be extraordinary enough, but remarkably it was a skill that ran in the family. Marius's brother Henri Casadesus (1879-1947) was also a phenomenally talented violinist and player of the viola d'amore, a now-obsolete six- or seven-stringed musical instrument with sympathetic strings that was popular in the baroque period. With Camille Saint-Saëns (1835-1921), Henri had founded the Society of Ancient Instruments in 1901 – at a time when proponents of modern avant-garde and twelve-tone were attempting to drown out the music of the old masters, Henri and his circle were reinvigorating public interest in this music by drawing attention to lost and obscure masterpieces. Some of these resurrected classics included Concerto (Suite) in D major for viola of Carl Philipp Emanuel Bach (1714-88), fifth child of Johann Sebastian Bach, which was published in 1931 and remains the most frequently recorded concerto of C. P. E.

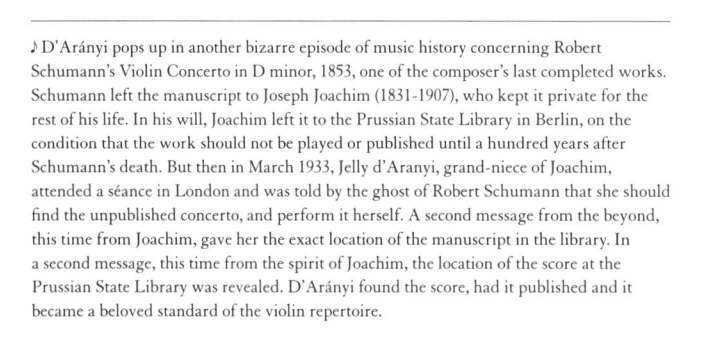

Jelly d'Arányi in 1926.

A publicity shot of Marius Casadesus.

♪ D'Arányi pops up in another bizarre episode of music history concerning Robert Schumann's Violin Concerto in D minor, 1853, one of the composer's last completed works. Schumann left the manuscript to Joseph Joachim (1831-1907), who kept it private for the rest of his life. In his will, Joachim left it to the Prussian State Library in Berlin, on the condition that the work should not be played or published until a hundred years after Schumann's death. But then in March 1933, Jelly d'Aranyi, grand-niece of Joachim, attended a séance in London and was told by the ghost of Robert Schumann that she should find the unpublished concerto, and perform it herself. A second message from the beyond, this time from Joachim, gave her the exact location of the manuscript in the library. In a second message, this time from the spirit of Joachim, the location of the score at the Prussian State Library was revealed. D'Arányi found the score, had it published and it became a beloved standard of the violin repertoire.

208 | *Madman's Orchestra*

Bach. So, too, did Casadesus find and popularise Quartet in A minor by C. P. E. Bach; Handel's Viola Concerto in B minor; Johann Christian Bach's (1735-82) Viola Concerto in C minor; and Luigi Boccherini's (1743-1805) Violin Concerto in D major. All of these are today believed to be the original and deliberately misattributed work of Henri Casadesus, though he would never admit to any forgery.

All of which leads to an interesting thought: just as art galleries around the world investigate fakes among their collections, how many celebrated classics performed and broadcast on continuous rotation today might actually be the work of a hoaxer? Because while Henri Casadesus's counterfeit discography is certainly impressive, it pales in comparative volume to that of the most prolific forger, the Austrian violinist and composer Fritz Kreisler (1875-1962), who in a bit of good fortune happened to stumble upon, he said, great piles of manuscripts of unknown and unpublished compositions by Arcangelo Corelli (1653-1713), François Couperin (1668-1733), Gaetano Pugnani (1731-98), Antonio Vivaldi (1678-1741) and others, in rural French monasteries and libraries. Some of the highlights include:

> Allegretto by Luigi Boccherin
> Andantino and Preghiera by Giovanni Battista Martini
> 'Aubade Provençale'; 'Chanson Louis XIII and Pavane';
>   and 'La Précieuse' by Louis Couperin
> Grave in C minor by Wilhelm Friedemann Bach
> 'La Chasse' ('Caprice') by Jean-Baptiste Cartier
> Menuett by Nicola Porpora
> 'Praeludium and Allegro' and 'Tempo di Minuetto'
>   by Gaetano Pugnani
> Scherzo by Carl Ditters von Dittersdorf
> 'Sicilienne and Rigaudon' by François Francœur
> 'Study on a Choral' by Johann Stamitz
> 'Variations on a Theme by Corelli' by Giuseppe Tartini
> Violin Concerto in C major by Antonio Vivaldi

Unlike the brothers Casadesus, Kreisler happily and proudly would eventually make sure that everyone knew he was the true author of the 'lost' works that he had popularised on stage for thirty years. He celebrated his sixtieth birthday on 2 February 1935 by unabashedly coming clean, after a *New York Times* critic wondered aloud whether Kreisler might be their originator. In the face of outrage, he argues that it 'should make

Henri Casadesus.

Franz Kreisler on the cover of TIME *magazine, 1925.*

no difference who wrote the works as long as people enjoyed them. The name changes, the value remains.' The works were retitled with the addendum of '… in the style of…', and the publicity (the scandal made the front page of *The New York Times*) only made Kreisler more popular.

David Popper (1843-1913) was not only one of classical music's last great cellists to play in the baroque style without an endpin (the rod at the base that supports its weight), but also a talented composer. At a concert at London's Crystal Palace on 1 December 1894, he made headlines by debuting a long-lost cello concerto by Joseph Haydn. The music had been shoved into his hands by an unidentified audience member at a concert in Vienna a few years earlier, on tattered sheets of manuscript paper. Popper claimed that he merely arranged piano and orchestral accompaniment. The story made for an electrifying premiere but started to fall apart under scrutiny when the sheets of original music could not be provided. Of Concerto for violoncello in C major (today catalogued as by David Popper, attr. J. Haydn), the *Musical Times* writes in 1895: 'Unfortunately, the evidence adduced is inconclusive, but the concerto is decidedly pleasing in character. If not written by Haydn, it is certainly thoroughly Haydnesque both in form and spirit.'

The same could have been said of more Haydn that came out of hiding in 1993, when the German musician Winfried Michel (b.1948) took the opening bars – recorded in a thematic index – of six lost Haydn works and successfully convinced prestigious music scholars that the six piano sonatas he had constructed from these scraps were genuine Haydn pieces. 'If these pieces are good enough to be thought to be by Haydn, then aren't they valuable on their own terms?' wonders a *New York Times* critic. 'Or is it only because of the aura of Haydn's authorship and historical context that they become meaningful? In which case, what is our criteria for judging the immanent qualities of musical works? Why can't works of brilliant pastiche be as good as the "real" thing, and valued as much by musical culture?'

Such classical musical hoaxes litter the early twentieth century: the Concerto in E minor, and a Concerto in A major, of the Italian double bass virtuoso Domenico Dragonetti (1763-1846), that turned out to have been written by the French double bass player Édouard Nanny (1872-1942) in 1925. The gorgeously sorrowful Adagio in G minor of Tomaso Albinoni (1671-1751) discovered in manuscript fragments in the bombed-

Cellist David Popper.

out Dresden State Library by the Italian musicologist and critic Remo Giazotto (1910-98), while researching a biography, seems to have actually been written by Giazotto in 1958.

With the subtlety and unlikeliness of their duplicity, these hoaxes are often hard to correct in the official record. As I write this, my speakers have filled the air around me with the music of Mykola Ovsianiko-Kulikovsky's Symphonie No. 21 in G minor, in a recording from 2005 of the Leningrad Philharmonic Orchestra, led by Evgeny Mvravinsky. It doesn't seem to matter to any involved that Mykola Ovsianiko-Kulikovsky never existed. He was invented by the Jewish Ukrainian composer Mikhail Goldstein (1917-89), in retaliation for a Ukrainian critic attacking his work and claiming a Jew could never understand the culture of Ukraine. In 1948, Goldstein concocted his fake composer, a forgotten figure of aristocratic stock, and announced that he had discovered an original Ovsianiko-Kulikovsky manuscript composition from 1809, Symphonie No. 21 in G minor (written by Goldstein), with the sly inscription 'for the dedication of Odessa Theatre'. The Soviet music world was ecstatic at the discovery, for here appeared to be Ukraine's answer to Joseph Haydn. The symphony was acclaimed and performed by the country's leading musicians, and Mykola Ovsianiko-Kulikovsky took his place in the *Great Soviet*

Musicologist H. C. Robbins Landon holding up the 'rediscovered' Haydn sonatas, 14 December 1993.

211 *Musical Hoaxes*

Encyclopaedia. Goldstein was horrified and came forward to admit the hoax. To his greater horror, he was ignored – only after a criminal investigation in the late 1950s was Goldstein's authorship confirmed; although if Spotify's database of recordings is anything to go by, the hoax persists.

Much of the hoaxing mentioned thus far are deceptions that were played on a specific type of audience, localised to specific fans of famous composers or roomfuls of attendees to live performances. But in the age of radio broadcast and recording, musical hoaxing explodes in scale. In England, a magnificent example would take place in 1961. By that time people were used to hearing surprising sounds emanating from their radio set tuning into the BBC radio service. On 18 April 1930, for example, those expecting to hear the fifteen-minute news bulletin were told instead that 'there is no news', and piano music was played for the rest of the slot. On 16 April 1939, via an international BBC broadcast, over 150 million people heard the two trumpets found in Tutankhamun's tomb sounded for the first time in over 3,000 years (see page 46). Radio hoaxing, too, had a precedence: a whole twelve years before Orson Welles (1915-85) gave his notorious *War of the Worlds* broadcast, on 16 January 1926, the BBC presenter and Catholic priest Father Ronald Knox cut into a talk about eighteenth-century literature with a live report that a murderous riot had broken out in central London. Big Ben had been destroyed with mortar fire, the Savoy Hotel had been burned to the ground and a government minister had been lynched. Subsequent broadcasts that the programme of dubious comic value had been a 'burlesque' did little to calm the public.

On 5 June 1961, the respected presenter Dr Hans Keller of the BBC Third Programme introduced 'the first performance in this country of a work by Piotr Zak, entitled "Mobile for Tape and Percussion" '. There were few grounds for suspicion. 'Piotr Zak, who is of Polish extraction but lives in Germany, was born in 1939', continues Keller. 'His earliest works are conservative, but he has recently come under the influence of Stockhausen and John Cage. This work for tape and percussion was written between May and September of last year. Within the precise and complex framework defined by the score, there is considerable room for improvisation.'

To the uninitiated, the experimental performance by percussionists 'Claude Tessier' and 'Anton Schmidt' sounds as though players are walking around a room full of musical

Mikhail Goldstein, creator of the non-existent Russian composer Mykola Ovsianiko-Kulikovsky.

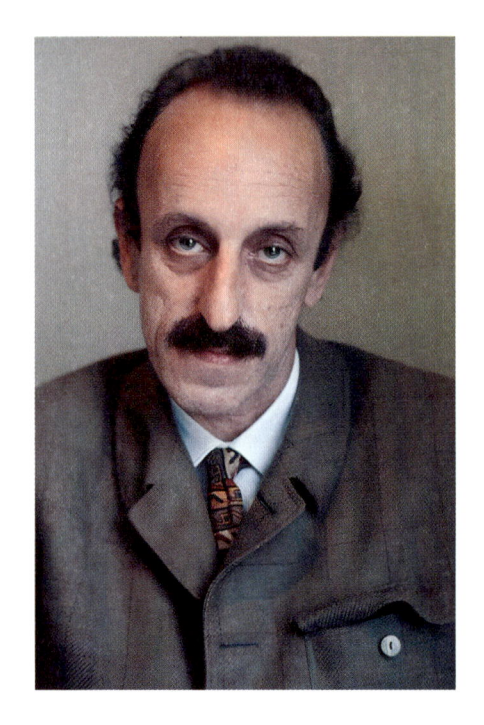

BBC executive Dr Hans Keller, co-creator of the fictional experimental composer Piotr Zak.

instruments and simply striking them at random. Which is, in fact, exactly what happened. Keller had grown so enraged by the acceptance of avant-garde music that he wanted 'to enquire how far a non-work could be taken for a work', and to compare how in the time of Mozart a work of such random noise would have immediately been dismissed as nonsense. Live on air, he and his colleague Susan Bradshaw walked around a studio of the BBC Music Department hitting various instruments, and used a microphone attached to an echo chamber to imitate electronic sounds. As was the custom of the programme, the 'recording' was then played a second time towards the end of the show to enable listeners to understand it better – this repeat was actually another impromptu, and quite different, live performance by the hoaxers. The critic Donald Mitchell deemed the Piotr Zak piece 'wholly unrewarding', writing: 'Zak exploited the percussion with only limited enterprise and his tape emitted a succession of whistles, rattles and punctured sighs that proclaimed, all too shamelessly, their non-musical origins.' The audacious scheme wasn't admitted until two months later.

In fact, the words 'audacious scheme' sweeps us onto a bizarre story that begins in 1976, when an English pianist of accomplished but unremarkable ability named Joyce Hatto (1928-2006) announced her retirement from public performance to wage a long battle with ovarian cancer. Unexpectedly, Hatto's name resurfaced in 1989 when she began releasing CDs of her dazzling performances of some of the most difficult piano pieces in history, produced by the small record label Concert Artist Recordings, which was run by her husband William Barrington-Coupe. First she tackled Liszt, then Bach, the Mozart sonatas and onto every Beethoven sonata, the Schubert, Schumann, Chopin and Liszt again. Over 120 CDs of her virtuoso performances were produced, in which she played with a chameleon-like mastery of every style and voice.

'Her legacy is a discography that in quantity, musical range and consistent quality has been equalled by few pianists in history', writes Jeremy Nicholas in her obituary for *the Guardian*. 'Most of her recordings date from the early 1990s, when she had reached an age at which many pianists are resting on their laurels…' Of her Schubert recordings, one critic writes: 'Think Schnabel and Curzon – and, dare I whisper it, better.' Other critics hailed Hatto as an overlooked genius: 'Joyce Hatto must be the greatest living pianist that almost no one has ever heard of,' writes Richard Dyer in *The Boston Globe* in 2005.

The first questions about Hatto were raised in 2005 by curious fans of her CDs, who gathered in online fora to discuss her work. At first, they were innocent musings: how was it that someone of such ill health and advanced years could perform and record such an enormous body of work? More than a hundred of her CDs were made in just the last ten years of her life. Several were released after her death. Why was so little known about her? And who was 'René Köhler', the conductor credited on some of her recordings, and what was the 'National Philharmonic-Symphony Orchestra' that occasionally accompanied her? A biography of Köhler suddenly popped up on the internet: a Polish-French-German Jew, he had survived the execution camp of Treblinka but then found himself in the Soviet Gulag for twenty-five years before embarking on a music career. But no other mention of Köhler, or the orchestra, could be found.

Then a very curious thing happened. A composer and fan of Joyce Hatto named Jed Distler inserted a CD of her 'Liszt *études*', and his iTunes library, which was linked online to the Gracenote catalogue of around four million CDs, identified the disc as a pre-existing recording by the Hungarian pianist László Simon (1948-2009). When Distler tested another CD, Hatto's recording of her 'Rachmaninov's Second and Third Piano Concertos', Gracenote identified the performer as Yefim Bronfman (b.1958).

A sound engineer named Andrew Rose compared the sound waves of Hatto's recording of Liszt's 12 *Transcendental Études* with those of a recording by Simon, and found ten of the études to be identical down to a measurement of '$\frac{1}{44}$, 100th of a second,' which would be an impossible imitation for a human to make. Rose also found that several Hatto recordings had been manipulated with altered tempos to create an artificial differentiation.

James Inverne, editor of the magazine *Gramaphone*, contacted William Barrington-Coupe, Joyce Hatto's husband, for an explanation. 'He was very charming', said Inverne. 'He sounded utterly puzzled. He said he could not explain it and asked to be informed if anyone shed any light on the affair.' But the evidence was building. Hatto's 'performances' were simply tracks copied from the albums of other performers and slapped with her name. 'As far as I know', remarked Inverne, 'the classical music world has never known a scandal like this. The art world has, but not classical music.'

Joyce Hatto.

Analysis of the Hatto CDs so far have found that, as well as her *Liszt's 12 Transcendental Studies* being the recording by László Simon, her *Godowsky's Complete Studies After the Chopin Études* was played by Carlo Grante. Her entire performance of the twenty movements of Olivier Messiaen's *Vingt regards sur l'enfant-Jésus* is actually that of the Korean-American classical pianist Paul Kim from 2002, slowed down by 2.4 per cent. Her CD *Maurice Ravel – Complete Piano Music* is a complete copy of the CD release by Roger Muraro from 2003. At least twenty-five of her sonata recitals from *Ludwig van Beethoven – Piano Sonatas, op. 2* are directly taken from the recording by John O'Conor. Felix Mendelssohn would have a few words to say about her CD *Felix Mendelssohn – Songs without Words, Vol. 1*, seeing as how eleven of the pieces are from Sergei Babayan's recording. Her *Camille Saint-Saëns – Piano Concerto No. 2* is a performance by Jean-Philippe Collard, conducted by André Previn, no less. And so on. 'It is a scandal unparalleled in the annals of classical music', writes Dennis Dutton in a *New York Times* op-ed on 26 February 2007.

William Barrington-Coupe, Joyce Hatto's husband.

So who was responsible? When the evidence was put to 76-year-old Barrington-Coupe by Martin Beckford of the *Daily Telegraph* on 20 February 2007, he insisted that his wife was the genuine performer of every recording: 'She was the sole pianist on those recordings. I was there at all the important sessions. I was the engineer on the jobs and I take full responsibility for everything released on my label Concert Artist. Twelve months ago she wasn't very well known… If it was all a fake, why would I put my wife's name on it? I would have put someone else, some Russian name, and we would have sold ten times as many.' He blamed the criticism on the English dislike of success, though admitted: 'I cannot explain some of the things that they say are there.' Two days later, when questioned by the *Washington Post* about the damning sound wave comparison, he responded with the magnificent line: 'Sound waves don't prove anything. If the sound waves are giving that impression, I'm at a loss.' His credibility then took a hit when the *Daily Mail* uncovered his 1966 conviction for tax fraud for which he served a year in prison after what the judge called 'blatant and impertinent frauds, carried out in my opinion rather clumsily, but such was your conceit that you thought yourselves smart enough to get away with it.'

Finally, several days later, Barrington-Coupe conceded in a letter of confession to Robert von Bahr, the head of BIS

Records, that he had, in fact, passed off recordings made by other pianists as the original work of his wife, but not for financial gain as all assumed. It was done, he said, in an effort to give his wife 'the illusion of a great end to an unfairly [as he put it] overlooked career'. As they re-recorded her repertoire on CD, she would grunt in pain from her illness, and so he would patch over these sounds with parts of others' recordings. He subsequently used longer patches, until it all got away from him. 'I don't consider I've hurt anybody', Barrington-Coupe told the *Daily Telegraph*. 'A lot of attention has been drawn to forgotten artists.'

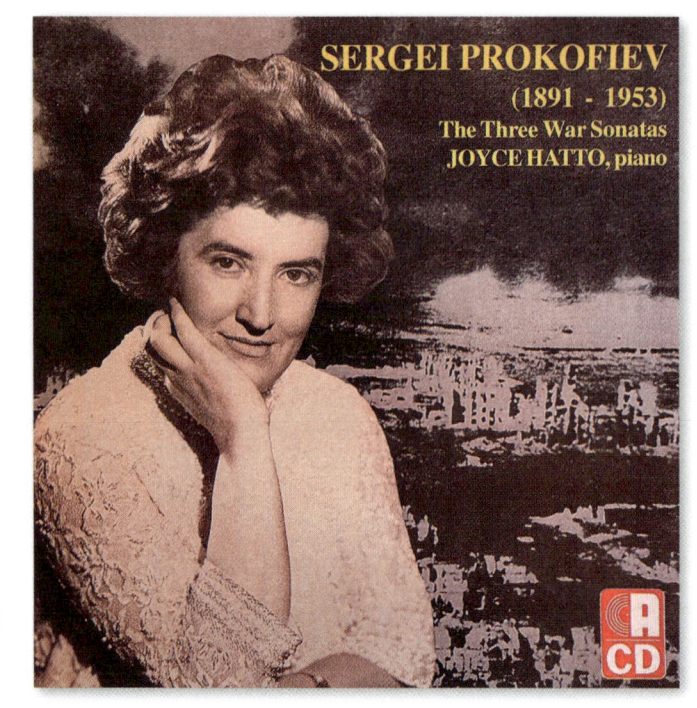

The cover of one of Joyce Hatto's many CD recordings.

An enormous amount of labour went into the deception. One Hatto collector told the BBC that, while buying around a hundred CDs in a 27-month period from Concert Artist Recordings, he had exchanged about 1,200 emails with over a dozen Concert Artist employees, each with a separate email address. All of them were actually Barrington-Coupe.

So, did Joyce Hatto herself know about the fraud? Her husband always insisted she was oblivious, but her credibility was also called into question when her claim of suffering cancer since 1976 was disputed by her consultant radiologist, who said she was first treated in 1992. The consensus is that it seems impossible that she wasn't a part of it. Would she not have wondered at some point, for example, why she didn't recall recording sessions with an eighty-piece orchestra? Jeremy Nicholas points to a smoking-gun of a letter he received from Hatto after writing a glowing article about her in 2006: 'I have re-worked the Godowsky, as I'm always trying to achieve the impossible and I hope you will enjoy the result. With all good wishes, Joyce.' Nicholas wonders: 'Why is she saying, "I have reworked the Godowsky" if she didn't play them in the first place?'

▶ PLAYLIST: MUSICAL HOAXES

'Bona Nox, Bist a Rechta Ochs', K. 561, 1788,
WOLFGANG AMADEUS MOZART

'Carl Nielsen – Our Great Composer',
BVN 355, 1948,
RUED LANGGAARD

'Город (Gorod)', 1986,
AKVARIUM

Concerto (Suite) in D Major for viola, 1750,
CARL PHILIPP EMANUEL BACH (FORMERLY ATTRIBUTED TO HENRI CASADESUS)

Concerto for violoncello in C major, 1894,
DAVID POPPER (ATTRIBUTED TO J. HAYDN)

'Dank sei Dir, Herr' ('Thanks Be to God'), late 19th century
SIEGFRIED OCHS (FORMERLY ATTRIBUTED TO GEORGE FRIDERIC HANDEL)

'Ein musikalischer Spaß', K. 522: IV, 1787,
WOLFGANG AMADEUS MOZART

Grave in C minor in the style of Wilhelm Friedemann Bach, 1911,
FRITZ KREISLER

'I. Introitus. Requiem aeternam', Requiem in D minor, K. 626, 1791,
WOLFGANG AMADEUS MOZART

'Intermezzo primo: Aria uberto', *La Serva Padrona*, 1733,
GIOVANNI BATTISTI PERGOLESI

'L'Enfance du Christ', op. 25, Deuxième Partie, *La Fuite en Égypte*: II. L'Adieu des Bergers,
HECTOR BERLIOZ

'Leck Mich im Arsch', K. 231, 1782,
WOLFGANG AMADEUS MOZART

Leopold Godowsky: *The Complete Studies after the Chopin Études*, released 2000,
JOYCE HATTO

Erster Teil: No. 1 'Kommt, ihr Töchter, helft mir klagen', *Matthäus-Passion*, BWV 244, 1727,
JOHANN SEBASTIAN BACH

'Mobile for Tape and Percussion', 1961,
HANS KELLER (FORMERLY ATTRIBUTED TO PIOTR ZAK)

Ouverture, *Les Trocqueurs*, 1753,
ANTOINE DAUVERGNE

'Se tu m'ami',
ALESSANDRO PARISOTTI (FORMERLY ATTRIBUTED TO GIOVANNI BATTISTI PERGOLESI)

'Study on a Choral' in the style of Johann Stamitz, 1930,
FRITZ KREISLER

Suite for String Orchestra, 1738-40,
HENRI CASADESUS (FORMERLY ATTRIBUTED TO CARL PHILIPP EMANUEL BACH)

Symphony No. 21 in G minor: I. Adagio, II. Romance, III. Minuet, IV. Finale, 1938-40,
MYKAILO GOLDSTEIN (FORMERLY ATTRIBUTED TO NIKOLAY OVSIANIKO-KULIKOVSKY)

Twelfth Mass, K. Anh. 232, date and composer unknown (FORMERLY ATTRIBUTED TO WOLFGANG AMADEUS MOZART)

'Variations on a Theme by Corelli' in the style of Giuseppe Tartini, 1910,
FRITZ KREISLER

Viola Concerto in B minor, 1924-25,
HENRI CASADESUS (FORMERLY ATTRIBUTED TO GEORGE FRIDERIC HANDEL)

Violin Concerto in D major, K. Anh. 294a 'Adélaïde': I. Allegro, II. Adagio and III. Allegro, 1933,
MARIUS CASADESUS (FORMERLY ATTRIBUTED TO WOLFGANG AMADEUS MOZART)

DECOMPOSITION: SOME CURIOUS DEATHS IN MUSIC HISTORY

French baroque master Jean-Baptiste Lully (1632-87) suffered a seemingly minor, self-inflicted injury when he struck his own foot with his conducting baton while leading a performance of *Te Deum* to celebrate Louis XIV's recovery from surgery. Gangrene set in, but Lully refused to have his toe amputated for fear it would impair his dancing. The gangrene swiftly spread until it killed him three months later, on 22 March 1687.

Henry Purcell (1659-95) died aged thirty-five or thirty-six at his home in Marsham Street, London. Some sources say he caught a chill after returning home late from a tavern, to find his wife had locked him out; while another rumour was that he had died from chocolate poisoning after drinking cocoa. The void left by his death led to England being labelled 'the land without music'.

The English composer Jeremiah Clarke (1674-1707) was so distraught after a beautiful noblewoman did not return his affections that, in a fit of melancholy, he flipped a coin to decide whether he should drown himself in a nearby pond or hang himself in the trees. The coin landed in the muddy bank on its edge, so he rode home to London and shot himself.

One night virtuoso violist and double-bassist František Koczwara (1730-91) paid a London prostitute called Susannah Hill to cut off his testicles. She refused, so Koczwara tied a ligature around a doorknob, fastened it around his own neck, and the two proceeded to have intercourse. When they had finished, Hill realised he had died during the act – one of the first recorded cases of auto-erotic asphyxiation.

Belgian composer César Franck (1822-90) was the first composer to die in a road traffic accident, when he was hit by a coach as he crossed the road in May 1890. Despite his injuries, he ignored medical advice and insisted on performing his 'Variations Symphoniques' that evening. His health deteriorated and he died six months later.

Franck's countryman and fellow composer Guillaume Lekeu (1870-94) died from dessert. After eating a contaminated sorbet, he contracted typhoid fever in October 1893, and died at his parents' home in Angers on 21 January 1894, one day after his twenty-fourth birthday.

The fate of the American music critic Gustav Kobbé (1857-1918) was an unusual case of death by seaplane. While sailing in the Great South Bay off Bay Shore, New York, in July 1918, a seaplane making its descent failed to see his boat and collided with it. Kobbé was killed instantly.

Loring McMurray (1897-1922) was a skilled and popular alto saxophonist with Sam Lanin's orchestra in the early 1920s; unfortunately, he was also a nose-picker. After a particular enthusiastic excavation, he gave himself a nosebleed. He died soon after from secondary complications via carotid arterial stenosis up to the brain.

Alban Berg (1885-1935) (introduced on page 169) was an Austrian composer of the Second Viennese School and one of the most important composers of the twentieth century. He died on Christmas Eve 1935 from blood poisoning after being stung by a bee.

Carroll Martin, a Chicago trombonist with Isham Jones's orchestra, was killed in 1940 in a car accident while holding his trombone, when the vehicle's sudden stop threw him forward with so much force that he was impaled by his own instrument.

American rhythm-and-blues singer Johnny Ace (1929-54) accidentally shot himself dead on Christmas Day 1954. 'It's okay!' he reassures his friends about the gun he was playing with. 'Gun's not loaded… see?' he says, pointing the loaded gun at his own head and pulling the trigger.

Morir, tremenda cosa! ('To die, a tremendous thing!') sang Leonard Warren (1911-60) on stage in New York as Don Carlo in *La Forza del Destino* ('The Force of Destiny') by Giuseppe Verdi (1813-1901), just before suffering a cerebral haemorrhage and falling face-forward, dead before he hit the floor.

On 20 July 1968, Joseph Keilberth (1908-68) died in the orchestra pit of the National Theatre, Munich, midway through conducting Wagner's opera *Tristan und Isolde* – the exact same spot where the conductor Felix Mottl (1856-1911) died in 1911; where the Italian conductor Giuseppe Patanè (1932-89) suffered a fatal heart attack during Rossini's *Barber of Seville* on 29 May 1989; and where the Hungarian conductor Stefan Soltész (1949-2022) collapsed and later died while conducting Richard Strauss's *Die Schweigsame Frau* in 2022.

In 1994, Mexican musician Ramón Barrero (1908-81), whose signature act was playing the world's smallest harmonica, accidentally inhaled his tiny instrument and choked to death.

THE HORNED SECTION; OR, THE DEVIL IN MUSIC

Long before Black Sabbath frontman and self-coronated 'Prince of Darkness' Ozzy Osbourne was snacking on bats, before the early twentieth-century bluesmen were marketing themselves with diabolic folklore, the Devil is mentioned in the Bible as a musician. In Ezekiel 28:13 the author writes of Satan: 'Thou hast been in Eden the garden of God; every precious stone was thy covering, the sardius, topaz and the diamond, the beryl, the onyx and the jasper, the sapphire, the emerald and the carbuncle and gold: the workmanship of thy tabrets and of thy pipes was prepared in thee in the day that thou wast created.' The mention of tabrets (a percussive instrument similar to a tambourine) and pipes 'being prepared in thee' has been interpreted both literally – that is, that Satan has musical instruments embedded in his angelic body – and figuratively, as a reference to his inherent musical ability, with which to charm with dark melody. From this begins the tradition known as the *Diabolus in musica* ('the Devil in music'), the infernal association and source of inspiration, that has crossed genres throughout the history of music.

Satan makes his musical debut in a German musical allegorical morality play composed in 1151. Hildegard of Bingen (1098-1179) was a German Benedictine abbess and scholar most famous for the mystic visions she recounts in *Scivias* ('Know the Ways of God'). At the end of this work is an early short version of her play *Ordo Virtutum* ('Order of the Virtues'), the only medieval musical drama to survive with an attribution for both text and music. The plot follows a chorus of Virtues, sung by seventeen female voices, battling the Devil for a human soul (another female vocal part) in a story of five sections. While the Virtues like Hope, Chastity and Innocence take turns in describing their merits, the Devil counters with promises of the material world, sung by a male performer. Eventually, the Soul is won over to the female side of Virtue, and together they bind the male Devil. Hildegard had no musical training – the music came to her in trances, just as her visions were delivered. While referring to *Ordo Virtutum* as being the world's first opera would be overstating things, it certainly played a tremendously significant role in the development of that later art form.

The Devil is also the subject of a short but beautiful antiphon by Hildegard called 'Sed Diabolus', otherwise known as 'Only the Devil Laughs'. This would likely have been

OPPOSITE: *Portraying monks as literal instruments of evil was a common form of attack by reformers against the Roman Catholic Church. In this c.1530 woodcut, the Devil hideously plays the head of a monk like bagpipes.*

Madman's Orchestra

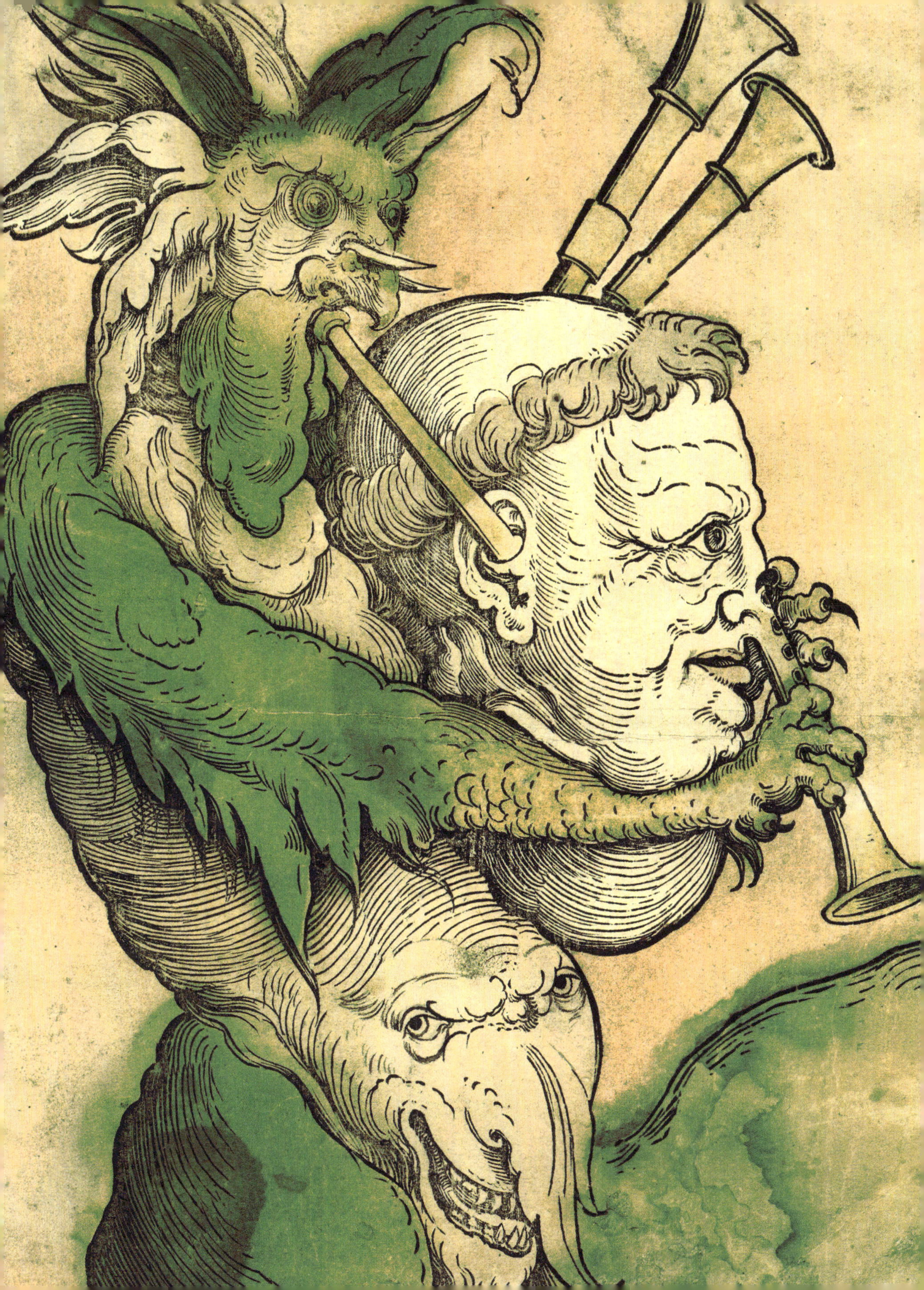

LEFT: *A miniature of Hildegard of Bingen's vision of the antichrist, from the lost Rupertsberg manuscript copy of her vision book* Scivias.

BELOW: *The short antiphon 'Only the Devil Laughs' by Hildegard of Bingen.*

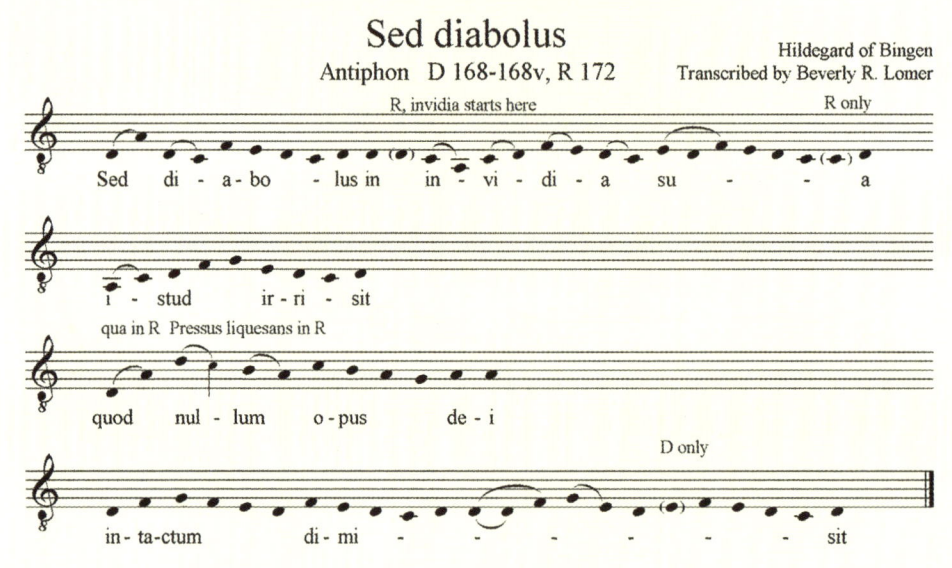

222 | Madman's Orchestra

The 'Drummer of Tedworth', a drum-playing devil said to haunt the cursed Wiltshire home of John Mompesson. From the witchcraft work Saducismus Triumphatus *by Joseph Glanvill, 1681.*

paired with Psalm 150 (which is thirteen lines of directions to praise God), the last of the final trio of psalms at festal lauds. The Devil mocks the virgin martyrs praising God, which becomes a mockery of the act of praising God, to which all are commanded to do by the psalm:

Sed Diabolus in invidia sua istud irrisit, qua nullum opus Dei intactum dimisit.	But envious, the Devil mocks, which leaves no work of God untouched.

Where the Devil as musical maestro really comes to the fore is in the eighteenth century, with the rise of the superstar violinists who took to centre stage and displayed such staggering ability that the only conclusion to be made was that, like Faust, a bargain struck with the Devil must be the only explanation for such talent. The Italian baroque composer Giuseppe Tartini (1692-1770) wrote over one hundred pieces for the violin, but he is best known for his devilishly difficult Violin Sonata in G minor for solo violin, more famously known as the 'Devil's Trill Sonata'. The story goes that, in conversation with the French astronomer Jérôme Lalande (1732-1807), Tartini revealed that the composition had come to him in 1713 in a dream, in which the Devil had appeared to him and, after taking the violin that Tartini offered him, performed an original

223 *The Horned Section; or, The Devil in Music*

composition that was unimaginably beautiful and impossible to play. When Tartini awoke, he frantically attempted to record as much of what he had heard as he could recall. 'How great was my astonishment on hearing a sonata so wonderful and so beautiful', he says, according to Lalande in his *Voyage d'un François en Italie*, 1765-66, 'played with such great art and intelligence, as I had never even conceived in my boldest flights of fantasy. I felt enraptured, transported, enchanted: my breath failed me, and I awoke. I immediately grasped my violin in order to retain, in part at least, the impression of my dream.'

But Tartini was never happy with the music he transcribed from the memory of the dream, because it couldn't compare with the Devil's supernatural skill. The sonata was written 'in vain! The music which I at this time composed is indeed the

Tartini's Dream, 1824, by Louis-Léopold Boilly.

224 | Madman's Orchestra

best that I ever wrote, and I still call it the "Devil's Trill", but the difference between it and that which so moved me is so great that I would have destroyed my instrument and have said farewell to music forever if it had been possible for me to live without the enjoyment it affords me.' The 'Devil's Trill Sonata' wasn't published until 1798 or 1799, almost thirty years after its composer's death.♪

Many diabolical rumours swirled around the tall, black-clothed, achingly gaunt figure of Niccolò Paganini (1782-1840), one of classical music's greatest showboaters. An habitual

The 'Devil's Trill Sonata' for violin.

♪ As well as inspiring the ballet *Le Violon du Diable*, 1743, you can also hear the 'Devil's Trill' as the basis for Chopin's Prelude No. 27, 1839.

225   *The Horned Section; or, The Devil in Music*

LEFT: *The* Violon du Diable *('Devil's Violin'), far right, built by Giuseppe Guarneri del Gésu (1698-1744) in 1734; as well as Stradivarius's 'La Pucelle' (far left) and his 'Le Messie' (centre) violins, exhibited in 1872 in the Exhibition of Ancient Musical Instruments at the South Kensington Museum, London. The* Violon du Diable *got its nickname after being played by Arthur Saint-Léon in the ballet* Le Violon du Diable *('The Devil's Violin') in 1848.*

drinker, gambler and womaniser, it was said that he'd granted his soul to the Devil, in exchange for his exceptional gifts. The impossible tones that sang from the strings of his instrument were said to be the screams of a woman whose soul Paganini had captured within it; it was even said that his strings had been fashioned from the intestines of a woman he'd murdered. He was nicknamed *Hexensohn* ('witch's son'). Music's first rock star, he moved and shook around the stage, earning the sobriquet 'rubber man', freed from the tether of sheet music which he abandoned, committing every piece to memory instead. His unusually long fingers allowed him to play three octaves with one stretched hand; and at one show he was officially recorded as playing twelve notes to the second. One audience member claimed to have seen lightning strike the tip of Paganini's bow.

While all of Paganini's *24 Caprices* for solo violin are often cited as the most difficult of all violin pieces to play, 'Caprice No. 13', known as 'Devil's Laughter' or 'Devil's Chuckle', is particularly noteworthy. Beginning with double-stopped passages at a moderate speed, it then falls into high-speed runs that demand extraordinary flexibility in the left hand, while the right-hand changes string with *détaché* bowing. The first noticeable theme uses a descending chromatic gesture in parallel thirds that gives the disturbing effect of demonic laughter, which is then returned to in a reprise towards the

ABOVE: *The Italian ballet dancer Fanny Cerrito (1817-1909) in devilish costume for the ballet* Le Violon du Diable *('The Devil's Violin'), 1848, a revival of Arthur Saint-Léon's (1821-70)* Tartini il Violinista *('Tartini the Violinist'), 1849, inspired by Tartini's sonata.*

Madman's Orchestra

end of the piece. Perhaps this is why one audience member at a performance in Vienna swore that he had seen the figure of a devil over Paganini's shoulder, spurring him on.

These pieces of Tartini and Paganini have at least part of their devilish nature amplified through the composers' unsettling use of the tritone, otherwise known as the 'Devil's Interval'. The harsh and sinister interval occurs between two notes halfway between a perfect fourth (for example, the opening two notes of 'Here Comes the Bride') and a perfect fifth (the opening two notes of 'Twinkle Twinkle Little Star'). Play a note on the piano, then play the next note three tones up, and you'll instantly recognise this almost threatening change from countless compositions across genres. Think of the first two notes that Jimi Hendrix repeatedly stabs out in the intro to 'Purple Haze', or the first two notes of the opening vocal line of 'The Simpsons Theme'. In contrast to the soothing quality of perfect fourths and fifths, the Devil's Interval is unresolved, violating our expectations with its dissonant question left unanswered.

ABOVE: *Portrait of Niccolò Paganini by Jean-Bernard Naudin.*

LEFT: *Frans Francken the Younger (1581-1642),* Death and the Miser, *1635.*

> # ▶ MINI PLAYLIST: SPOT THE DEVIL'S TRITONES
>
> 'Bitter Peace', 1998, SLAYER
>
> *Black Sabbath*, 1970, BLACK SABBATH
>
> 'Blues for Alice', 1951, CHARLIE PARKER
>
> 'Danse Macabre', 1874, CAMILLE SAINT-SAËNS
>
> 'Girl From Ipanema', 1962, ANTONIO CARLOS JOBIM
>
> 'Mars, the Bringer of War', *The Planets*, op. 32, 1917, GUSTAV HOLST
>
> 'Prelude to the Afternoon of a Faun', 1894, CLAUDE DEBUSSY
>
> 'Purple Haze', 1967, JIMI HENDRIX
>
> 'Station to Station', 1976, DAVID BOWIE
>
> 'The Simpsons Theme', 1989, DANNY ELFMAN
>
> 'Woo Ha!! (Got You All In Check)', 1996, BUSTA RHYMES

A widespread and seemingly unkillable myth about the tritone is that it was banned by the church from compositions in the medieval era for fear that it summoned the Devil. While the tritone is, indeed, largely absent from the body of sacred music, this is more likely attributed to the inappropriateness of its tonal mismatch, and there is no evidence of any stated ban, nor any composer or performer suffering any form of punishment for its use. In fact, you can find examples of tritones in medieval compositions, such as 'Viderunt omnes', a haunting Gregorian chant based on Psalm XCVII (97) traditionally sung as the gradual at the Masses of Christmas Day and historically on its octave, the Feast of the Circumcision. It is a particularly famous musical text as two of its early settings are some of the earliest pieces of polyphony, by composers of the Notre Dame school,

The music of Pérotin's 'Viderunt omnes', written in 1200, with a tritone or Devil's Interval highlighted.

228 | Madman's Orchestra

Léonin (*fl.* 1135-1201) and his successor Pérotin (*fl.* 1200). Their style of music, *organum*, brought polyphonic colour to the Gregorian intonation, in part by drawing on tritones.

For spectacular tritonal usage, though, a Devil's playlist should, of course, include 'Danse Macabre', op. 40, the symphonic poem written in 1874 by the French composer Camille Saint-Saëns, which makes full use of the disconcerting tone. Saint-Saëns even applies it to the tuning of the solo violin (which was originally a vocal line in the piece's earlier incarnation), loosening the E-string down to E flat in *scordatura* ('discordant') tuning. This shifts the open intervals of the double stop A and E to the tritone (A and E flat) for the violin, which launches into the disquieting opening motif of the work.

Immediately, the image of a violin-laying devil waltzing around the stage is conjured, as the xylophones launch into their theme to represent the rattling bones of the skeletons that come alive and whirl around in their annual Hallowe'en dance, luring the living to join them in the 'Totentanz' ('death dance'). Only in the final section does the rhythm and texture break and the discordant features fall away, as the dawn arrives and the cockerel crows (represented by the oboe), signalling the time for the dead to return to their graves. Saint-Saëns's 'Danse Macabre' debuted on 24 January 1875, and it did not meet with the popularity it enjoys today. The tritones were disturbing, the shrieking violin and the unusual use (at the time) of the xylophones, with the morbid imagery and references to the 'Dies irae', a sequence from the Mass for the dead, leaving audiences cold.

Devil's Intervals, dancing skeletons (played with strings, this time) and dancing witches fill the climactic fifth and final movement of Hector Berlioz's *Symphonie fantastique:* 'Épisode de la vie d'un artiste… en cinq parties' (*Fantastic Symphony* 'Episode in the Life of an Artist… in Five Sections'), op. 14,

ABOVE: *The 'Dance of death' illustration, the earliest printed image of an animated skeleton, from the* Nuremberg Chronicle, *1493, by Hartmann Schedel.*

BELOW: Danse Macabre *by the Estonian artist Bernt Notke (1440-1509). This 7.5m (24ft) fragment of a painting originally 30m (100ft) wide is the only surviving medieval* Danse Macabre *in the world painted on canvas.*

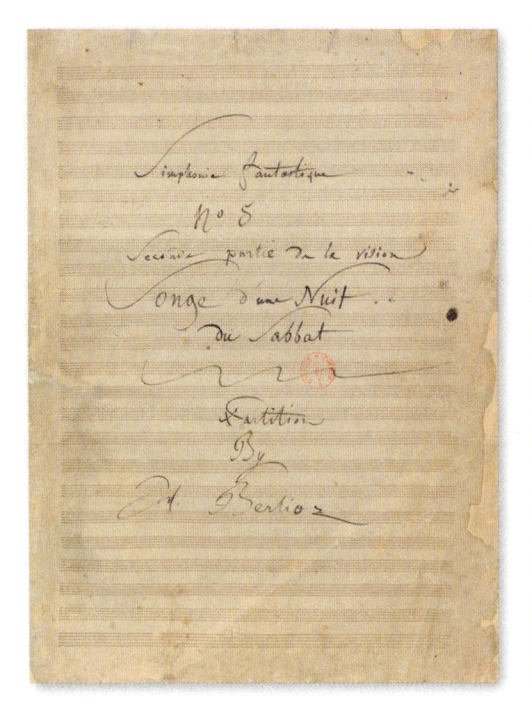

'Songe d'une nuit du Sabbat' ('Dream of a Witches' Sabbath'). The symphony tells the story of a talented artist who is tortured by his unrequited love for a beautiful and captivating woman 'who unites all the charms of the ideal person his imagination was dreaming of', writes Berlioz in the notes for the 1830 premiere at the Paris Conservatoire. The artist can no longer take his advances being rebuffed, and attempts to commit suicide by opium overdose. This leads to Gothic drug-fuelled hallucinations that eventually culminate in a march to the scaffold, and the artist then finding himself at a horrifying satanic dance in the fifth movement: the 'Witches' Sabbath'.♪

> He sees himself at a sabbath [writes Berlioz] in the middle of a horrible troop of ghosts, sorcerers and monsters of all kinds gathered together for his funeral. Strange noises, moans, bursts of laughter, distant cries to which other cries seem to respond. The beloved melody reappears again, but it has lost its character of nobility and timidity; it is no more than a dance tune – ignoble, trivial and grotesque; it is she who

The title page of the fifth movement, and first page of musical notation, of Hector Berlioz's 1830 autograph manuscript of his 'Symphonie fantastique'.

♪ For another wonderful musical rendition of the 'Witches' Sabbath', play also 'Night on Bald Mountain', 1867, by the innovative Russian composer Modest Mussorgsky (1839-81). One of the first tone poems by a Russian composer, it was never performed in any form during Mussorgsky's lifetime – his mentor, Mily Balakirev (1836-1910), refused to perform it, which disheartened Mussorgsky, and it wasn't even published until 1968. Surprisingly, though, audiences around the world got to hear it in 1940, when an arrangement of it by Leopold Stokowski (1882-1977) was used in the Disney film *Fantasia*, 1940.

is coming to the sabbath… Roar of joy as she arrives… She joins in the diabolical orgy. Funeral knell, burlesque parody of the 'Dies irae', witches' round dance. The round and the 'Dies irae' together.

Funerary bells chime, and the 'Dies irae' is performed with low brass, a combination of bassoons and tubas (although Berlioz first scored this for an ophicleide, a mostly obsolete brass instrument that tubas have replaced). Dry raspy strings paint the skeletons' dance in a distorted and jagged form of the main theme – this is achieved in accordance with unusual instructions from Berlioz, who divided each violin section into three parts to thin out the sound. In certain parts, the strings are told to play *col legno*, when notes are tapped out with the wooden part of the bow against the strings (string players will often bring a second bow when playing under these instructions, as the technique can damage it). The woodwinds are also required to slide their notes, souring the music. Combine all of this with the use of tritones and the effect on a contemporary audience was that there was something disturbingly unnatural about the piece. (Gioachino Rossini once remarked of the symphony: 'It's lucky it's not music.') The story of the *Symphonie fantastique* is thinly disguised autobiography – Berlioz had become infatuated with the Irish actress Harriet Smithson (1800-54) after seeing her Ophelia in a performance of Shakespeare's *Hamlet* on 11 September 1827. Berlioz pursued her for years, bombarding her with love letters, but she refused to meet him. Eventually, however, she would attend a performance of a revised version of the *Symphonie fantastique* in 1832, and the two would marry the following year. Leonard Bernstein (1918-90) considered the symphony, with its hallucinations and dream imagery, to be the first piece of psychedelic music. 'Berlioz tells it like it is', he said. 'You take a trip, you wind up screaming at your own funeral.'

The Devil and the Hell described by Dante (1265-1321) in *The Divine Comedy*, 1321, served as a significant source of inspiration for Franz Liszt, via Victor Hugo's (1802-85) poem *Après une Lecture de Dante* ('After a Reading of Dante'), 1836. In 1849, the Hungarian composer wrote a piano sonata in one movement titled 'Après une lecture du Dante: Fantasia quasi Sonata' (commonly referred to in English as the 'Dante Sonata'). It's a fascinating piece to listen to how Liszt vividly paints the settings of Heaven and Hell. Like Dante, he divides the piece into sections, first plunging the listener headlong

The Irish actress Harriet Smithson, the inspiration for the Symphonie fantastique, *in a nineteenth-century portrait by George Clint.*

LVCIFER

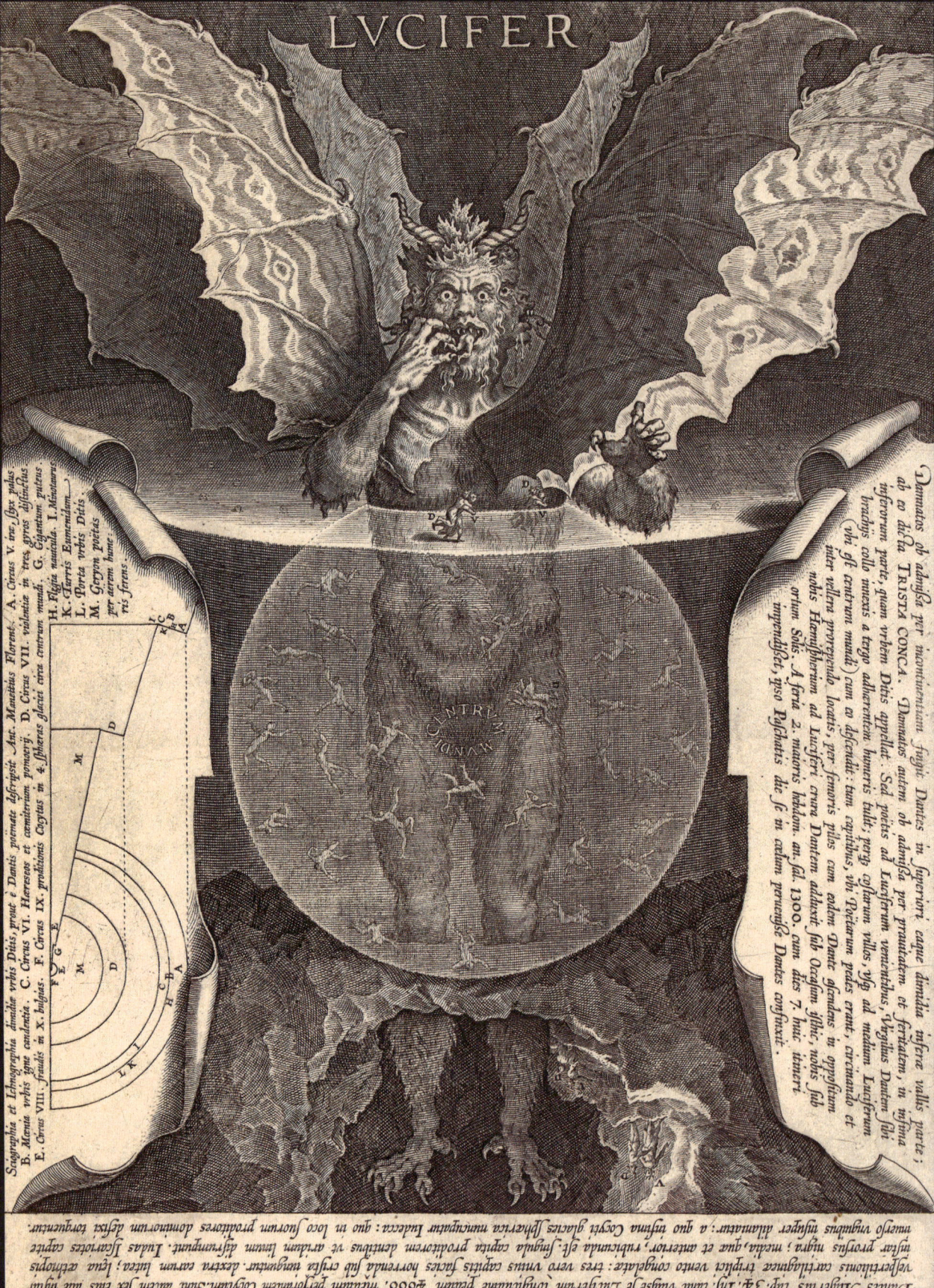

into the rings of Hell by drawing on the key of D minor, which was commonly used for deathly pieces (hear also Liszt's 'Totentanz' ('Dance of Death'); or the terrifying climactic scene of Mozart's opera *Don Giovanni*, when the phantom of the Commendatore offers Don Giovanni a last chance to repent, which the latter rather ill-advisedly rebuffs, and so is dragged to Hell by demons). Tritones stab through this first section of the 'Dante Sonata' like pitchforks, evoking the cries of Hell's black soul choir. The second theme of the piece blazes in the key of F sharp major, beaming like a beatific vision of God in Heaven. Again, it's a device that Liszt has used before for uplift, in works like 'Benediction of God in Solitude', 1847-52, and 'Les Jeux d'eaux à la Villa d'Este', 1877. In the glow of the major key walks the character of Beatrice, until towards the end of the piece, played at frantic speed, it splits into three dramatic different themes, representing Dante's description of the enormous figure of Satan at the centre of Hell, with his three faces perpetually munching on the three great traitors of history: Brutus and Cassius, betrayers of Julius Caesar; and Judas, betrayer of Christ.

OPPOSITE: *The three-headed Lucifer as described by Dante, depicted by the printmaker Cornelis Galle the Elder (1590-1600), Italy. The figures of Dante and Virgilius (marked D and V) are shown in three separate places: hurrying past him on the ice surface; diving down through the sphere of floating souls, past the demonic genitals that form the centre of the world (a discovery that certainly would have livened up Jules Verne's* Journey to the Centre of the Earth); *and inspecting his feet in the cave at the bottom.*

BELOW: *Handwritten cast list in the notes of one of the earliest operas of the story of Faust, Ignaz Walter's* Doktor Faust, *1797.*

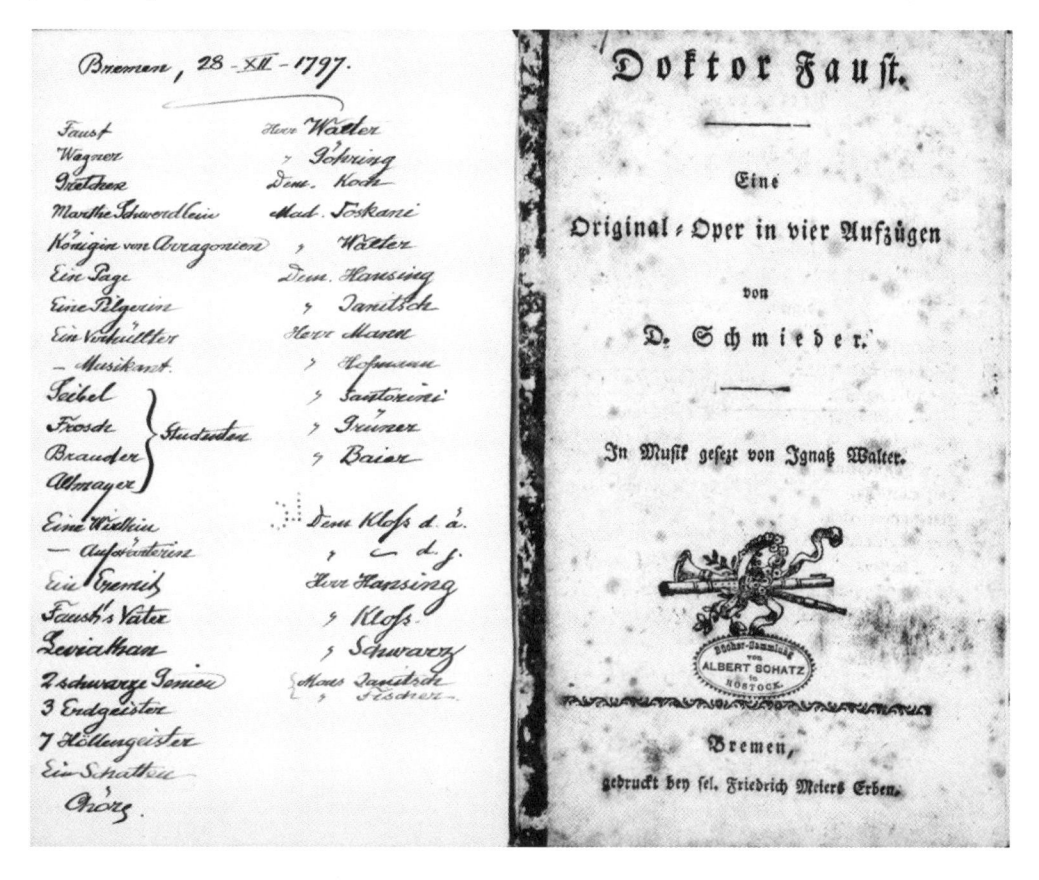

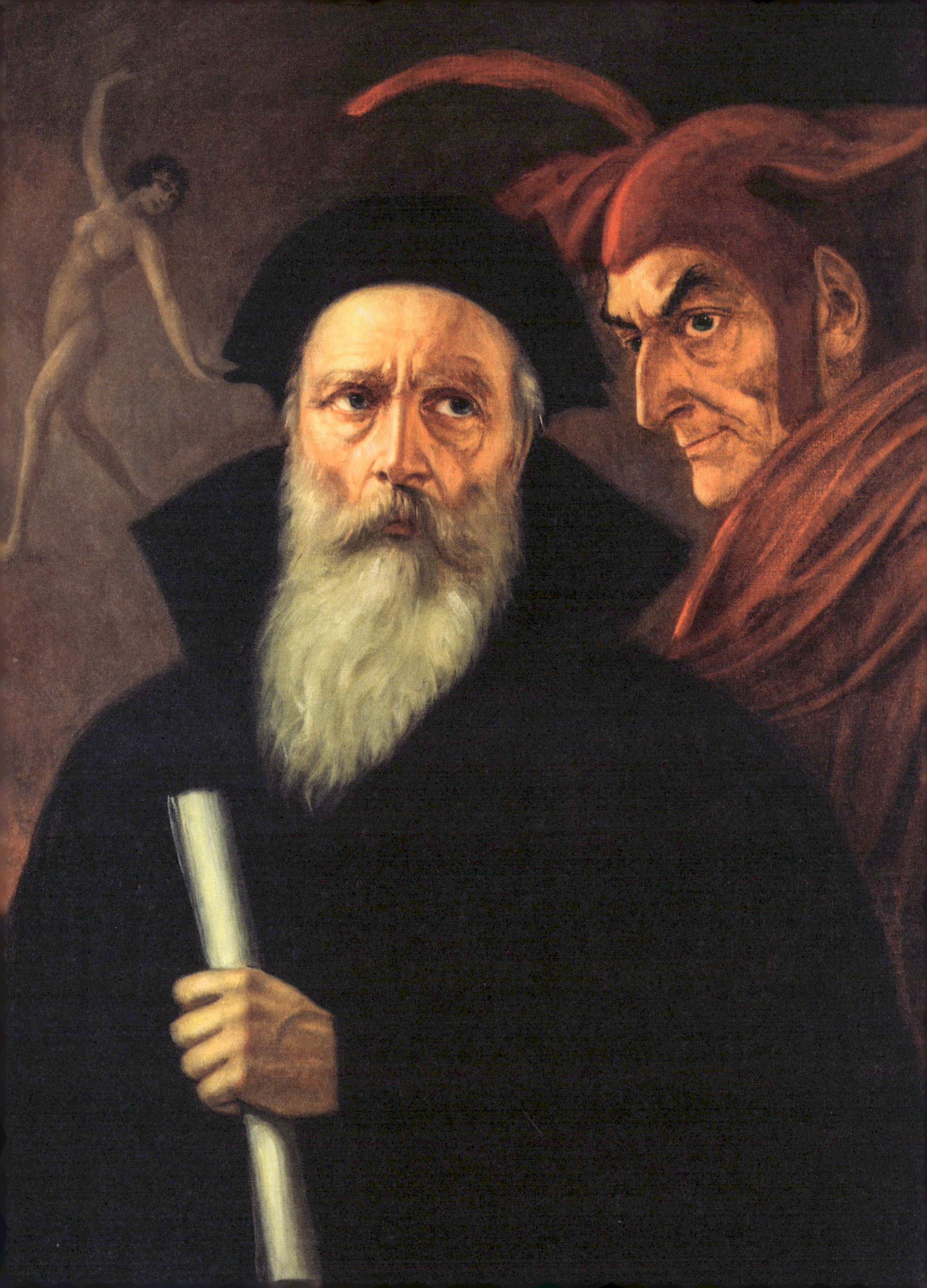

Throughout the remainder of his career, between 1859 and 1885, Liszt continued composing with the theme of the Devil, but for source material he moved away from Dante and turned instead to the popular legend of Faust. 'Der Tanz in der Dorfschenke: Erster Mephisto-Walzer' ('The Dance in the Village Inn: First Mephisto-Waltz'), 1859-62, the first of what would be a fold of four *Mephisto Waltzes*, took as its programme not the two-part *Faust* tragedy, 1831, of Johann Wolfgang von Goethe (1749-1832), but Nikolaus Lenau's 1836 verse drama *Faust*. With just a frenzy of piano notes the storytelling is vivid enough, but Liszt had the following note added to the printed score to help conjure up the imagery:

> There is a wedding feast in progress in the village inn, with music, dancing, carousing. Mephistopheles and Faust pass by, and Mephistopheles induces Faust to enter and take part in the festivities. Mephistopheles snatches the fiddle from the hands of a lethargic fiddler and draws from it indescribably seductive and intoxicating strains. The amorous Faust whirls about with a full-blooded village beauty in a wild dance; they waltz in mad abandon out of the room, into the open, away into the woods. The sounds of the fiddle grow softer and softer, and the nightingale warbles his love-laden song.

The Faust legend – in which the eponymous scholar makes a blood-pact with Mephistopheles (Satan) to gamble his soul for an experience of true transcendence on Earth – has provided huge musical inspiration. 'Scenes from Goethe's *Faust*' (completed in 1853) is considered the magnum opus of German composer Robert Schumann, although Schumann never lived to see all three parts of his musical-theatrical work performed, nor published together. Richard Wagner's 'Faust Overture', 1840, is one of the few works by the composer written for the concert hall, not the theatre.

In opera, the most famous iteration of all is Charles Gounod's (1818-93) *Faust*, 1859, but as early as 1797, the composer Ignaz Walter (1755-1822) and the librettist Heinrich Gottlieb (1763-1811) were staging *Doktor Faust* in the German city of Bremen. German composer Louis Spohr (1784-1859) had his adaptation of *Faust* performed at the Estates Theatre in Prague on 1 September 1816 after years of unsuccessful pitching of the project, which certainly wouldn't have been helped by the fact that, when singing his pieces with his limited vocal range to prospective backers, he supplemented the (many) notes he couldn't reach with whistles.

OPPOSITE: Faust and Mephisto, *painted by Anton Kaulbach (1864-1934) at the turn of the twentieth century.*

Hector Berlioz's *The Damnation of Faust*, 1846, which is actually somewhere in between opera and cantata, was received with indifference on its debut at the Opéra Comique, on 6 December 1846. 'Nothing in my career as an artist wounded me more deeply than this unexpected indifference', he later recalls. But it built in popularity over the years, until culminating most notably and most curiously in 2015 at the Opéra National de Paris, which staged a reimagining of Berlioz's *Faust* as the wheelchair-bound English scientist Stephen Hawking (1942-2018). Adapted in collaboration with NASA, the dilemma faced by this Faust was not a metaphysical journey, but the space journey of a man leaving Earth to populate the planet Mars as part of the Mars One project.

Mefistofele, 1868, based on Goethe's *Faust*, is the only completed opera with music by the Italian composer Arrigo Boito (1842-1918), who considered Gounod's *Faust* too light and shallow a treatment of the source material. Boito decided to do something almost unheard of in Italian opera at the time – he wrote the libretto himself, a modus operandi he had admired in Richard Wagner. The opera debuted on 5 March 1868 at La Scala, Milan, with the composer-librettist himself wielding the conductor's baton, but the hissing response of the audience was so overwhelming that the show was closed after just two performances.

Into the twentieth century and the Faust story is famously absorbed into American folk opera by the composer Douglas Moore (1893-1969), with *The Devil and Daniel Webster*, the libretto of which was written by Stephen Vincent Benét (1898-1943), who also penned the 1937 short story that served as source material for the opera, and, later in 1941, the Hollywood film adaptation of the same title. Though the story is often referred to as an American Faust, its notoriety pales in comparison to how the legend itself crossed over into the bones of American folklore, becoming part of the fabric of the story of the blues and rock and roll. While the blues originated in the 1860s among African-Americans in the Deep South of the United States, the most famous bluesman of all time, Mississippi-born Robert Johnson (1911-38), came to prominence with recordings made in 1936 and 1937.

Just like Faust, who inscribed magic circles at a crossroad to summon the Devil to strike a deal, so too, according to the legend that surrounded him, did Robert Johnson, meeting the Devil at midnight on a crossroads near the Dockery plantation

Portrait of Edward Reszke (1853-1917), singer, in stage costume in 1893 as Mephisto in the opera Faust *by Charles Gounod at the Grand Theatre of Warsaw.*

Set design for the 'Prologue in Heaven' of Mefistofele*, by Carlo Ferrario (1833-1907), 1881.*

236 | *Madman's Orchestra*

where bluesman Charley Patton (*c.*1891-1934) was raised, to sell his soul for superlative musical ability.♪ Like Paganini, how else could one explain the astonishingly skilful playing that Johnson casually exhibited? (Interestingly, as we can see in the few contemporary photos of the blues player, just like Paganini, Johnson also wielded supernaturally long fingers to his great advantage.) Nothing pours more petrol on the fire of legend than an early and mysterious death, and Johnson's death on 16 August 1938 at the age of twenty-seven remains a mystery – his passing was never reported publicly, no autopsy was performed and his death certificate lists only time and place. The rumour goes that, after flirting with a married woman at a dance, he drank a bottle of whiskey that had been secretly poisoned by the aggrieved husband. The true location of his grave also remains unknown.

'Oh my brother, take this warning / Don't let old Satan take your hand / You'll be lost in sin forever / You'll never reach the promised land', warns the bluegrass master Bill Monroe (1911-96) in 'The Old Cross Road', 1947, as part of the response of those who found the romanticising of 'Devil's music' to be troubling. Even before Johnson's time, blues had already garnered a reputation, among both its proponents and critics, as the 'Devil's music' (one of the many things that rock and roll took with it as it grew out of the blues). In Johnson's style and repertoire you can hear the influence of Peetie Wheatstraw (1902-1941), born William Bunch, who called himself 'the Devil's Son-in-Law' and 'Peetie Wheatstraw, the High Sheriff from Hell', boasting of his demonic nature in his 'stomp' compositions. A month after he recorded 'Mister Livingood' and 'Bring Me Flowers While I'm Living', Wheatstraw died in a high-speed car collision with a freight train, in December 1941.

Jazz had the same reputation. Jelly Roll Morton (1890-1941) boldly claimed to have invented jazz in 1902 (to which the American composer Gunther Schuller (1925-2015) once suggested there was 'no proof to the contrary'). Nearly a decade before Johnson was recording 'Hell Hound on My Trail', Morton recorded the devil-inspired song 'Boogaboo' (1928),

Self-Portrait with Death Playing the Fiddle, 1872, by the Swiss symbolist artist Arnold Böcklin (1827-1901). According to Gustav Mahler's wife Alma, the composer was 'under the spell' of the painting when writing the Scherzo of his Fourth Symphony.

♪ The idea of a crossroads as a junction between worlds has a long history. In medieval Europe, the fact that crossroads were a common place to exhibit the bodies of executed criminals would certainly explain its morbid association. But it also calls to mind the afterlife belief of the Maya, in which the underworld Xibalba ('Place of Fright') can only be reached by crossing a river of scorpions, a river of thick blood, then an oozing river of pus, before you must navigate a crossroads of four roads. The catch here is that each road speaks aloud, telling lies to lead you down the wrong path.

at a time when jazz was the music of bars, brothels and other dens of iniquity. 'When my grandmother found out that I was playing jazz in one of the sporting houses', he recalls, 'she told me that I had disgraced the family and forbade me to live at the house… She told me that Devil music would surely bring about my downfall, but I just couldn't put it behind me.'

The accusatory association of jazz and blues with the Devil has also been a charge levelled at, and enjoyed by, rock and roll, heavy metal and hip-hop artists keen to play with the moral panics stirred up by the occult. Little Richard (1932-2020) once claimed his rock career was 'directed and commanded by the power of darkness', with his family considering rhythm and blues (R&B) music to be 'Devil music', and his strict religious upbringing instilling a feeling of conflict between God and his profession, and his sexuality, throughout his life. While on tour in Australia in October 1957, he looked up and saw a fireball racing across the sky. Unaware this was the Sputnik 1 satellite falling to Earth, he took it as a sign that God was ordering him to change his ways and so became a preacher, abstaining from secular music until being tempted back in 1962.

John Lennon (1940-80) once joked to a press conference that the Beatles were successful because he had sold his soul; and heavy metal bands of the 1970s went farther, like Ozzy Osbourne talking about the 'devil-worshipping' songs of Black Sabbath, and calling himself 'The Prince of Darkness'. 'I was convinced I truly was possessed by the Devil', he said in an interview. 'I remember sitting through *The Exorcist* a dozen times, saying to myself, "Yeah, I can relate to that".' At the same time, in America in 1979, the Charlie Daniels Band was having success with 'The Devil Went Down to Georgia', about the Devil failing to beat a young fiddle player in a contest of musical skill, which is a narrative theme found in other cultures also. In Columbian folklore, for example, Francisco el Hombre ('Francisco the Man') is a legendary *juglar* (a kind of wandering minstrel), who wandered the country playing in *piquerias* ('improvised musical duels') with his accordion.♪ Legend has it that one night as Francisco travelled through the countryside, playing to himself, Satan countered with a song so powerful that it snuffed out the stars and Moon. Francisco fell to his knees, prayed to Heaven and proceeded to play the most

Robert Johnson, photographed at the Hooks Bros photographic studio in Memphis, 1935. Note his extraordinarily long fingers.

A photograph of Robert Johnson discovered in 2007, and authenticated in 2013 by forensic analyst Lois Gibson of the Houston police department, who found the identity of the sailor kissing the nurse in the Life *magazine photo of Times Square on Victory Japan (VJ) day, when the Second World War ended.*

♪ 'A gentleman', American musician, singer-songwriter and actor, Tom Waits (b.1949) once muttered, 'is someone who can play the accordion, but doesn't.'

238 Madman's Orchestra

beautiful melody ever created, which brought the Moon and stars back to life. The Devil screamed in defeat, and fled to the mountains.

In the 1980s came satanic panics about messages hidden in music through the use of 'backmasking', which could be heard by playing the record backwards. This is largely attributed to the American televangelist Paul Crouch, in 1982, who claimed on his Trinity Broadcasting Network (TBN) show that playing Led Zeppelin's 'Stairway to Heaven' backwards revealed the message: 'Here's to my sweet Satan / The one whose little path would make me sad, whose power is Satan / He will give those with him 666 / There was a little toolshed where he made us suffer, sad Satan.' The band rubbished the claims, with the audio engineer Eddie Kramer deeming it 'totally and utterly ridiculous. Why would they want to spend so much studio time doing something so dumb?' The Eagles were accused of hiding the message 'Yes, Satan organised his own religion' in their song 'Hotel California', a title that was suggested by the same paranoiacs to refer to the headquarters of the Church of Satan. AC/DC were similarly accused, but singer-songwriter Brian Johnson laughed it off: 'They'd say, "If you play the record backwards, you can hear evil things like Grrrr!" And I would think, geez, I didn't know the devil sounded like that. I thought he was coherent like the rest of us.' Never mind the fact that there's no evidence such phonetic reversals influence behaviour, nor that the mind can even detect them. Perhaps this can all be traced back to the English occultist Aleister Crowley (1875-1947), who in his 1913 book *Magick (Book 4)* recommended playing records in reverse as a practice for students of black magic to learn how to think and speak backwards.

The first musical satanic panic of the twenty-first century was introduced not by a rock band but by the rapper Lil Nas X with his song 'Montero (Call Me by Your Name)', which was fronted by a publicity-generating scandal campaign as sharply multipronged as a trident. First came the music video, which not even the most generous critic would label ambiguous in its imagery, culminating in the rapper sliding down a stripper pole to Hell, where he gives Satan a lap dance while wearing only Calvin Klein boxer briefs. He seduces the Father of Lies, murders him and steals the horned crown of Hell to wear himself. As these images drew opprobrium from every conservative Christian public figure in America, the fervour was ramped up by the announcement that Lil Nas X had

Monument to Francisco el Hombre defeating the Devil in a musical duel, in the centre of Riohacha, Columbia.

English occultist Aleister Crowley in the dress of the Hermetic Order of the Golden Dawn in 1910.

TORMENTO DOS OVVIDOS

teamed up with the art collective MSCHF to sell 666 pairs of specially adapted black Nike Air Max 97 trainers labelled 'Satan Shoes', which each carried a bronze pentagram on the laces and were infused with human blood in the air bubble of the sole. The asking price was US$1,018, a reference to the Bible passage Luke 10:18: 'I saw Satan fall like lightning from heaven.' The evangelical pastor Mark Burns called the shoes 'evil' and 'heresy'. Today, the shoes are, of course, a highly sought-after collectors' item.

Torment of the Ears, *an illustration from* Desenganno dos Peccadores *('Disillusion of Sinners') by the Jesuit priest Alexandre Perier (1651-1730), first published in Rome in 1724. Sense-based tortures that await sinners in Hell include demons blasting Hell's trumpets directly into one's ears.*

▶ RECOMMENDED PLAYLIST: THE DEVIL IN MUSIC

Faust Symphony, 1854,
FRANZ LISZT

Angels and Devils, 1931,
HENRY BRANT

Blue Spirit Blues, 1929,
BESSIE SMITH

Boogaboo, 1928,
JELLY ROLL MORTON

'Caprice No. 13', 1817,
NICCOLÒ PAGANINI

'Chased Old Satan Through the Door', 1931,
WOODIE BROTHERS

'Danse Macabre', 1874,
CAMILLE SAINT-SAËNS

'Der Erlkönig', 1815,
FRANZ SCHUBERT

Der Freischütz, 1821,
CARL MARIA VON WEBER

'Devil Got My Woman', 1968,
SKIP JAMES

'Devil or Angel', 1955,
THE CLOVERS

Doktor Faust, 1797,
IGNATZ WALTER

Faust, 1887,
HEINRICH ZÖLLNER

'Faust Overture', 1840 (revised 1855),
RICHARD WAGNER

'Get Behind Me Satan', 1955,
THE ALMANAC SINGERS

Hildegard: Visions, 2025,
NWANDO EBIZIE

Kate and The Devil, op. 112, B. 201, 1899,
ANTONÍN DVOŘÁK

Le Petit Faust, 1869,
music by HERVÉ

'Le Streghe' ('Witch's Dance'), op. 8, 1813,
NICCOLÒ PAGANINI

'Little Demon', 1956,
SCREAMIN' JAY HAWKINS

Me and the Devil, 2010,
GIL SCOTT-HERON

'Me and the Devil Blues (Take 1)', 1937,
ROBERT JOHNSON

Mefistofele, 1868,
ARRIGO BOITO

'Mephisto Waltz No. 1', 1881,
FRANZ LISZT

'Montero', 2021,
LIL NAS X

'Must Have Been the Devil', 1954,
OTIS SPANN

'Night on Bald Mountain', 1867,
MODEST MUSSORGSKY

'Old Devil', 1938,
BO CARTER

'Pagin' the Devil', 1938,
THE KANSAS CITY SIX

Piano Sonata No. 9, op. 68, 'The Black Mass', 1913,
ALEKSANDR SCRIABIN

'Scenes from Goethe's *Faust*', 1853,
ROBERT SCHUMANN

Schwanda the Bagpiper, 1927,
JAROMÍR WEINBERGER

Symphony, op. 12, No. 4, 'La Casa del Diavolo', 1771,
LUIGI BOCCHERINI

The Damnation of Faust, 1846,
HECTOR BERLIOZ

The Devil and Daniel Webster, 1939,
DOUGLAS MOORE

'The Devil Has Thrown Him Down', 1960,
SISTER ROSETTA THARPE

'The Devil Went Down to Georgia', 1979,
CHARLIE DANIELS BAND

The Rake's Progress, 1951,
IGOR STRAVINSKY

'The Seventh Enochian Key', 1976,
EDWARD SHIPLEY

'There's Going to Be the Devil to Pay', 1935,
FATS WALLER

'Tying a Knot in the Devil's Tail', 1931,
POWDER RIVER JACK AND KITTY LEE

'Up Jumped the Devil', 1940,
BYRON PARKER AND HIS MOUNTAINEERS

SOME FINAL WORDS OF GREAT MUSICIANS

J. S. Bach (1685-1750) – 'Don't cry for me, for I go to where music is born.'

Jean-Philippe Rameau (1683-1764) – 'What the devil do you mean singing to me, Priest? You are out of tune!'

Wolfgang Amadeus Mozart (1756-91) – 'His last movement was an attempt to express with his mouth the drum passages in the *Requiem*. That I can still hear.' From the memoirs of his wife's sister, Sophia.

Ludwig van Beethoven (1770-1827) – 'Pity, pity, too late', after receiving a case of wine from his publishers and realising he'd never recover enough to drink it.

Franz Schubert (1797-1828) – 'Here, here is my end.'

Frédéric Chopin (1810-49) – 'The earth is suffocating… As this cough will choke me, I implore you to have my body opened, so that I may not be buried alive.'

Hector Berlioz (1803-69) – 'They are finally going to play my music.'

Johannes Brahms (1833-97) – 'Ah, that tastes good', after his doctor gave him some wine.

Franz Liszt (1811-86) – 'Tristan'. Presumed to be a reference to his daughter Cosima's husband, Richard Wagner, who had recently died and who had written the famous opera *Tristan und Isolde*.

Edvard Grieg (1843-1907) – 'Well, if it must be so.'

Gustav Mahler (1860-1911) – 'Mozart, Mozart!'

Béla Bartók (1881-1945) – 'The sad thing is I leave with so much to say.'

Arnold Schoenberg (1874-1951) – 'Harmony'.

Igor Stravinsky (1882-1971) – 'How lovely. This belongs to me, it is my home.' As recalled by his personal manager, Lillian Libman, after she wheeled the 88-year-old around his new ten-room apartment at 920 Fifth Avenue in New York City.

Harry 'Bing' Crosby (1903-77) – 'That was a great game of golf, fellas. Let's go have a Coca-Cola.'

Elvis Presley (1935-77) – 'I'm going to the bathroom to read.'

Terry Kath (1946-78) of the band Chicago – 'Don't worry about it… Look, the clip's not even in it. What do you think I'm gonna do? Blow my brains out?', before pressing his revolver to his temple and pulling the trigger, having forgotten about the round in the chamber.

Bob Marley (1945-81) – 'Money can't buy life.'

Buddy Rich (1917-87) – 'Yeah, country music', replying to a nurse prepping him for surgery who asks: 'Is there anything you can't take?'

Leonard Bernstein (1918-90) – 'What's this?'

George Harrison (1943-2001) – 'Love one another.'

Barry White (1944-2003) – (to his nurse) 'Leave me alone, I'm fine.'

Adam Faith (1940-2003) – 'Channel 5 is all shit, isn't it? Christ, the crap they put on there.'

Michael Jackson (1958-2009) – 'I'd like to have some milk. Please, please give me some more.'

Amy Winehouse (1983-2011) – (on Twitter, now X) 'Oinka Oinka Oinka why you awake.'

Some Final Words of Great Musicians

SELECT BIBLIOGRAPHY

Abraham, Gerald (1979) *The Concise Oxford History of Music*, Oxford: Oxford University Press

Blanning, T. (2008) *The Triumph of Music*, London: Allen Lane

Bohlman, P. V. (2020) *World Music*, Oxford: Oxford University Press

Burton-Hill, C. (2017) *Year of Wonder: Classical Music for Every Day*, London: Headline Home

Burton-Hill, C. (2021) *Another Year of Wonder: Classical Music for Every Day*, London: Headline Home

Cook, N. (1998) *Music: A Very Short Introduction*, Oxford: Oxford University Press

Cooper, B. (2009) *Child Composers: Their Works*, Lanham, Maryland: Scarecrow Press

Dearling, R.; Dearling, C.; Rust, B. (1976) *The Guinness Book of Music*, London: Guinness Superlatives

Djossa, C. A. (2018) 'With Musical Cryptography, Composers Can Hide Messages in Their Melodies', *Atlas Obscura*; https://www.atlasobscura.com/articles/musical-cryptography-codes

Franssen, M. (1991) 'The Ocular Harpsichord of Louis-Bertrand Castel: The Science and Aesthetics of an Eighteenth-Century *Cause Célèbre*', *Tractrix: Yearbook for the History of Science, Medicine, Technology, and Mathematics*, Vol. 3, Amsterdam: Editions Rodopi

Gant, A. (2021) *Five Straight Lines: A History of Music*, London: Profile Books

Goodall, H. (2013) *The Story of Music*, London: Vintage

Green, J. (2005) *Rock 'n' Pop Music Trivia*, London: Wise Publications

Grout, D.J. (1973) *A History of Western Music*, New York: W. W. Norton & Company

Hankins, T. L.; Silverman, R. J. (1995) *Instruments and the Imagination*, Princeton: Princeton University Press

Henley, D.; Jackson, S. (2009) *Classic Ephemera: A Musical Miscellany*, London: Elliott and Thompson Limited

Henley, D.; Lihoreau, T. (2004) *Stephen Fry's Incomplete & Utter History of Classical Music*, London: Macmillan

Holder, N. (2020) *Why Is My Piano Black and White?*, London: Holders Hill

Hoppin, R. (1978) *Medieval Music*, New York: W. W. Norton & Company

Isserlis, S. (2001) *Why Beethoven Threw the Stew*, London: Faber

Isserlis, S. (2006) *Why Handel Waggled His Wig*, London: Faber

Key, J. A. (2016) 'My End Is My Beginning: "Popular" (?) Music from Fourteenth-Century France: Part 3', Gainesville, Florida: https://www.jordanalexanderkey.com/single-post/2016/08/13/popular-music-from-14th-century-france-part-3-guillaume-de-machaut-c-1300-1377-rondea

Krull, K.; Hewitt, K. (1993) *Lives of the Musicians*, New York: Clarion

Latham, A. (ed.) (2002) *The Oxford Companion to Music*, Oxford: Oxford University Press

Latham, A. (ed.) (2004) *Oxford Dictionary of Musical Terms*, Oxford: Oxford University Press

Leonard, L. (2000) *1812 and All That*, Toronto: Sound and Vision

Levison, B.; Farrer, F. (2007) *Classical Music's Strangest Concerts and Characters*, London: Robson Books

Lihoreau, T. (2004) *Stephen Fry's Incomplete & Utter History of Classical Music*, London: Macmillan

Maloney, A. (2018) *Last Night of the Proms*, London: BBC Books

Pauly, R.G. (1988) *Music in the Classic Period*, Englewood Cliffs: Prentice Hall

Pearsall, R. (1975) *Edwardian Popular Music*, Newton Abbot: David & Charles

Philip, R. (2003) *A Little History of Music*, New Haven, Connecticut: Yale University Press

Reese, G. (1940) *Music in the Middle Ages: With an Introduction on the Music of Ancient Times*, New York: W.W. Norton & Company

Ross, A. (2007) *The Rest Is Noise: Listening to the Twentieth Century*, London: Fourth Estate

Sachs, C. (1940) *The History of Musical Instruments*, London: J. M. Dent & Sons Ltd

Sacks, O. (2008) *Musicophilia*, London: Picador

Sams, E. (1979) 'Musical Cryptography', *Cryptologia*, Vol. 3, No. 4; https://ericsams.org/index.php/on-cryptography/333-musical-cryptography?limitstart=0

Schonberg, H. (1970) *The Lives of the Great Composers*, New York: W.W. Norton & Company

Slonimsky, N. (2000) *Lexicon of Musical Invective*, New York: W. W. Norton & Company

Spiegel, F. (1997) *Musical Blunders and Other Off-Beat Curiosities*, London: Robson Books

Spitzer, M. (2021) *The Musical Human: A History of Life on Earth*, London: Bloomsbury

Sullivan, P. (2003) *Sullivan's Music Trivia*, London: Sanctuary

Swafford, J. (1992) *The Vintage Guide to Classical Music*, New York: Vintage Books

Taruskin, R. (2005) *Oxford History of Western Music*, Oxford: Oxford University Press

INDEX

Page numbers in *italics* refer to illustrations; page numbers followed by an 'n' refer to footnotes.

AC/DC 239
Ace, Johnny 219
Adams, John 186
Adams, John Luther 49n
Akutagawa, Yasushi 190, 198
Alarm Will Sound 197
Albinoni, Tomaso 210–11
Albrechtsberger, Johann Georg 182–3, 198
Allais, Alphonse 194–5, 198
Anderson, J. H. 152
Antheil, George 165
appoggiatura 14
Aquinas, St Thomas 129, 147–8
Arányi, Jelly d' 208, *208*
archicembalo 188, *188*
Arcimboldo, Giuseppe 88
Aristotle 20, 22, 84
Aristoxenus of Tarentum 22
Arnold, Malcolm 190, *190*, 198
Astley, Rick 9, 184
astronomy 19, 20
Attwood, Thomas 204

Babayan, Sergei 215
Baburen, Dirck van *183*
Bach, Carl Philipp Emanuel 175, 208–9, 217
Bach, Johann Christian 209
Bach, Johann Sebastian 129, *175*, 208, 242
    cryptographic music 144–5, *145*, 151
    experimental oddities 199
    mathematical sequences 33–4, *35*, 38
    musical hoaxes 207, 217
    The Musical *Offering* 174–5
    Voyager Golden Record 37, 39
Bach family 118
Bacon, Francis 27n
Bacon, Roger 132
badgermin 9, 67
Bahr, Robert von 215
Balakirev, Mily 230n
balnaphone 51
barcarolle 14
Barnum, P. T. 92
Barrero, Ramón 219
Barrington-Coupe, William 213, 214, 215–16, *215*
Bartók, Béla 242
BBC 149, 150
Beach, Amy 83, *83*, 111

The Beatles 14, *148*, 238
Beckford, Martin 215
Bedford, David 190
Beethoven, Karl van 156
Beethoven, Ludwig van 78, 121, 131, *156*, 183, 242
    cryptographic music 145, 149–50, 151
    experimental oddities 198
    Fifth Symphony 13, 149–50, 151, 166
    glass armonica 52, 77
    'Grosse Fuge' 118–19, *118*, 129, 168
    String Quartet No.12 in E flat major, op.127 155–6, 165
    Symphony No. 6 'Pastoral' 32n, 38
    visible music 81, 96, *97*, 111
Bellini, Vincenzo 112–13, *113*, 129
Benét, Stephen Vincent 236
Berg, Alban 165, 169n, 219
Berio, Luciano 190
Berkeley Theory Manuscript 172
Berlioz, Hector 78, 165, 242
    curious instruments 71
    The Damnation of Faust 236, 241
    musical hoaxes 205–7, *206*, *207*, 217
    'Symphonie fantastique' 229–31, *230*
Bernstein, Leonard 11, 231, 243
Berry, Chuck 37, 39
Besant, Annie 99, *100*, *101*
Between Music 197
Beyoncé 84, 111
Biber, Heinrich Ignaz Franz 180, 181–2, *182*, 198, 199
bicycle, musical 75
Big Bang 16
Binconi, Philippe 194
bird bone flutes 42, *42*
birdsong 32, *32*
bisbigliando 14
Bishop, Bainbridge 91–2, *92*, 95
Bizet, Georges 129, 165
Björk 59, 77
black holes 16–17
Black Sabbath 220, 228, 238
Blades, James 150
Błażusiakówna, Helena Wanda 128
blues 236–7, 238
Boccherini, Luigi 209, 241
Böcklin, Arnold *81*, 237
Boethius 20, 22, *23*
Bogoslowski, Ruslan *148*
Boilly, Louis-Léopold *224*
Boito, Arrigo 236, 241

Boomerang telescope 16
Bosch, Hiëronymus 124–5, *125*
Boulez, Pierre 162, *163*, 165
Bourgeois, Derek 190–1, 199
bowafridgeaphone 76, *76*
Bowie, David 38, 228
Bradshaw, Susan 213
Brahe, Tycho 22
Brahms, Johannes 78, 79, 145–6, 151, 242
British Secret Intelligence Service 139
Britten, Benjamin 79
Bronfman, Yefim 214
Bruno and His Swinging Tigers 148–9
Bry, Johann Theodor de 26, *64*
Bücking, J. 141, *143*, 144
Buckvich, Daniel 167
Buonanni, Filippo 66, *68–9*, 70
Burney, Charles 183
Burns, Mark 240
Busoni, Ferruccio 145, 185–6

cactus instruments 56
Cage, John 166, 186, 212
    4'33" 79, 168, 194, 195
    curious instruments 56, 77
    experimental oddities 187, 199
Campanella, Tommaso 179
Carafa, Fabrizio 178–9
Cardew, Cornelius *191*, 199
Carney, Harry 84
carnyx 49
Carrillo, Julián 188
Carter, Howard 46, 48
Caruncho, Manuel Vázquez 156
Cary, Tristram 190, 198
Casadesus, Henri 208–9, *209*, 217
Casadesus, Marius 208, *208*, 217
Castel, Louis-Bertrand 88, 90–1, *90*, 92, 93, 95
caves 40, 41–3, *41*, *44*, 77
Celentano, Adriano 136n
Cellarius, Andreas *19*
Celts 49
Cerrito, Fanny *226*
Chailly, Riccardo 153
Chandra X-ray Observatory 16
Chappell, Eric 17
Charles Stuart *141*
Charlie Daniels Band 238, 241
Charlie and His Orchestra 13, 148–9, *150*, 151
Chauvet-Pont-d'Arc Cave 40, 41–2, *41*
cheese paradiddle 14
chicharra 14
chicken pickin' 14
Chisholm, Erik 162
Chladni, Ernest *106*, 107, *107*
Chladni figures 104, *106*, 107

Chopin, Frédéric 14, 78, 145, *156*, 242
    études 186, 199, 215, 217
    lost music found *128*, 129
    Piano Sonata No. 2 in B flat minor 156, 165
Chumbawamba 36n, 38
Churchill, Winston 149
Ciconia, Johannes *136*
Cimarosa, Domenico 152
Clarke, Jeremiah 218
Claudian 49
Coates, Albert 159
Collard, Jean-Philippe 215
colour of music 80–111
colour organs 91–7
composers 78–9, 166–7
condom, sound-playing 75
Content Creator Man 184, 198
Copernicus, Nicolaus 22
Copland, Aaron 79
Cordier, Baude *170–1*, 172, 198, 199
Corelli, Arcangelo 209
Cornelius, Peter 183–4, *183*, 198
Cornetti, Paulo 121, 129
Costa, Marco 34
Cotton, Margaret *189*
couesnophone 74, *74*
Couperin, François 209
Covent Garden Theatre 152
Cowell, Henry 158, 159–60, *159*, 165
crab canons 168, 174–5
Cranmer, David *67*, 74
Crispi, Giovanni Pietro Maria 183
Crofts, J. 65
Cromwell, Oliver *141*
Crosby, Harry 'Bing' 243
Crouch, Paul 239
Crowley, Aleister 239, *239*
Crumb, George 182, 199
Cruz, Jorge 44–5
cryptographic music 132–51
Cryptomenytices et Cryptographiae Libri IX 140
Ctesibius of Alexandria 49
Cui, César 79, 157
cutlery, musical 56

da Fabriano, Gentile *122–3*, 124
Dante 231, *232*, 235
d'Arezzo, Guido 115
Dauvergne, Antoine 201, *202*, 217
De La Soul 36n
deaths in musical history 218–19
Debussy, Claude 79, 130, *131*, 147, 186, 228
Declercq, Nico 45
Deep Purple 16, 38
Deldevez, Édouard 137
della Porta, Giambattista 138, *138*

Demetrius Gallitzin, Prince 155
    the Devil in music 220–41
Dies, Albert 154
Dirjec, Janez 42
Distler, Jed 214
Divje Babe flute 42, *42*
Dixon, Laurinda S. 124–5
Donizetti, Gaetano 52, 77
Dorabella cipher 147, *147*
Dossi, Dosso 174, *174*
Dowland, John 179–80, 198
Dragonetti, Domenico 210
drums 55
Druyan, Ann *36*, 37
Duc, Pierre 206
Ducré, Pierre 205–7, *206*
duende 15
Dukas, Paul 147
durchkomponert 14
Durko, Zsolt 191, 198
Dutton, Dennis 215
Dvořák, Antonín 111, 241
Dyer, Richard 213

The Eagles 239
Egyptians, ancient 46–8
eidophone 107, *107*, *108–9*, *110*
Eilish, Billie 84, 111
Eleanor of Aragon, Queen of Castile *173*
Elgar, Edward 139, 146–7, *147*, 151
    Cello Concerto in E minor 158–9, 165
Ellington, Duke 83–4, 111
enigma canons 172–8
Ešenvalds, Ēriks 20n, 38
Etna, Mount 112
experimental oddities 168–99
eye music 172–8

Faber, Johann Christoph 144, 145
Faith, Adam 243
Faraday, Michael 99, 101
Fauré, Gabrial 145, 147
Faust *234*, 235–6
Ferdinand III 61
Ferdinand IV *179*
Ferguson, Maynard 71, 77
Ferrari, Luc 190
Ferrario, Carlo *236*
Fibonacci sequence 33–4
Field, George *85*
Field, John 145, 151
Fillmore, Henry 74
Fine, Oronce *18*
fire organs 9, 99, 101–5
Fleury, Charles *179*
Fludd, Robert *16*, 24, 26–7, *26*, *28*, *29*

flutes 82
    bird bone flutes 42, *42*
    witch flute 9, *9*
Fontana dell'Organo *50*
Frances-Hoad, Cheryl 16n, 38
Franciolini, Leopoldo *201*
Francisco el Hombre 238–9, *239*
Franck, César 218
Francken, Frans the Younger 227
Franklin, Benjamin 51
Frederick, King of Prussia 174–5, *175*
Frescobaldi, Giralomo 31–2
Froberger, Johann Jakob 32, 61, *179*, 199
Fusco, Renata 132

Gaffurius, Franchinus *21*
Gagarin, Yuri 36
Galileo 19
Gallagher, Liam 79
Gallagher, Noel 79
Galle, Cornelis the Elder *232*
Gay, Noel *150*
Geissenklösterle Cave 42, *42*
General Electric 95n
Gesualdo da Venosa, Carlo 178–9, 199
Gesualdo da Venosa, Donna Maria 178–9
Giazotto, Remo 211
Glanvill, Joseph 223
glass armonica 51, 52, *52*, *53*, 77
glass harp 51
Glasspiel 51
Glazunov, Aleksandr 157
Gluck, Alma 184
Glynn, Christopher 120
Godowsky, Leopold Sr 186, 199, 215, 216
Goebbels, Joseph 149
Goethe, Johann Wolfgang von 13, 86, 235, 236
golden ratio 34, *35*
Goldstein, Mikhail 211–12, *212*, 217
Goléa, Antoine 162
goofus 74, *74*
    The Goofus Five 74, 77
Górecki, Henryk 127–8, 129
Goss, Samuel 75
Gottlieb, Henrich 235
Gounod, Charles *100*, 101, 111, 235, *236*
Graham, Harry *150*
Grainger, Percy 166
Grante, Carlo 215
Great Continuous Organ 58, *58*, *60*, 77
The Great Stalacpipe Organ 43, *44*, *45*, 77
Greeks, Ancient 15, *18*, 19, *19*
Grieg, Edvard 130, 242
Guarneri del Gésu, Giuseppe 226
Guido d'Arezzo 56, *57*
Guidonian hand 56–7, *57*

248 *Madman's Orchestra*

Guillemin, Amadeo 105
Gye, Frederick 152

Hába, Alois 188
Habermann, Michael 162
Hahn, Reynaldo 147
Hallock-Greenewalt, Mary 95–6, *96*, *97*
Hamrick, Amelia 124–5
Handel, George Frideric 78, 178, 198, 207, 209, 217
Hanslick, Edvard 130
harmonicas 74
harps 51, 60
harpsichords 40, 90–1, *90*, 92
Harrison, George 243
Harrison, Lou 181, 198
Hassan, Hala 48
Hatto, Joyce 213–16, *214*, *216*, 217
Haussmann, Elias 175
Havré, Duke of 144
Hawking, Stephen 16n, 236
Hay, David Ramsay 86–7, *86*, *87*, *88*
Haydn, Joseph 211
    The Creation 18–19, 38
    experimental oddities 181, 199
    'Miracle' 154, *154*, *155*, 165
    musical hoaxes 210, 217
    Symphony No. 93 125n, 129
Haydn, Michael 138–9, *146*
Heisenberg, Werner 20
heksenfluit 9, *9*
Helicopter Quartet 9, *197*
Henderson, William James 161
Hendrix, Jimi 227, 228
Herrmann, Timo Jouko 121
Herschel, William 18
Herzog, Anton 202
hexachords 32–3, 56, *57*, 60, 146
Higgins, Bryan 99
Higley, Sarah 135–6
Hildegard of Bingen 133–6, *135*, 220–3, *222*
Hill, Susannah 218
Hillier, Lejaren 189–90, 198
Hindemith, Paul 38, 169n
hippopotamus tusk clappers 48
hoaxes, musical 200–17
Hodges, Johnny 84
Hoffman, E. T. A. 82n
Hoffnung, Gerard 189
hog harmonium 9
Holst, Gustav 31, 38, 181, 228
Hooke, Robert 102, 104, *106*, 107
Hugo, Victor 231
Hurrian Hymn 116–17, *117*
hydraulic organs *50*, *63*
hydraulis 49, *50*
hydraulophone *50*

Ibert, Jacques 190, 198
ice instruments 52
Ice Music Festival 55
Indy, Vincent d' 147
instruments, curious 40–77
Inverne, James 214
Isungset, Terje 52, *54*, 55, 77
Ives, Charles 181, 189, 198, 199

Jackson, Michael 243
Janzen, Ryan *50*
jazz 237–8
Jerome of Bologna 40
Jew's harp 182n, *183*
Joachim, Joseph 208n
Johnson, Brian 239
Johnson, Robert 236–7, *238*, 241
Jones, Isham 219
junkstrument 74

Kagel, Mauricio 190, 198
Kandinsky, Wassily 80, *80*
Karel, Rudolf 125n
Karlsson, Robert *197*
Kastner, Georges Frédéric Eugène 101, 102, *102*
Kath, Terry 243
Katzenorgel 61, *64*, 65, 67
Kaulbach, Anton *234*
Keilberth, Joseph 219
Keller, Dr Hans 212–13, *212*, 217
Kepler, Johannes 27, 29, *29*, 31
Kerman, Joseph 119
keyboard instruments 40, 49
Khunrath, Heinrich 25
Kilian, Korina *121*
Kim, Paul 215
King, Ray Stanton 8
The King's Theatre 154, *154*
Kipsigis tribe 9n
Kircher, Athanasius 70, 138
    Arca musarithmica 60–1
    magic lanterns 88, *89*
    Musurgia Universalis 31–3, *32*, *33*, 60–6
klangfarbenmelodie 15
klaxophone 74
Klüber, Johann Ludwig 136
Knox, Father Ronald 212
Kobbé, Gustav 219
Koczwara, Frantisek 218
Köhler, René 214
Kramer, Eddie 239
Kraus, Joseph H. 70
Kreisler, Fritz 209–10, *209*, 217
Kreutzer, Léon 207
Kurtág, György 82n, 111
Kuryokhin, Sergey Anatolyevich 200

Lablache, Luigi *12*
Lack, Theodore 102
Lady Gaga 34, 38
Lalande, Jérôme 223–4, *224*
Landon, H.C. Robbins *211*
Lane, Jane *141*
Langgaard, Rued 38, 205, *205*, 217
Langton, Hugh Gordon *112*
Lanin, Sam 219
Larsonneur, Charles 137
Laveleye, Victor de 149
Leadbeater, Charles 99, *100*, *101*
Led Zeppelin 239
Lee, Dai-Keong 191
Lehrman, Henri *185*
Leibnitz, Gottfried 136
Lekeu, Guillaume 218
Lenau, Nikolaus 235
Lenin, Vladimir 200
Leningrad Television 200
Lenman, Jamie 116, 129
Lennon, John 238
Leonardo da Vinci
    cryptographic music 132, *132*, 133, *133*, *134*, 151
    curious instruments 58–9, *58*, *60*
    Portrait of a Musician *126*, 127, *127*, 132
Léonin 229
Leopold II, Emperor 152
Levit, Igor 187
Libetta, Francesco 186
Ligeti, György 82, 111, *197*
Lil Nas X 239–40, 241
Liszt, Franz 15, 79, 145, *185*, 242
    the Devil theme 231, 233, 235, 241
    experimental oddities 185, 186, 198
    visible music 82, 111
lithophones 43–5, *43*, 77
Little Richard 238
Locke, John 80
Lonardi, Massimo 132
Lorges, Duke of 144
lost music 112–29
Lott, Felicity 184
Louis XI 65
Louis XIV 218
Lucas, Alfred 48
Lucca (Mancini) Codex 136
Lucretius 32n
Lully, Jean-Baptiste 218
Luons, Paul 75
Luray Caverns 42–3, *44*, *45*, 77

McCall Smith, Alexander 8
McClellan, Dr Robinson *128*
Machaut, Guillaume de 168–9, *168*, *169*, 172, 174, 199

McMurray, Loring 219
magic lanterns 88, *89*
Mahler, Alma *237*
Mahler, Gustav 166, 181, *237*, 242
Maier, Michael *24*
Mancini, Henry 167
Marconi, Guglielmo 36
Marian antiphon *122*, 124
Marie Antoinette 52
Marley, Bob 243
Mars 31, 36n, 236
Martin, Carroll 219
Martini, Giovanni Battista 175
Martirano, Salvator 190
Maslanka, David 167
Maternianus, Bishop of Reims 114
Matthews, David 119
Maximilian I *10*
Mayan pyramids 44–5, *46*
Medici family 117
melisma 15
Mendelssohn, Felix 78, 207, 215
    lost music found 119–20, *119*, 129
Menuhin, Yehudi 208
Menzel, Adolf von *175*
Merian, Matthäus 26
Mersenne, Marin 60
Merz 20n
Mesmer, Franz 52
Messiaen, Olivier 32n, 38, 79, 81, 111, 215
    cryptographic music 147–8, 151
Metallica 15
Michel, Winfried 210
microtones 187–8
Miller, Henry 160–1
Missy Elliot 35–6, 38
Mitchell, Donald 213
Mögling, Daniel *30*
Monnet, Jean 201, *202*
Monroe, Bill 237
Moore, Douglas 236, 241
Morley, Thomas 174
Moroney, Davitt 117–18
Morton, Jelly Roll 237–8, 241
Moscheles, Ignaz *184*, 199
Mottl, Felix 219
Moyreau, Christophe *182*, 199
Mozart, Constanze 203, 203n
Mozart, Wolfgang Amadeus 77, *121*, 242
    cryptographic music 144
    Don Giovanni 233
    experimental oddities 198
    music of the Universe 34, 37, 38, 39
    musical disasters 153, 165
    musical hoaxes 202–5, *204*, 207, 208, 217
    musical puzzles 175, 178

Requiem in D minor 202–3, *203*
and Salieri 120–1, 129
MSCHF 240
Müller, Wenzel 207
Muraro, Roger 215
musica mundana 22, 24
musica universalis 20, 22, 32
musical disasters 152–65
musical terms, unusual 14–15
Mussorgsky, Modest 230n, 241
Mvravinsky, Evgeny 211

Nancarrow, Conlon 194, *195*, 199
Nanny, Édouard 210
NASA 35–6, *36*, 37, *37*, 39, 236
Nasello, Riccardo 112
Naudin, Jean-Bernard *227*
Newman, Ernest 159
Newton, Isaac 84, *84*, 86
Nicholas, Jeremy 213, 216
Nielsen, Carl 38, 205, *205*
Nikkal 116
notation knives 56, *56*
Notke, Bernt *229*

Oasis 79
occult works 139–40
Ochs, Siegfried 207
O'Conor, John 215
octobass *17*
ocular harpsichord 90–1, *90*, 92
organs *89*
  colour organs 91–7
  fire organs 99, 101–5
  Great Continuous Organ 58, *58*, 60
  Great Stalacpipe Organ 43, *44*, 45
  hydraulic organs *50*, 63
  Katzenorgel 61, 65, 67
  perfume organ *70*
  water organs 49, *50*
Osbourne, Ozzy 220, 238
Ouseley, Frederick *13*
Ovsianiko-Kulikovsky, Mykola 211–12, *212*
Ovsianiko-Kulikovsky, Nikolay 217

Paganini, Niccolò 155, 181, 225–7, *227*, 237, 241
Paisiello, Giovanni 155, 165
Pala, Giovanni Maria *134*
palindromes 168–9
Parisotti, Alessandro 207
Partch, Harry 188–9, *189*, 198
Patanè, Giuseppe 219
Patton, Charley 237
Penny, Dora 147, *147*
Pepys, Samuel 61
perfume organ 9, *70*

Pergolesi, Giovanni 200, 207, 217
Perier, Alexandre *240*
Perlman, Itzhak 84
Pérotin 229, *229*
pesantissimo 15
piangendo 15
pianos 17n
Pierson, Alan *197*
piganino 65, *66*, 67
Pires, Maria João 153
Plato 49
playlists
  cryptographic music 151
  curious instruments 77
  the Devil in music 228, 241
  the Devil's tritones 228
  experimental oddities 198–9
  lost music found 129
  music of the Universe 38–9
  musical disasters 165
  visible music 111
plop 15
Plotkin, Fred 112–13
The Pogues 203n
polyphony 31, 113–17, *114*, 179, 228–9
Popovych, Pavlo 36
Popper, David 210, *210*, 217
Poulenc, Francis 186
Pousseur, Henri 191, 198
Powell, Jonathan 194
Presley, Elvis 15, *148*, 243
Previn, André 215
Prez, Josquin des 174, *174*, 198
Prokofiev, Sergei 79
proslambanomenos 15
psychedelic music 11, 231
Ptolemy, Claudius 84
Puccini, Giacomo 130, 157–8, *157*, 165
Pugnani, Gaetano 209
Purcell, Henry 218
Purser, Edward 115–16
Pushkin, Aleksandr 121
Pyramid of the Moon, Teotihuacán 45, *46*
pyrophone 99, 101–5
Pythagoras 20, 27, 84, 87
Pythagoreans 20–2, *21*, 22, 24–7, *26*

Rachmaninoff, Sergei 79, *81*, 157, 165
Raff, Joachim 82, 111
Rameau, Jean-Philippe 242
Ramirez, Larry 71
Ramsay, Sir W. M. 115–16
Ravel, Maurice 32n, 38, 147, 151, 186
The Really Terrible Orchestra (RTO) 8–9, *8*
rebuses 132, *132*, *133*
Rees, Abraham *142*

Reger, Max 131
Reich, Steve 163–4, 165
Reil, Johann Christian 65
Reszke, Edward *236*
Reznikoff, Iegor 41
rib music (jazz on bones) *148*
Rich, Buddy 15, 243
riddle canons 172–8
Rig Veda 17–18
Rimington, Alexander Wallace 93–5, *93*, *94*, *95*
Rimsky-Korsakov, Nikolay 81, 82, 111, 145
Roberts, Tim S. 147
Robinson, Thomas 180
Rochlitz, Johann 52
Rodgers, Jimmie 9n
Rodrigo, Olivia 111
Rollini, Adrian 74, 77
Romans 19
Roosevelt, Franklin D. 149
Rose, Andrew 214
Rosicrucian Order 27, *30*
Rossini, Gioachino 78, 165, 182, 199, 231
    The Barber of Seville 155, *155*, 219
Rubenstein, Arthur 186

Sachs, Georg Tobias Ludwig 81n
Sagan, Carl *36*, 37
Saint-Léon, Arthur *226*
Saint-Saëns, Camille 208
    The Carnival of the Animals 52, *53*, 77
    and the Devil 228, 229, 241
Salieri, Antonio 120–1, 129
Salmond, Felix 159
Sand, George 156
Satie, Erik 165, 166, *186*
    experimental oddities 186–7, 198, 199
    Parade 189–90
Satina, Natalie 157
Sax, Aldolphe 71, *72–3*
saxhorn 71
saxtuba 73
Scelsi, Giacinto 9, 184, 198
Schandflöte 57–8, *58*
Schedel, Hartmann *229*
Schneider, Louis 79
Schnyder von Wartensee, Franz Xaver Joseph Peter 52, 77
Schoenberg, Arnold *80*, 146, 151, 243
Schoenberg hexachord 146
Schonberg, Harold C. 186
Schott, Gaspar *64*
Schubert, Franz 121, 129, 242
    the Devil theme 241
    experimental oddities 168, 199
    visible music 81–2, 111
Schulhoff, Erwin *187*, 194, *196*, 198, 199

Schuller, Gunther 237
Schumann, Clara 79
Schumann, Robert 82n, 111, 208n
    cryptographic music 138–9, 145, 151
    the Devil in music 235, 241
Schuppanzigh, Ignaz 156
Schwedler, Karl 149
Schweitzer, Vivien 56
Scriabin, Aleksandr 81, 82, 111, 199, 241
    Mysterium 184–5, *184*
    'Prometheus: The Poem of Fire' 97–9, *98*, *99*
Scudo, Pierre 205
Second World War (1939–45) 148–50
Seikilos epitaph 115–16, *115*
Selenus, Gustav 139–40, *139*
Senleches, Jacob *173*
Shkreli, Martin 120n
Sholokhov, Sergey 200
Shostak, Dean *52*, 77
Shostakovich, Dmitri 36, 38, 131, 146, 151
Sibelius, Jean 84, 111
Siebold, Agathe von 145–6
Siepi, Cesare 162–3, 165
Siklós, Albert 181, 199
Simon, László 214, 215
Simon and Garfunkel 194
Sloane 351 (f.15b) 139
smite 15
Smith, Erik 178
Smithson, Harriet 231, *231*
Soldier, Dave 167
Solomon, Yonty 162
Solrésol 137
Soltész, Stefan 219
Sorabji, Kaikhosru Shapurji *161*
    experimental oddities 191, 194, *194*, 199
    musical disasters 161–2, 165
The Sounds of Earth (Golden Record) *36*, 37, *37*, 39
soundwaves 16, 45
Souster, Iner 74, 76, *76*, 77
Spohr, Louis *145*, 235
Spring, Matthew 180
Sprinkle, Leland W. 42–3, 77
Stevenson, Peter 8
Stockhausen, Karlheinz 167, 191, *197*, 198, 212
Stoessel, Jason 124
Stokowski, Leopold 230n
Stonehenge 43–4
Storchio, Rosina 158
Stradivari, Antonio 34, *226*
Strauss, Johann II 152
Strauss, Richard 38, 52, 78, 219
    experimental oddities 180–1, 199
    musical unappreciation 130, 131
Stravinsky, Igor 79, 129, 140, 165, 168, 241, 243
Striggio, Alessandro 117, 129

stripper ending 15
Stump, John *192–3*, 198
Sudanese drums 55
Sudre, Jean-François 137–8
superbone 71
Süssmayr, Franz Xaver 202–3
Swift, Taylor 49n
Sylvestre, Loic 34
synaesthesia 81–4

Tagg, Philip 15
Tang, Muhai 164, *164*
Tappern, James 46–8
Tartini, Giuseppe 138, 151, 223–5, *225*, 227
Tchaikovsky, Pyotr Ilyich 78, 130, 166
Telemann, Georg Philipp 90–1, *181*, 198
tessitura 15
Thicknesse, Philip 141
Tilson, Michael 164
tirade 15
Tobin, John 161–2, 191
Toch, Ernst 189, *189*, 199
Tool 34, 38
Tooley, Sarah 94–5
Tracey, Hugh 9n
Treuting, Jason 56
tritones 227–33
Trnka, Wenzel 203n
trombones 71n, *72*, 73
trumpets 71, *72*, 80, 82
    Tutankhamun's cursed trumpets 46–9, *47*, 212
tubo cochleato 68, 70
Turk, Ivan 42
Tutankhamun, King 46–9, *47*, 212
Twain, Mark 131
Tyndall, John 101

unappreciation, musical 130–1
the Universe, music of the 16–39

Vaardt, Jan van der *201*
Vado, Juan del *176–7*
Varelli, Giovanni 114, 117
Varèse, Edgard 131, 160–1, *160*, 165
Várez, Antonio Roca *43*
vegetable instruments 55–6, *55*
The Vegetable Orchestra 77
Venus 29, 31, 35–6
Verdi, Giuseppe 130, 165, 219
verrillon 51
Vezzosi, Alessandro *134*
Vicentino, Nicola 188, *188*
Viel, Edmond 206–7
Vienna Vegetable Orchestra 55, *55*
viola organista 59, *59*, 77
violins *226*

visible music 80–111
Vivaldi, Antonio 32n, 38, 129, 181, 209
voice flowers 107, *108–9*, *110*
Volmar 136
Vostrák, Zbynek 125n
Voyager 1 36–7, *36*, *37*, 39
Vuillaume, Jean-Baptiste 17

Wagner, Richard 71n, 131, 165, 219
    composers on 78, 242
        the Devil in music 235, 236, 241
    visible music 80, 84, 93–4, 98, *101*, 111
Waits, Tom 238n
Waldmüller, Ferdinand Georg *156*
Walpole, Horace 201
Walsegg, Count Franz von 201–3, *203*
Walter, Ignaz *233*, 235, 241
Warren, Leonard 219
water organs 49, *50*
Watts, Robert 182, 198, *199*
Watts Hughes, Megan (Margaret) 107, *107*, *108–9*, *110*
Weber, Carl Maria von 182, 198, 241
Webern, Anton 131
Weißheimer, Wendelin 101–2, *103*
Welles, Orson 212
Wheatstraw, Peetie 237
White, Barry 243
Wilkins, John 136
Will Wood and the Tapeworms 167
Williamson, Amy 120
Winehouse, Amy 243
witch flute 9, *9*
Wolff, Christoph 118
Wooding, Kevin 167
woodshedding 15
Wren, Sir Christopher 104
Wu-Tang Clan 120n

Yesenin, Sergey 200
Young, La Monte 167, 195, 198

Zak, Piotr 212–13, *212*, 217
Zappa, Frank 167
Zarlino, Gioseffo 17
Zubrzycki, Sławomir 59
Zulehner, Carl 207

PICTURE CREDITS

P1, P221 British Museum; P2 Getty Center; PP4-5 Prado Museum; P6 Palais des Beaux Arts de Lille; P9 Museum aan de Stroom, Antwerp; P10 National Library of Spain; P11 Wellcome Collection; P12 British Museum; P13 Wikipedia.co.uk; P16 Wellcome Collection; P17 (top) The George Peabody Library, The Johns Hopkins University Sheridan Libraries; P17 (bottom) Orchestre symphonique de Montréal (Antoine Saito); P18 Houghton Library, Harvard; P19 Barry Lawrence Ruderman Antique Maps; P21 Biblioteca Nazionale Centrale di Firenze; P22 Jossifresco, Wikipedia.co.uk; P23 Cambridge University Library; P24 Roy G. Neville Historical Chemical Library; P25 Beinecke Rare Book and Manuscript Library; P26 Courtesy of Science History Institute; P28, P29 (top) Beinecke Rare Book and Manuscript Library; P29 (top), P30 Courtesy of Science History Institute; P29 (bottom) Det Kongelige Bibliotek; P30 AF Fotografie / Alamy Stock Photo; P32 St Andrews University Special Collections; P33 St Andrews University Library; P35 Bach Digital; PP36-37 (all images) NASA/JPL-Caltech; P40, P41 HTO, wikipedia.co.uk; P42 (top left) Petar Milošević; P42 (bottom right) Thilo Parg, Wikipedia.co.uk; P43 Carles Garcia-Roca; P45 Jon Callas; P46 Gorgo, Wikipedia.co.uk; P47 The Cairo Museum; P48 Metropolitan Museum of Art; P49 Amazonenkrieger, wiki commons; P50 (top left) Sinyo, Flickr; P50 (top right) Glogger, wikipedia.co.uk; P50 (bottom) British Museum; P51 Glogger, Wikipedia.co.uk; P52 Tonamel, Wikipedia.co.uk; P53 National Library of France; P54 Laurence Harvey / Alamy Stock Photo; P55 Imago / Alamy Stock Photo; P56 Koller Auktionen AG, Zurich, Switzerland; P57 (top) Jpascher, Wikipedia.co.uk; P57 (bottom) Kislak Center for Special Collections, Rare Books and Manuscripts, University of Pennsylvania; P58 (top) Peter Schmelzle; P58 (bottom) Biblioteca Nacional de España; P59 Bibliothèque de l'Institut de France; P60 California Science Center; P61 St Andrews University Special Collections; P62 Bavarian State Library; P63 (top) Bavarian State Library; P63 (bottom) St Andrews University Special Collections; P64 (top) University of Illinois Urbana-Champaign; P66 British Museum; P67 (all images) David Cranmer; PP68-69 Oberlin College Library; P72 (all images) Henri Selmer, Paris; P73 (both images) Metropolitan Museum of Art; P74 Museo del Saxophono; P75 (bottom) Google Patents; P76 Wiki Commons; P80 Städtische Galerie im Lenbachhaus and Kunstbau, München, Germany; P81 (both images) Alte Nationalgalerie Berlin; P83 Library of Congress; P84 Boston Public Library; P85 Beinecke Library, Yale University; P86 Getty Research Institute; P87 Getty Research Institute; P88 Getty Research Institute; P89 (bottom) Wellcome Collection, London; P90 Waddesdon Image Library; P94, P95 (all images) Whitney Museum of American Art, Frances Mulhall Achilles Library; P97 (both images) United States Patent and Trademark Office; P98 Daderot, Wikipedia.co.uk; P102 Wiki Commons; P103 Family May-Weißheimer, Thomas Goller; P105 Biblioteca de la Universidad de Sevilla; P106 Exhibit made by Estes Objethos Atelier, photo by Rodrigo Tetsuo Argenton; P108, P109, P110 (all images) Cyfarthfa Castle Museum and Art Gallery, Rob Mullender and Louis Porter; P113 (top left) National Library of Spain; P113 (top right) Museo Teatrale alla Scala, Milan; P113 (bottom) Triquetra, it.wikipedia; P114 (both images) British Library; P115 (top) Artem. G, wikipedia.co.uk; P115 (bottom) Wikipedia.co.uk; P117 (top) Françoise Ernst-Pradal; P117 (bottom) Disdero, wikipedia.co.uk.jpg; P118 Juilliard Manuscript Collection; P119 Christie's; P120 (left) Gesellschaft der Musikfreunde; P121 dpa picture alliance / Alamy Stock photo; P122 Metropolitan Museum of Art; P123 The J. Paul Getty Museum, Los Angeles, 77.PB.92; P125 Prado Museum; P126, P127 Biblioteca Ambrosiana; P128 The Morgan Library & Museum; P132, P133 Royal Collection Trust; P134 Wikipedia.co.uk; P135 Wiesbaden State Library; P136 Archivio di Stato Lucca, Lucca, Italy; P138 SCD – Université – Poitiers; P139, P140 Bayerische Staatsbibliothek; P141 (both images) British Library; P143 Massachusetts Institute of Technology, Libraries, Institute Archives and Special Collections; P148 Swales92, reddit.com; P150 Bonhams; P152 British Museum; P155 (bottom) Metropolitan Museum of Art; P156 (top) Kunsthistorisches Museum; P156 (bottom) Chopin Museum; P157 (bottom) The Morgan Library; P158 New York Public Library; P160 Sevela.p, Wikipedia.co.uk; P163 Dutch National Archives; P164 Imago / Alamy Stock Photo; P168, P169 (all images) National Library of France; P170, P171 Chantilly, Bibliothèque du Château; P172 Berkeley Library, University of California; P173 Newberry Library; P174 Horne Museum, Florence; P175 (top) Alte Nationalgalerie, Staatliche Museen zu Berlin; P175 (bottom) Museum of City History Leipzig; P176, P177 Biblioteca Digital Hispánica; P178 Gopes, Wiki Commons; P182 (top) Bavarian State Library; P183 (top) Centraal Museum, Utrecht; P183 (bottom) ibiblio.org; P184 (bottom) Wikipedia.co.uk; P185 Musée Carnavalet, Todeswalzer

Wikipedia.co.uk; P188 Lunlunta99, Wikipedia.co.uk; P189 (bottom) Popperfoto; P190 Lebrecht Music & Arts / Alamy Stock Photo; P191 Faber Music; P192, P193 John Stump archive; P195 Conlon Nancarrow; P197 (top) PA Images / Alamy Stock Photo, P197 (middle) Hiroyuki Ito / Contributor; P197 (bottom) Associated Press / Alamy Stock Photo; P201 (top) Mum's taxi, Wikipedia.co.uk; P201 (bottom) Aldercraft, Wikipedia.co.uk; P202 (top) University of Western Ontario; P203 (both images) Austrian National Library; P204 British Library; P205 (bottom) Georg Lindstrøm, Adam Cuerden; P206 National Library of France; P207 Paris Musées; P208 (top) British Library; P208 (bottom) casadesus.com; P209 (top) Volgi Archive; P209 (bottom) TIME Magazine; P210 Wiki Commons; P211 Denzil McNeelance; P212 (top) Museum-digital Berlin; P212 (bottom) BBC; P214 William Barrington-Coupe, John Miller Crawford, wikipedia.co.uk; P215 Shutterstock; P222 (bottom) Beverly Lomer; P224 Collections du Musée de la musique – Philharmonie de Paris; P226 (top) Benjamin Hebbert; P227 (top) Library of Congress; P227 (bottom) Galerie Lowet de Wotrenge; P229 (bottom) Art Museum of Estonia; P230 National Library of France; P231 Sotheby's; P232 Rijksmuseum; P233 Library of Congress; P234 Hempel Auctions; P236 (top) National Museum, Warsaw; P236 (bottom) Archivio Storico Ricordi; P237 Alte Nationalgalerie; P240 John Carter Brown Library
All other images are the author's own or public domain.

Every effort has been made to find and credit the copyright holders of images in this book. We will be pleased to rectify any errors or omissions in future editions.

ACKNOWLEDGEMENTS

I would like to express my deep appreciation to all who provided such indispensable help in the creation of this book: to Charlie Campbell at Greyhound Literary; to Alison Macdonald at Simon & Schuster UK; to Laura Nickoll and Keith Williams for yet another beautiful design, and to Joanna Chisholm. With many thanks to my family for all their support; and to Alex, Alexi, Luca and Winter Anstey; Matt, Gemma, Charlie and Wren Troughton; and to Dan Schreiber, Andy Hunter Murray and Jason Hazeley.

First published in Great Britain by Simon & Schuster UK Ltd, 2025

Copyright © 2025 by Edward Brooke-Hitching

The right of Edward Brooke-Hitching to be identified as the author of this work has been asserted by him in accordance with sections 77 and 78 of the Copyright, Designs and Patents Act, 1988.

Editorial Director: Alison MacDonald
Project Editor: Laura Nickoll
Design: Keith Williams, sprout.uk.com

1 3 5 7 9 10 8 6 4 2

Simon & Schuster UK Ltd
1st Floor
222 Gray's Inn Road
London WC1X 8HB

For more than 100 years, Simon & Schuster has championed authors and the stories they create. By respecting the copyright of an author's intellectual property, you enable Simon & Schuster and the author to continue publishing exceptional books for years to come. We thank you for supporting the author's copyright by purchasing an authorized edition of this book.

No amount of this book may be reproduced or stored in any format, nor may it be uploaded to any website, database, language-learning model, or other repository, retrieval, or artificial intelligence system without express permission. All rights reserved. Inquiries may be directed to Simon & Schuster, 222 Gray's Inn Road, London WC1X 8HB or RightsMailbox@simonandschuster.co.uk

Simon & Schuster strongly believes in freedom of expression and stands against censorship in all its forms. For more information, visit BooksBelong.com.

www.simonandschuster.co.uk
www.simonandschuster.com.au
www.simonandschuster.co.in

Simon & Schuster Australia, Sydney
Simon & Schuster India, New Delhi

The authorised representative in the EEA is Simon & Schuster Netherlands BV, Herculesplein 96, 3584 AA Utrecht, Netherlands. info@simonandschuster.nl

The author and publishers have made all reasonable efforts to contact copyright-holders for permission, and apologise for any omissions or errors in the form of credits given. Corrections may be made to future printings.

A CIP catalogue record for this book is available from the British Library

Endpapers: Front: Piganino. Credit British Museum. Back: Harmonia organica. Credit Beinecke

Hardback ISBN: 978-1-3985-3240-3
Ebook ISBN: 978-1-3985-3241-0

Printed in Dubai by Oriental Press

Tintiñabl.